Fred Halliday was born in Dublin and studied at Queen's College, Oxford, and the School of Oriental and African Studies, London. He is the author of *Arabia without Sultans* (London 1974), *Iran: Dictatorship and Development* (London 1978) and *Soviet Policy in the Arc of Crisis* (Washington 1981). He is a Fellow of the Transnational Institute, an editor of *New Left Review* and a contributing editor of *MERIP Reports*.

Maxine Molyneux was born in Karachi and studied at Essex University. She is the author of *State Policies and the Position of Women in South Yemen* (Geneva 1981) and *Women and Socialism* (Amsterdam 1981), as well as of several articles on the theory of women's subordination. She is a Lecturer in Sociology at Essex University and a member of the editorial collective of *Feminist Review*.

Fred Halliday
Maxine Molyneux

Verso

The Ethiopian Revolution

First published, 1981
© Fred Halliday and Maxine Molyneux, 1981

Verso Editions and NLB,
15 Greek Street, London W1

Typeset in Monophoto Imprint by
Servis Filmsetting Ltd, Manchester

Printed in Great Britain by
Unwin Brothers, Woking

British Library
Cataloguing in Publication Data
Halliday, Fred
  The Ethiopian revolution.
  1. Ethiopia – Politics and government
  2. Ethiopia – History – 1889–
  I. Title   II. Molyneux, Maxine
  963'.06   DT387.95

ISBN 0–86091–043–1
ISBN 0–86091–741–X Pbk

Contents

Preface	9
1 Revolution in the Third World	11
Social Revolution in the Post-Colonial World	13
Revolution From Above	25
Dynamics of Military Rule	31
Nationalism in Post-Colonial Societies	38
International Determinations	43
2 The Fall of the Ancien Régime	51
A Legendary Land	51
The Historical Background	54
Prelude to Revolution	62
The Imperial State	69
Opposition Forces	74
The 1974 Revolution	82
Main Characteristics of the Revolutionary Movement	88
3 Revolution From Above: (i) Policies and Problems	96
The Dynamics of Transformation	96
The Major Enactments	99
Land Reform	104

The Ambiguity of the Reforms 110
The Derg: Division and Consolidation 112
Civilian Opposition 119
Assassination and Red Terror 122

4 Revolution From Above: (ii) The Post-Revolutionary Order 128

Civilian-Military Alliances 128
Ideological Innovations 135
The Elusive 'Proletarian Party' 139
The Post-Revolutionary State 145

5 The Regional and National Questions 156

A Fragmented Society 156
PMAC Policies 159
Region in Revolt: Eritrea 171
The Political Character
  of the Eritrean Guerrillas 182
Nationalities in Movement:
  Oromo, Somali, Tigrean 193
The Responsibilities of the Centre:
  Past and Future 207

6 The International Dimensions 211

The Horn in International Politics 211
US Policy: Who Lost Ethiopia? 214
The Somali Connection 225
Middle Eastern Coordinates 231
The USSR and the Ethiopian Revolution 237
Cuba's Interventions 250
Interested Spectators:
  China and the Communist Movement 256
Ethiopia in World Affairs:
  Object and Subject 264

**7 Conclusions:
A State of Socialist Orientation?** 268

Abbreviations 284
Short Bibliography 286
Maps 291
Index 297

Preface

This study draws on research carried out over the four years from mid-1977 to 1981. First-hand observation of the situation in Ethiopia was possible during visits to the country in 1977 and 1978, and we have supplemented this with a wide range of interviews in the Middle East, Western Europe and the USA. In addition to meeting with officials of the Ethiopian government, we have been able to talk with many members of the Ethiopian opposition and of the Eritrean movements. We have also talked with representatives of the US, British, Swedish, Russian, Cuban, South Yemeni, Somali, Egyptian, Sudanese and Iraqi governments. We would like to take this opportunity to thank all those who set time aside to answer our questions and to provide information that we requested. We owe a special debt of thanks to Patrick Gilkes, whose knowledge of Ethiopia, combined with great generosity and patience, has been of invaluable assistance; to John Duggan, who allowed us to consult his unpublished reports on Eritrea; to Perry Anderson, who read the text at manuscript stage; and to all those friends from the Horn of Africa who guided and stimulated our investigations. We would also like to thank those members of staff of the Sociology Department, Essex University, and of the Politics and Sociology Department, Birkbeck College London, who helped in retyping the manuscript, and the Fellows of the Transnational Institute, Amsterdam, for their constant and loyal support.

Fred Halliday and Maxine Molyneux
London, July 1981

1

Revolution in the Third World

This study discusses a particular social revolution within the context of social upheaval and political change in the contemporary Third World. It is not intended to be a comprehensive study of contemporary Ethiopia. What follows is, rather, an analysis of the *main features* of the Ethiopian revolution: we attempt to disentangle it from the controversies that often surround any contemporary event and to identify its causes, course and consequences. At the same time, we seek to relate the events of the Ethiopian revolution to certain more general theoretical and political questions that arise in the study of the Third World and of the revolutions it has recently undergone.

The subsequent chapters resume the main empirical material relevant to the discussion of the topic in hand: the revolution itself, the policies of the post-revolutionary regime, the regional and national questions, and the international dimensions of the revolution. The final section discusses the possible post-revolutionary outcomes. The intention is to focus on those issues that are both central to the course of the revolution and which have a broader, comparative, relevance, whether of a theoretical or a political kind. The present chapter discusses how the pattern of revolutionary upsurge in the Third World changed in a number of surprising ways during the 1970s. Whilst no analytic account can keep fully abreast of such transformations, we will attempt cautiously to identify some of the features of this new revolutionary pattern in conjunction with a study of the Ethiopian revolution.

The author of a recent comparative study of three revolutions has written as follows: 'Social revolutions are rapid, basic transformations of a society's state and class structures; and they are accompanied and in part carried through by class-based revolts from below. Social revolutions are set apart from other sorts of conflicts and transformative processes above all by the combination of two coincidences: the coincidence of societal structural change with class upheaval; and the coincidence of political with social transformation.... What is unique to social revolution is that basic changes in social structure and in political structure occur together in a mutually reinforcing fashion. And these changes occur through intense socio-political conflicts in which class struggles play a key role.'[1] The author emphasizes, on the basis of her criteria, that revolutions of this kind are comparatively rare events, to be distinguished from mere rebellions or political revolutions; but it is our contention that the transformations undergone by Ethiopia in the 1970s merit its inclusion in the list of social revolutions of the twentieth century. Whatever the final pattern of political rule in the post-revolutionary order, or the ultimate territorial boundaries of the republican state, a revolutionary change of political, social and economic structure has come about through a process in which mass movements played an important part. The political and social power of an entrenched ruling dynasty has been broken, those who held social and economic sway in the countryside have been expropriated, and a long-established pattern of particularist ethnic domination has been shattered. Certainly, this process has had its limits. The post-revolutionary order has established neither full equality between social groups nor equality between nationalities, and it has not set up anything that might be termed a democratic political order. Yet such failings are not unique to the Ethiopian revolution: they should not obscure the import of what has occurred in Ethiopia, a socio-political transformation of a depth rare in the contemporary Third World.

[1] Theda Skočpol, *States and Social Revolutions*, Cambridge 1979, p. 4.

Social Revolution in the Post-Colonial World

We will try, in this analysis, to ascertain the causes of the 1974 revolution, and to delineate the structural crisis the *combination* of factors that undermined the existing order. Such a concept of crisis is of particular relevance to revolutions such as the Ethiopian, where a variety of individual causes, on different time-scales and with extremely divergent particular courses, combined to produce a situation in which the *ancien régime* was overthrown.[2] No single factor, or revolutionary agent, produced this end result. The theorists of structural crisis may have gone too far in devaluing the role of conscious political action by revolutionary agents, in both historic and contemporary revolutions, but they are justified in emphasizing the prior importance of the structural crisis without which purposive action has only limited import. Such a crisis may itself produce sudden and unexpected change in the plans of small groups; it turns them into agents they would not otherwise have expected to become and invests them with new political capacities. Only this kind of approach can uncover the unity of the apparently disparate pre-revolutionary factors that precipitate the final crisis. It is an essential antidote to the tendency of post-revolutionary victors to write history as if they had planned and executed its course from the beginning. This restoration of purposive action to its appropriate place is equally relevant for analysing the pattern of the post-revolutionary settlement and for disengaging the study of revolutions from the schemas of disappointment and deviation that so many seek to project. While revolutions can transform for the better the lived conditions of the oppressed, no revolution produces a perfect society, or the one that most of those who participate in it expect at first to see: the Ethiopian revolution is no exception to this generalization. But it is mistaken to see the course of revolution as a series of betrayals and usurpations; they are not voluntaristic enterprises capable of yielding a wide variety of outcomes. The concept of structural crisis helps to

---

[2] Skočpol's formulation of the Marxist theory of structural crisis is contained in ibid., pp. 14–18.

identify those elements in the pre-revolutionary order that established the political capacities of different actors and so helped to shape the post-revolutionary settlement. These elements make other, perhaps more desirable results either impossible or far harder to attain than their proponents would accept. While the result of the Ethiopian revolution may not have corresponded to the aspirations of the majority of those who helped bring about the crisis of 1974, it did reflect the relative strengths of the different revolutionary forces. In particular it reflected their capacity to acquire and retain state power, and to implement a programme of revolutionary change.[3]

In a comparative perspective, the Ethiopian revolution of 1974 would appear to have little in common with most other recent Third World social upheavals. It took place in a country still dominated by pre-capitalist social and political institutions and with only the briefest overall experience of colonial rule. State and society diverged from the normal colonial and post-colonial models. There was a nationalistic or anti-imperialist element in both causation and ideology, but this was subordinate to that of internally generated contradictions. Moreover, unlike all post-1945 social revolutions in the Third World, apart from Iran, it was not made in the countryside, let alone by peasants, although rural contradictions and a variety of rebel forces that recruited peasants contributed to weakening the *ancien régime*. Nor were revolutionary parties present in the revolutionary upsurge: Ethiopia had to an extreme degree been innocent of the organizational and theoretical currents of modern revolution. The Ethiopian revolution was reminiscent not of the recent upsurges in the Third World but of the classic revolutions of Europe – France in 1789 and the February 1917 revolution in Russia – and it took place in a country

[3] For a cogent statement of the 'revolution betrayed' thesis see John Markakis and Nega Ayele, *Class and Revolution in Ethiopia*, Nottingham 1978; see also John Markakis, 'Garrison Socialism: The Case of Ethiopia', *MERIP*, no. 79, June 1979, and Jan Valdelin, 'Ethiopia 1974–7: From Anti-Feudal Revolution to Consolidation of the Bourgeois State', *Race and Class*, spring 1978. For analyses arguing that only the military could have carried out the revolutionary transformation, see Marina and David Ottaway, *Ethiopia, Empire in Revolution*, London 1978, and René Lefort, *Ethiopie, la révolution hérétique*, Paris 1981.

displaying many of the features of these two societies on the eve of their revolutions. The transition to capitalism was far from complete, but it had already weakened the traditional bases of social and political power. This transition, combined with a protracted agrarian crisis, was forcing ever-greater sections of the peasantry into destitution, and the agrarian crisis was depriving other sectors of the economy of the resources needed for expansion. At the centre sat a monarchy debilitated in personal and political terms, and increasingly separated both from the traditional aristocracy and from a new bureaucratic and military elite intent upon social modernization and greater influence. Outside the state apparatus itself there developed a clamorous coalition of urban oppositions. None of these groups was able to organize a concerted drive against the monarchy or possessed a clear idea of where the protest was going. Yet their combined impact seriously weakened the monarchy and so precipitated a revolution.

As in France and Tsarist Russia, there was no direct causal correlation between the fall of the monarch himself and the wider crisis in the society as a whole. Yet the gradual decomposition of the old order, accelerated by certain specific immediate causes, brought about an explosion in the cities in which the monarch was forced to step down. This individual act of abdication itself paved the way for further social radicalization. Ethiopia shared with these European revolutions the apparent confusion of revolutionary actors – dissident aristocrats, combative democratic tendencies, interventionist military personnel. As in the earlier cases, those who began the process did not complete it. But among those actors one – the radical military – was able to displace its political competitors and consolidate a new post-revolutionary order. If such resulting conditions were not the product of some original intentionality, they cannot be seen either as purely contingent and haphazard, or as betrayals of some alternative post-revolutionary system that would otherwise have been easily attainable. It is precisely in the balance of structural causation and purposive action that the outcome of these revolutions can be discerned.

France in 1789 and Russia in 1917 were absolutist states and the Ethiopia of 1974 was, in its main features, comparable to them. The absolutist states were pre-capitalist political systems, feudal monarchies, ruling over societies in transition to capitalism: in response to the challenges of this transition, and of increasingly organized contestation with other states, they sought to adjust the political arrangements of their societies to preserve their thrones. They created new, centralized monarchies with 'standing armies, a permanent bureaucracy, national taxation, a codified law, and the beginnings of a unified market':[4] whilst these were changes that would promote a transition to capitalism, they were nonetheless designed to preserve the feudal monarchies of Europe from displacement by the socio-economic changes occurring in their countries.

In the period of Haile Selassie's rule, similar measures were taken: in response to the Italian occupation, US pressure and Somali rivalry, a new military and civilian machinery was established, while attempts were made to tax rural sectors and promote changes in agricultural output and trade. As in Europe, it was the failure of these reforming measures combined with the pressures exerted by the new social groupings associated with the transition to capitalism that produced the revolutionary crisis. As we shall see, Ethiopia can be termed 'feudal' only in a qualified sense of the term; but there is sufficient congruence between Ethiopia and the absolutist states for an identification to be made between them. Over a period of three centuries the absolutist monarchies of Europe were swept away: yet Ethiopia prolonged the time-scale of such pre-capitalist monarchies longer than almost any other, until the eve of the final quarter of the twentieth century.[5]

[4] Perry Anderson, *Lineages of the Absolutist State*, London 1974, p. 17.

[5] A comparable case was that of Afghanistan: the Mohammadzai monarchy was overthrown in July 1973, but the state remained under the control of members of the royal family and the related nobility until April 1978. Nepal is another state where a monarchy established in a pre-capitalist epoch retains state power, as do the assorted royal families of the Persian Gulf. In none of these was the articulated structure of monarchy and aristocracy so developed, and comparable to that of European absolutism. If the social formation rather than the state system is taken into consideration, then Ethiopia would also be one of the countries where the transition to capitalism had, in the 1960s and 1970s, gone less far than in almost all other Third World countries. An illuminating study of this issue is contained in Addis Hiwet, *Ethiopia: From Autocracy to Revolution*, London 1975.

However, if the Ethiopian revolution belonged to the time of European absolutism, it occurred in a world of a very different kind, one in which the capitalist mode of production had to a considerable extent transformed production relations in the Third World and begun to integrate the poorer countries into new economic and political orders. Ethiopia had not been subjected to colonial rule – with the exception of Eritrea, and the brief six years of Italian occupation between 1935 and 1941. Yet in the post-war epoch a transition to capitalism was affecting ever-larger areas of Ethiopian society. This was an exogeneously powered transition, resulting from the pressures upon Ethiopia of the capitalist world order without, rather than from the kind of internal maturation of capitalism that had transformed feudal Europe. This exogenous dynamic had two important effects.

First, by providing the state with a source of external financial and military support, it enabled the monarchy to prolong its existence beyond the time when it might otherwise have been able to survive. The very availability of US support in an era of cold war and strategic rivalry with the USSR therefore prolonged the time of pre-capitalist monarchy in the highlands of Ethiopia. One can see here a political counterpart of the preservation – and even creation – of pre-capitalist economic sectors in colonial societies that has accompanied the spread of the capitalist market across the globe.[6] Second, Ethiopia did not produce a bourgeoisie – in Europe the motor for the transition to capitalism. There existed a small mercantile class, but much of it was composed of foreign merchants. There was no class to play the social or political role of the bourgeoisie under European absolutism. The main social impact of this exogenous capitalism was not on the mercantile class but on the state machine itself – on the civil servants, including teachers, and army officers. These sectors of the expanded state apparatus were recruited from intermediate social strata and were most exposed to alternative ideas and political models; their ideology and social position within a still autocratic regime cast them in a central

---

[6] Ernesto Laclau, 'Feudalism and Capitalism in Latin America', *New Left Review*, 67, May–June 1971; Harold Wolpe, ed., *The Articulation of Modes of Production*, London 1980.

role in the 1974 revolution. Thus, the exogenous dynamic of the Ethiopian transition to capitalism was central both to the regime's improbable survival into the 1970s and to the course of its dissolution.

This very different international context is not merely a corrective to what would otherwise be a purely internal and historical presentation of Ethiopia's pre-capitalist system as, in a qualified sense, absolutist. It also introduces what is an equally striking feature of Ethiopia's revolution: if it belongs to the time of European absolutism prior to the anti-colonial revolutions, it simultaneously belongs to another time, one *posterior* to the latter. If it is the last of the upheavals that overthrew absolutist states, it can also be seen as one of those social revolutions of a Third World freed from the direct domination of colonialism and from the need to overthrow it. Many of the revolutionary upheavals of the 1970s continued in the pattern of earlier anti-colonial movements, even if they included strong socially revolutionary components. This was true in Africa of Angola, Mozambique, Guinea-Bissau, and Zimbabwe. In Indo-China, the movements in Vietnam, Cambodia and Laos were as socially revolutionary as that in Ethiopia, but they developed within the context of a struggle against foreign domination. However, there have been other Third World revolutions that have followed a different pattern and which, for all their differences, form an identifiable and separate category: these are 'post-colonial revolutions', social revolutions in societies no longer under direct colonial rule, or that never experienced transformation by colonial domination. In these, the primary target of the upheavals was not foreign domination but the political and social system of an indigenous ruling class and its allies. Although often supported from outside, this class alliance was internally rooted, and its overthrow, therefore, involved a correspondingly greater and deeper transformation of the society in question. The underlying contradiction behind these revolutions was not that between a national movement and the armies of a foreign occupying power. Hence it was the strength of internal structures that determined the manner in which external forces could participate to block or assist the revolutionary movement.

As such, these revolutions were located in a new revolutionary time, one that began only with the post-colonial era. Like the end of absolutism, the advent of this era has not been in any sense synchronic: Latin America, where direct colonialism ended in most countries at the beginning of the nineteenth century, contrasts with Asia and Africa, where decolonization was completed only in the 1960s and 1970s. Hence it is not surprising that two of the first post-colonial revolutions should have been in the new world: in Mexico (1910–20) and Cuba (1956–9). These were social revolutions that destroyed the pre-existing ruling classes and systems of political power, and introduced far-reaching changes in the systems of social and economic organization. One Asian country that avoided complete domination by colonialism experienced social revolution in the earlier half of the twentieth century: China, where the upheaval lasted from the fall of the monarch in 1911 until the establishment of the post-revolutionary order in 1949. In Thailand, which also escaped colonial rule, a coalition of radical officers and intellectuals seized power in 1932 but was ousted before implementing revolutionary measures.

The Cuban revolution was perhaps the clearest instance of such a revolution in the post-war period. There were, however, other revolutions initiated in the 1970s that can be included in the same category: those in Iran, Afghanistan, Nicaragua and Ethiopia. The regimes of these four countries were not isolated from the international system, or from the supports that international assistance could provide. Three had been either installed or re-installed with the assistance of the West (the Nicaraguan in 1937, the Ethiopian in 1941, the Iranian in 1953), whilst the Afghan regime, long reliant on assistance from the USSR, had in its last phase become increasingly dependent on the support of the Shah of Iran. More significantly, however, the sources of external assistance available to these regimes in a polarized international climate had helped to detach the repressive state from its social base; this was an essential component of the structural crisis and a condition for the triumph of the revolutions themselves. Whilst external assistance granted short-term relief and a stay of execution to these states, it encouraged them to ignore the social and economic forces maturing beneath them. They were able to dispense with structural reforms, and political confirmations such as the organization of internal bases of support, to which other more internationally autonomous regimes would have been forced to pay attention. The pattern and effect of exogenous support was, however, quite distinct from that which operated in colonial conditions: in the latter, it was the direct presence of foreign domination, combined with a greater or lesser incidence of economic exploitation, that forged an insurrectionary climate; in the former, post-colonial, situation, the availability of exogenous support exacerbated a conflict *internal* to the social formation itself.

Ethiopia and Afghanistan provide strikingly parallel cases of the way in which external support produced that detachment of the state which was to foster a revolutionary climate.[7] In both, the pre-capitalist monarchies had over-run the normal life-span of their kind. This was partly because of their sensitive strategic locations, and partly because their countries presented no great economic attractions that would, in other circumstances, have brought about their integration into the world market and the international system of capitalist production. The main index of their condition was that neither regime was willing or able to mobilize the rural surplus for economic growth by instituting new systems of taxation or reorganizing land tenure. Rather, the resistance of the landed proprietors to reform led to a stagnation in rural output, a growing threat of famine, substantial migration of marginalized peasants and a fall in rural taxation. Yet these regimes were able to dispense with such reforms and even to forgo domestically generated income precisely because they came increasingly to rely on support from abroad. In Ethiopia this was from the West, of course, but Afghanistan's contrasting dependence on the

[7] Two-thirds of the Ethiopian state's capital expenditure was financed by foreign sources in the last decade of imperial rule. The Afghan state budget for 1975–6 derived only 36 per cent of its income from local sources; the remainder was from foreign aid. ('Interview with an Afghan Marxist', *Pakistan Progressive*, New York, March–April 1980, p. 36.) See also Louis Duprée, *Afghanistan*, Princeton 1980 and Fred Halliday, 'Revolution in Afghanistan', *New Left Review*, 112, November–December 1978.

USSR had no more effect on the internal social structures there, which remained remote from any inclination towards socialism. At the same time, both monarchies were encouraged and enabled by foreign aid to expand their state apparatuses, drawing the graduates of new educational establishments into expanded civil services and developing modern and permanent armies where they had, until the 1930s, relied on provincial levies.[8] It was precisely the underlying agrarian crisis, resulting from the failure of monarchical transformation from above, that produced a context in which radicalized sections of the state apparatus, influenced by foreign ideas, took power. Given the enormous bloodshed in both countries since the start of their respective revolutions, in 1974 and 1978, it is relevant to recall that the regimes themselves were overthrown with almost no resistance whatsoever, so isolated had they become from the social forces over which they had ruled. The objective disjuncture of society and state brought about by exogeneous state support had the same paradoxical effect in both cases. It enabled these archaic regimes to prolong their suspension in the historical time of pre-capitalist monarchy, then wrenched them forward into the historical time of social revolution in the post-colonial Third World.

Iran and Nicaragua were societies in which the transition to capitalism had gone much further than in Ethiopia or Afghanistan, and Western, particularly US, support for their regimes was all the greater. The Somoza family had issued from the National Guard, the local military unit left behind when the US Marines withdrew in 1932. The Pahlavi monarchy, although established through largely endogenous factors in the 1920s, had come increasingly to rely on US political and military support in the 1940s and 1950s. In Iran, however, the key disjuncture opened up by trans-national assistance was produced not by direct state-to-state support but by oil revenues, which served, far more than direct US government aid, to exempt the Pahlavi regime from reforms

[8] On the recruitment of Ethiopian school graduates see below p. 71; in 1971 it was estimated that 51 per cent of all Afghans with nine years of education or more were working for the Ministry of Education. *Area Handbook on Afghanistan*, Washington 1973, p. xviii.

and political initiatives that it would otherwise have been forced to consider. Oil output generated a large state revenue, but it made virtually no demands upon Iranian society itself and so could in practical terms be seen as an income from outside the formation.[9] It produced considerable prosperity in the towns; but this was accompanied by widespread corruption, growing inequality of income, and social tensions out of which grew the revolution of 1978–9. The subjective consequences of oil revenues – royal delusions, palace corruption – combined with the objective social dislocations to produce the structural crisis of the late 1970s. Despite the resources and international backing apparently available to the Shah, his regime collapsed unexpectedly quickly in the face of the popular protest movement, neither the army nor the prosperous middle class associated with his regime trying in any decisive way to halt the revolutionary process. Once again, a flood of support from without masked and effectively furthered the erosion of the regime's internal social and political foundations.

The Somoza family was not a monarchy, although it acted like the most rapacious and arrogant of dynasties.[10] The institutions that sustained the Somoza dictatorship – above all, the National Guard – were much more the direct product of imperialist intervention than any in the other three instances. But Nicaragua had been formally independent for nearly half a century by the time the revolution of 1979 occurred. The Somoza regime had implanted itself as an indigenous one in no way comparable to some merely colonial administration. For this reason, the revolutionary movement that developed in the 1970s was directed not just against a certain level of foreign interference, but against an economic system of ownership and exploitation that permeated the rural and urban economies – against a *Nicaraguan* ruling class. International support was crucial to the regime's

---

[9] Oil revenues have been considered by some writers as a form of rent in the sense of 'a free gift of nature or . . . a grant from foreign sources', Hossein Mahdavy, 'The Patterns and Problems of Economic Development in Rentier States: the Case of Iran', in M.A. Cook, ed., *Studies in the Economic History of the Middle East*, London 1970, p. 429; and H. Katouzian, *The Political Economy of Modern Iran*, London 1981.

[10] H. Jung, 'The Fall of Somoza', *New Left Review*, 117, September–October 1979.

survival. Somoza relied for a considerable part of his appropriations on money exacted from foreign ventures, whether foreign firms or the funds brought into Nicaragua after the 1972 earthquake. But it was not the quasi-colonial relationship of the early 1930s, so much as the post-colonial support relationship of the early 1970s, that defined the international dimension of the Nicaraguan revolution. It was this that fostered the critical disjuncture, the detachment of Somoza and his associates from Nicaraguan society that reproduced the weakness of the Shah and Haile Selassie. The Sandinist forces had to fight fiercely and heroically to dislodge the Somoza government, yet here too the level of assistance received by the regime from its patrons in the USA was far less than would have been the case in a colonial situation; and the very force of the revolution was such that it could not end merely with the destruction of a particular political regime but had to continue to a substantive reorganization of Nicaragua's social and economic structures.

It was the curious fate of the Ethiopian revolution, as of that in Afghanistan, that it participated in this post-colonial revolutionary process and yet was also placed in the earlier time of revolutions against a decaying pre-capitalist order. The world into which it was drawn then had its own impact. As with the internal so with the external characteristics of the revolution: these influenced the genesis of the revolution *and* the direction of the post-revolutionary order. The discussion of the international dimensions in chapter 6 shows that it was not merely the pre-revolutionary strategic significance of Ethiopia to the West that influenced its political system, but to an even greater extent the post-revolutionary significance of such a country for East and West alike. If Ethiopia had felt to some extent exempted from the conflicts of world politics in the period up to 1974, this ceased to be so in the subsequent years. Its enemies were to recruit substantial external assistance in their attempts to destroy it, whilst the very course of the Ethiopian revolution itself was to be shaped, positively and negatively, by the character of the assistance it received from the USSR and its allies. This international dimension, and the encouragement it gave to political radicalization within, belonged quintessentially to the time of post-colonial revolutions in which, after 1974, Ethiopia found itself abruptly immersed.[11]

The pattern of international response provides a significant insight into the difference between colonial and post-colonial revolutions. In the colonial cases the dominant external powers fought tenaciously to defend their own implanted systems of domination. The results were the Algerian and Vietnamese wars, and the agonized conflicts of Portuguese-speaking Africa, in all of which metropolitan armies participated directly. In the non-colonial cases the Western patrons, who might have been expected to intervene to support their clients, were unable or unwilling to do so: the Shah, Somoza, Batista and Haile Selassie were all abandoned to their fates, not a single NATO soldier intervening to help them. The West lost interest in Afghanistan in the 1950s and the Afghan regime's fall in April 1978 took the West and the Shah of Iran by surprise.[12] This asymmetry also operated in the post-revolutionary period, but in reverse. The defeated interventionist powers accepted the verdicts of conflict in Vietnam, Algeria and Portuguese Africa: only in Angola, where the succession was disputed and the West supported its own candidate for power, was this not the case. No such acceptance was accorded to the post-colonial revolutions: the want of full-scale support for the old regimes was made good by active support for the counter-revolutions that were later instigated by those whose interests were expropriated. The Bay of Pigs invasion of Cuba, the encouragement of Somalia's invasion of Ethiopia, and the promotion of the Afghan resistance operating from Pakistan testified to the refusal of the Western states to accept these new Third World revol-

---

[11] This was also true in the realm of ideas: although, prior to the 1970s, there had been no significant socialist movement in the Horn, socialist ideas of a generically Marxist and Leninist character had become almost obligatory by the end of the decade in Ethiopia, Somalia and amongst the majority of Eritreans. These were often used to compound, rather than alleviate, existing disputes.

[12] Inadvertence at the time of the revolution's triumph tended to produce a later 'Who Lost?' literature, designed to draw lessons from these defeats. Emphasis upon the need for, and possibility of, such 'hard-line' policies on the part of American administrations confronted with Third World revolution was a stock-in-trade of the right-wing foreign policy establishment after the Iranian revolution.

utions.[13] It would also appear that, whilst Washington had learnt from the Cuban case of the dangers of premature counter-revolution, it was keeping the possibility of similar ventures in mind for both Nicaragua and Iran, an option partly dependent on how far these revolutions went in transforming society. This pattern of intervention and apparent acceptance focuses attention upon what is one of the central differences between colonial and post-colonial revolutions. The former pose a political challenge to the dominating power, but they do not necessarily threaten the capitalist social system. The latter present no such obvious political challenge and may even initially escape the closest attention of the West; but the longer-term consequences of social transformation, combined with the rise of an internal opposition to revolutionary change, tend to draw the major capitalist powers into new counter-revolutionary initiatives.

Revolution From Above

Chapters 3 and 4 analyse the development of the post-revolutionary regime: the policies of the PMAC, the divisions within it, the relationship between the military and the various civilian political forces, and the extent to which the state has been reorganized, the course of the major reforms implemented by the regime, and the process by which more and more sections of the civilian political movement were separated from the PMAC and adopted positions of open opposition. Much of what has been written to date on these issues has been of a clearly partisan character, involving either direct hostility to the post-revolutionary regime or various forms of apologia for it. We consider it relevant to assess some of these arguments, and, where appropriate, to register disagreement with the accounts of both tendencies. Yet, beyond these particular disputes, the post-revolutionary experience of Ethiopia bears on more general issues of

---

[13] In all of these cases the precondition for such foreign involvement was the existence of an internal opposition which was able successfully to internationalize the social conflicts developing within each society. This internationalization on the right inevitably produced a countervailing internationalization on the left, in the form of increased Soviet support for the regime in question.

relevance to contemporary debate on the Third World as a whole, two of which merit some discussion here. They are the questions of revolution from above and of the role of the 'progressive' military – that is, of the direction from which revolutionary change originates and the institution that carries it out.

The central thesis of the concept 'revolution from above' is that profound transformations of social and political structures can occur in a particular country, meriting the term 'revolutionary' yet initiated and controlled not by a mass movement but by a sector of the pre-existing state apparatus. The concept is designed to identify a particular set of historical phenomena and to distinguish them both from coups d'etat – a transfer of power between state personnel – and from mass revolutions, 'revolutions from below'. In the catalogue of major bourgeois revolutions the clearest instances of this kind of revolution would be the German, through which Bismarck transformed a reunified state in the 1870s, and the Japanese, instituted and realized after the Meiji restoration of 1868. Other examples would include the Atatürk revolution in Turkey in 1921 and, some would argue, the Nasserite revolution in Egypt in 1952. Certainly the question of which historical cases can legitimately be included here is secondary to the major, theoretical question of whether the category is itself justifiable; it can be argued that there is something inherent in any definition of the word revolution that requires it to be effected by a substantial measure of mass action independent of and directed against the existing state apparatus. But the justifications advanced for this category of elite revolutions appear to us legitimate. The German and Japanese transformations were effected by radical sectors of the state apparatus and at the same time effected the transition of their respective societies to a new mode of production.[14] The concept of revolution from above is therefore one which, sparingly used, has a valid application: whether such revolutions can be socialist as well as capitalist, and whether Ethiopia's revolution can legitimately be included in either category, are separate matters.

[14] The tensions produced in both cases by this form of transition are examined in Barrington Moore Jr, *Social Origins of Dictatorship and Democracy* London 1967.

On the basis of her study of Japan and Turkey Ellen Kay Trimberger proposes five criteria for revolution from above:[15]

1. the revolution is organized and led by high military and sometimes high civilian bureaucrats of the old regime;
2. 'there is little or no mass participation in the revolutionary takeover or in the initiation of change';
3. the takeover and change are accompanied by little violence or resistance;
4. the change is undertaken in 'a pragmatic, step by step manner, with little appeal to radical ideology';
5. 'military bureaucrats who lead a revolution from above destroy the economic and political base of the aristocracy or upper class'.

If the fifth criterion specifies why the process can be called revolution, the other four identify what its specific operational features are. Some of these features may be deemed desirable, in the light of other revolutionary experiences: the lack of terror, and the cautious piecemeal approach facilitate a greater degree of consent than may be possible in other processes. But Trimberger also stresses that there are limits inherent in any such process. One reason for this is the failure on the part of state officials to mobilize popular forces, which necessarily limits the process of rupture with surviving sections of the ruling class. She adds a more questionable limit, namely the capacity to break the ties of dependence on foreign capital.[16] While suggesting that the incidence of revolution from above may increase, given the tensions within the Third World and the increasingly nationalistic

---

[15] Ellen Kay Trimberger, *Revolution from Above: Military Bureaucrats and Development in Japan, Turkey, Egypt and Peru*, New Brunswick, New Jersey, 1977, p. 3.

[16] Trimberger particularly stresses the fact that such limits are likely to have greater effect in later instances of revolution from above, such as Egypt and Peru, than in earlier cases, because of what she sees as the much greater strength of ties of dependence in the late twentieth century. This approach to the international dimensions of revolution from above is debatable. She stresses the need for autarky, economic self-sufficiency, and cites Egypt's continued reliance on foreign capital as one of the reasons for its failure to industrialize (pp. 164–7). This poses certain problems. First, very few Third World countries can hope for sustained growth

character of the military, she argues that such transformations must in the end be more limited than their apparently less radical predecessors.[17]

Analysing the genesis of revolution from above in the Japanese and Turkish instances, Trimberger identifies five salient factors. First, using a particular version of the concept of autonomy, she argues that the officer class, or at least one segment of it, should be autonomous or independent of those who control the means of production. Where, for example, an *ancien régime* has recruited its officers from previously disfavoured sectors, who do not own land, then such an autonomous group can emerge. Second, the military must 'develop political cohesion' by championing a nationalist cause against foreign domination, or by championing economic development and social change in arrested societies. Third, such revolutions from above are precipitated 'in response to movements in the country demanding an end to national degradation by foreign powers'. The military bureaucrats respond to the 'push of violence and disruption from below'. Fourth, such military radicals take advantage of favourable international circumstances: either the major powers are less able to intervene than would otherwise be the case, or the threat of outside intervention itself fosters a revolutionary climate. Finally, successful revolutions in Japan and Turkey were made possible by the creation of 'counter-governments' in provincial areas which then successfully challenged the centralized states.

Whilst all such political typologies tend to abstract specific

---

through autarky: even China, with one billion people, has had to abandon that path. The international precondition for consolidating such revolutions is not self-sufficiency, but rather substantial economic aid from alternative sources. This is something the post-capitalist states have found themselves unable to provide in adequate quantities, the case of Cuba being the one exception. Second, Egypt under Nasser did not remain 'dependent' on international capitalism; it was tied to the economy of the USSR, but was unable to take advantage of the (limited) advantages that this presented. Third, the thesis that 'dependence' on international capitalism prevents industrial growth is questionable: the average annual growth rate of Egyptian manufacturing in the Nasserite period (1960–70) was 4.7 per cent; the rate under Sadat, when 'dependency' grew (1970–78), was 7.6 per cent (*World Development Report* 1980 p. 112).

[17] Trimberger, pp. 173–5.

features of a historical process from the context of the formation within which it occurs, it is relevant to note how Ethiopia is in certain respects a vindication of this model. At the same time it poses certain problems that highlight difficulties in the concept itself. The five criteria of genesis certainly apply to the Ethiopian instance and seem to allay Trimberger's caution about how far the full Japanese-Turkish model can apply in the late twentieth century. First, the revolution in Ethiopia was carried through precisely by such an autonomous and radical sector of the state apparatus, the officers of the PMAC. Second, the ideology of the military was both nationalist and modernizing – directed against the corruption of the Solomonic regime, against US domination and, so the officers claimed, against the weakening of the state by 'secessionist' movements. It was this ideology that provided the PMAC's 'political cohesion'. Third, the military framed their programme and seized power precisely in a context in which several years of student unrest, and then weeks of civilian mobilization in early 1974, had created a new political conjuncture in the country. Fourth, the international circumstances were favourable in both the respects that Trimberger identifies: the USA was weakened by its experience in Vietnam and its disagreements with Haile Selassie and so was unwilling to intervene to save him; moreover, the Somali invasion of 1977 and the persistent image of an Arab-Muslim assault upon the Christian highlands was used by the military to rally public opinion.

Trimberger notes that in the later-twentieth-century cases of Egypt and Peru her fifth condition of a provincial 'counter-government' did not apply, and indeed nothing comparable to Atatürk's rising in Anatolia or the revolt of Choshu province in Japan occurred in Ethiopia. But one essential component of the revolution was a series of mutinies amongst the provincial military that broke out in early 1974, spotlighting the weakness of the imperial government at the centre. In a more limited sense, the weakening of the monarchy through the summer of 1974 took place as the mutinous barracks in the Addis Ababa region defied the ailing monarch in his palace. They formed a 'counter-government' in a striking instance of dual power within the apparatus itself.

However, while it confirms many of Trimberger's specifications and her general argument that such revolutions may become more frequent, the Ethiopian case appears to diverge from the given model of revolution and to pose certain problems for it. The most obvious empirical divergences concern the question of terror and violence, and the depth of social transformation involved. The Ethiopian revolution faced almost no direct resistance from the *ancien régime*, and in this might be thought to conform to Trimberger's model. But the land reform did provoke widespread resistance in the countryside, and the consolidation of the regime involved repression and calculated terror on a substantial scale, both against dissident left-wing guerrillas in the capital and against the revolts in Eritrea and other provinces. At the same time, the scope of the reforms was far more sweeping than in the other cases she cites. These empirical divergences reflect a deeper theoretical ambiguity in the model, concerning the place of mass action in such revolutions from above. For pressure from below plays a more important part than Trimberger indicates, and this is suggested by a shift of emphasis in what she herself proposes. In her account of what defines a revolution from above, she writes: 'There is little or no mass participation in the revolutionary take-over or in the initiation of change'. However, she adds, 'mass movements and uprisings may precede and accompany revolution from above . . . .' Later, she asks why a military bureaucracy becomes politicized, an important question in the case of Ethiopia, where officers exhibited virtually no dissidence in the pre-1974 period and certainly no sympathy for socialism.

The answer is that movements among the people help to alter the consciousness of the military. If one surveys the Ethiopian or Egyptian revolutions, or such others as the Peruvian of 1968, the Iraqi of 1958 or the Afghan of 1978, it becomes clear that mass action can play a major role in preparing for revolutions from above. It both weakens old regimes and politicizes the actual agents of change, the military bureaucracy. The two forms of challenge to the *ancien régime* are more closely related than a pair of contrasted models might suggest, and it is mass action from below that has a prior, instigatory, role. Revolution from above is not so much an alternative to revolution from below as an extension or fulfilment of a mass movement from below, where the latter is, for a variety of reasons, unable to go beyond the stage of creating an atmosphere of national dissidence and to overthrow the established regime.

In the Ethiopian case the greater degree of revolutionary pressure from below correlates with the other empirical divergences: a greater depth of reforms put through by the military and a greater level of repression. Both are consistent, mutually reinforcing aspects of the same process. It was not just counter-revolutionaries in the provinces who challenged the new regime, nor was it the 'moderate' opposition Trimberger discusses in the case of Japan and Turkey: it was rather the far left and the nationality movements that played a role in creating the revolutionary crisis that faced the PMAC. The irony of the Ethiopian revolution was that this most radical of revolutions from above owed its revolutionary transformation to the crisis of Ethiopian society and the force of the movement for change. But by the same token the new military rulers felt compelled to crush these competitors for power who had helped create the conditions in which they sought power and to do so with comparably greater ferocity. The force of the terror, far from indicating the incomplete nature of the revolution or its links to untransformed sectors of the former ruling class, indicated the opposite – the degree to which revolutions from above are prepared by mass actions from below, and the degree to which they then have to assert control over their precursors.

Dynamics of Military Rule

The importance of the military in post-colonial societies needs no elaboration here. Nearly all the countries of the Third World experienced military rule at some point in the 1960s and 1970s and this proliferation has bred a large specialist literature.[18] On the basis of the many available

---

[18] Ruth First, *The Barrel of a Gun*, London 1970; Jack Woddis, *Armies and Politics*, London 1977; Roger Murray, 'Militarism in Africa', *New Left Review*, 38, July–August 1966; S.E. Finer, *The Man on Horseback*, London 1962; Robin Luckham, 'Militarism: Force, Class and International Conflict', in M. Kaldor and A. Eide, *The World Military Order*, London 1979.

examples, certain general characteristics of such rule have been noted: their access to the means of coercion gives the military an ability to take power, especially in societies where civilian political and social organization are weak; the availability of foreign arms supplies and administrative models lends the military in Third World societies material and social support disproportionate to the endogenous resources of the society itself; their structure and ideology as 'modern' bureaucratic institutions give them a privileged ability to assume and administer state power; their supposed major function, that of defending the country against external attack, provides a basis for their adherence to an ideology of the national interest, devoid of class or other sectional representations; their hierarchical and secret command structures preclude democratic interaction with civilian political forces, or with the population as a whole. These are virtually universal features of military rule, yet they do not provide the elements for a socio-political theory of military rule – either its causes or its subsequent character. Indeed no such general theory of the political and social character of military rule is possible, because of the variety of such regimes, and the many different kinds of government they have established. Beyond the stipulation of these behavioural generalities, analysis of the military must debouch into analysis of the social and political conditions in which an army takes and administers power. It is often said that the military take power because there is a vacuum left by civilian forces: yet beyond being a tautology, in that any situation in which the army takes control can on some definition be called a vacuum, this is rather misleading. It conceals the truth that underlies such seizures: the military take power in determinate social and political conditions, in specific contexts that on closer analysis turn out to be the opposite of vacuums. These contexts determine both the nature of the seizure of power itself and the direction of policy thereafter.

One of the most simple distinctions relating to military regimes is that between 'conservative' and 'progressive' ones: between those designed to prevent or reverse changes in social relations, and those designed to initiate or advance such changes. Since virtually all military regimes claim to be doing the latter, it is on the basis of their policies, not their proclamations, that a judgement on this matter must be made. The coups in Iran in 1953, in Indonesia in 1965 and in Chile in 1973 fall into the former category. Those in Egypt in 1952, in Peru in 1968 and in Afghanistan in 1978 fall into the latter. The Ethiopian military took power in 1974 in a series of advances sometimes characterized as 'a creeping coup', but the net result was similar to what it would have been had the army taken power in a single day. Their advent to power can be included in the 'progressive coup' category, given the reforms they subsequently implemented. Yet the very category of the 'progressive coup' can itself be disaggregated, so that, on the basis of the varying social and political factors surrounding such coups, at least four distinct kinds of progressive coup can be identified.

1. There are cases of sudden seizures of power by conspiratorial groups within the armed forces dedicated to social change and greater national independence. Whilst all coups take place in social situations that can, in some measure, be termed ones of social crisis, and are preceded by some mass opposition and unrest, they are not carried out in any direct liaison with opposition political groups or coincidentally with mass protests. The Egyptian coup of 1952, the Iraqi of 1958, the Yemeni of 1962, and the Somali of 1969 are all cases in point. Whilst they could not have happened without a previous history of wider opposition to the regime, the military struck to a considerable extent in separation from the civilian opposition.

2. There are coups that occur after substantial weakening of the previous regime by civilian opposition action, and in which the military have a working alliance with civilian political forces but which are not part of a socially revolutionary process. The Peruvian coup of 1968 was one such case. So too was that in the Congo, where in 1963 the government of the Abbe Youlou was overthrown by urban civilian opposition and where, in 1969, following years of social and political unrest, a 'Marxist-Leninist' military regime took power.

3. There can be coups in which the military take power, but on the direct orders of a civilian political organization here acting through its military network. This was the case with the Afghan coup of 1978, carried out by the army and air force at the behest of the People's Democratic Party of Afghanistan, an underground communist organization committed to revolutionary change. The Afghan upheaval furnishes the one clear case of a 'revolutionary coup'.

4. There are coups that occur in conjunction with a process of social revolution. In cases 1. and 2., the society in question may be in some generic form of 'crisis', and there may be a level of mass opposition: but it would be inaccurate in either case to speak of 'a revolutionary situation'. The third type of coup may initiate a revolution, but does not occur as part of one. In this fourth category, however, much higher levels of mobilization and transformation – accurately termed revolutionary – have been reached and the military intervene as one of the candidates for the assumption of post-revolutionary power. The military do not on their own overthrow the pre-existing regime; they confront a regime already weakened by revolutionary upheaval or overthrow this regime in conjunction with such an upsurge. The conflicts of society as a whole may reproduce themselves within the military through mutinies and rebellion by lower ranks. The Ethiopian coup of 1974 can, legitimately, also be included in this category: it was not the military alone that overthrew the *ancien régime*, nor were the transformations accompanying military rule mere adjustments of the social order. This was a coup in the context of social revolution. It arose from and to some degree consolidated the achievements of the mass movements, whilst the upheavals that threatened the old order were mirrored within the ranks of the armed forces.[19]

---

[19] The claim that the conflicts within the armed forces are in some measure related to broader conflicts within society is self-evident. This does not, however, validate the implication that such conflicts, for example a mutiny by junior officers, or the emergence of a Derg, can in effect *substitute* itself for broader processes of transformation. Lefort (p. 112f.) is somewhat ambiguous on this point, as is the Soviet Ambassador to Ethiopia, Ratanov (p. 250n below).

If the context of widespread political unrest is essential to explain the advent of 'progressive' coups and to suggesting certain differences between them, it also pertains to the evident limits of military regimes that have come to power in this manner. For the greater the level of mass mobilization by organized and spontaneous oppositions prior to the coup, the greater the sense of these civilian forces that the military has cheated them of a triumph they would otherwise have enjoyed. Such speculation is a recurrent element in the critical literature on progressive coups: there are those who saw the July 1952 coup in Egypt as a pre-emption by the military of a socialist revolution that would otherwise have been attainable; similar analyses have been made of the Iraqi coup of 1958, and of the Sudanese coup of 1969.[20] Comparable retrospective analysis is common in the Ethiopian case, made all the more plausible by the fact that the level of mass mobilization and consequent weakening of the *ancien régime* had gone so much further before the military took over. Once progressive coups are seen in their socio-economic context, they appear illegitimate almost by definition; any of the civilian forces that helped to form the context can itself claim that the military robbed it of victory. Here again, the 'vacuum' concept is misleading. Only an observer unduly hostile to the attractions of counter-factual history would deny that *no* such situation ever existed; and it shows undue indulgence to the claims of the losers in the contest for post-revolutionary power to assume that all such arguments are valid. A judgement of probability has to be made in each case, in the light of the relative strength of the forces involved in the competition for power.

With all their particularities, these progressive military regimes are marked by certain constitutive weaknesses dictated by the ways in which they are formed and the contexts in which they wield power. There is, first, the fact that unless guided by a political leadership, military regimes tend to proceed in an empirical manner, from a set of vague if deeply held political aims, to more concrete social programmes, the latter often reflecting the local and international alliances they

---

[20] Anouar Abdel-Malek, *Egypt: Military Society*, New York 1968, pp. 34–46.

are led to make. The historical accounts of the Nasserite regime in Egypt demonstrate beyond reasonable doubt how rudimentary the Free Officers' perspectives were when they assumed power in July 1952 and how they only gradually came to adopt something they called 'socialism'. One of the determining factors in such cases is the growth of an alliance with the USSR which, for reasons both cosmetic and substantive, encourages a radical nationalist military regime to present its policies in the guise of socialism, however this is locally interpreted. But if this process of radicalization and policy development can be inflected to the left, by internal and external causes, it can also be inflected in a more conservative direction, as the later histories of Egypt and of such countries as Somalia and Iraq have made clear. The relative independence of military regimes in matters of policy may arise from an initial social and ideological imprecision that renders them ductile in ways that civilian regimes, more specific in their initial political orientations and in their internal commitments, less often are. In the Ethiopian case a similar initial vagueness was, over time, replaced by concrete policy orientations and the adoption of 'socialism' as the ideology of the regime. Again, it is possible to identify at least some of the internal and international factors that led to its policy changes. It would be mistaken to argue that the PMAC had conceived of its policy development from the very beginning, and equally mistaken to see its later decisions as purely contingent or as mere opportunist disguises with which to cloak its authoritarian rule. The ductility of the policies adopted by military regimes is a two-way process. The professions of socialist rectitude proclaimed at one time may, in different conjunctures, be replaced by appeals of a rather different kind.

The second major weakness of military regimes is that, despite their popular and often populist rhetoric, they tend to resist measures that would lessen their monopoly of power. As one writer has observed, 'their attitude towards democracy is at worst negative, at best paternal. Trained to issue orders, to carry through the line of command, to instruct rather than to listen, their whole outlook presses against any disposition to discuss with others or to accept democratic, collective decisions. In particular, their whole training and social upbringing makes them hostile to the idea of accepting the will of those whom they have been taught to regard as socially beneath them'.[21] In Ethiopia this tendency has been extreme, leading to terror and repression of appalling dimensions. Yet it would be mistaken to assume that, for this reason alone, no social revolution has taken place in Ethiopia or that, if one has taken place, it has occurred in spite of the military regime. The fact of the Ethiopian terror, for which the PMAC bears a considerable measure of responsibility, is not in itself inconsistent with the major transformation of social and economic power. What it has indicated is the highly fragmented and factional character of the combination of forces that overthrew the *ancien régime* and the violations of legality to which authoritarian governments are prone.

The pattern of military rule in Ethiopia cannot be derived uniquely from the authoritarian structures of power that the military project from their own formation on to the society they rule: it lies in a more fundamental and pervasive aspect of military rule, namely the pattern of class formation attendant upon the development of a post-revolutionary order. It is here, rather than in policy variation as such or in the command structures of the officer corps, that the greatest reservation about the potentiality of 'progressive' military rule has continued to lie. The class character of post-revolutionary military regimes cannot be derived from the origins of those directing the regime, even if this factor plays a certain role. For almost all army officers who come to power in progressive coups are likely to come from some intermediate social sector of urban petty bourgeois or medium-scale landowners, and their subsequent radicalization cannot follow automatically from any class-based intentionality. What is far more important is the distribution of social and political power under the military regime, and particularly the new patterns of ownership and accumulation that are created. However much such regimes profess 'scientific socialism' or some local variety thereof, the practical effects of

[21] Woddis, pp. 88-9.

state policies rarely amount to securing the conditions for a transition to socialism. Some states do proceed to a socialist transition from such a starting point, but it is more often the case that what has occurred is the forging of a capitalist order, one in which capitalist social relations are at least as important, if not more so, than socialist ones. The mere facts of nationalization and a substantial state sector in industry do not necessarily alter this pattern. And when an appropriate time comes, such regimes can reopen their doors to foreign capital and abandon the term 'socialism' altogether. This was the pattern followed by Egypt, and it is an example with wider application. The post-1952 transformations in that country were real enough, and created a new social and political order; yet it was the underlying processes of class formation rather than formal espousals of 'socialism' that indicated the underlying direction of the post-revolutionary system. If military rule is not the only means by which such processes can occur, it is nonetheless especially suited to such a venture. The Ethiopian revolution has been a far more profound process than the experience of Nasserist Egypt: but the possibility of an 'Egyptian outcome' is nonetheless present in post-revolutionary Ethiopia.

Nationalism in Post-Colonial Societies

The fifth chapter of this book is concerned with the place of the national and regional question in the Ethiopian revolution. Much of the international discussion of Ethiopia has focused uniquely on this issue, and in particular on the conflict in Eritrea. Whatever the motives involved, this has had certain distorting analytic effects. First, it has led to a distinct idealization of the Eritrean movement itself; this is so in the sense that analysis of its development is ideal*ist* because abstracted from the specific social conditions in which it arose, and in the sense that it is ideal*ized*, presented in a purely vindicatory light. The analysis presented here is an attempt to assess the PMAC's policies in a critical light, but at the same time to present a materialist and critical analysis of the Eritrean movement. This involves locating the specific socio-political context in which it arose and gathered strength, rather than presenting it as the inevitable expression of some eternal Eritrean national entity. Second, the focus on the national and regional question alone has implied that because of the PMAC's repression in Eritrea, no social revolution has occurred in Ethiopia itself – a bias that ignores the general historical tendency of all social revolutions to pursue centralizing policies. Conflict between a revolutionary central government and ethnic or regional forces is by no means peculiar to Ethiopia: such conflicts are common in modern social upheavals. Revolutionary regimes in multinational states have only rarely made concessions to ethnic and regional opponents in the midst of such processes. This resistance to decentralization was evident in the earlier bourgeois revolutions: the French revolution was strongly centripetal, and Cromwell repressed dissent in Ireland. In the twentieth century, both the Russian and Chinese revolutions combined the overthrow of their central governments and associated social systems with a reassertion of central control over minority areas. Whilst the Bolsheviks conceded independence to Finland, they were less indulgent towards those seeking separation elsewhere. This was so even where, as in the case of Georgia, the separatist movements enjoyed popular support and were socialist in orientation.[22] The Chinese Communists took over the nationalities policy enunciated by Kuomintang founder Sun Yat-sen, whilst allowing a degree of cultural diversity to the five ethnic groups supposed to make up the Chinese nation. His essentially nationalist theory formed the basis for undisputed central control.

In the late 1970s the revolutions in Iran and Afghanistan underlined the manner in which the dissolution of an old social system tends to strengthen centrifugal forces, even when these have played no leading role in the revolution itself.[23] A variety of Third World capitalist states – India,

---

[22] Nonetheless, the practice of the early Bolsheviks and even later Soviet policy diverged from that of the PMAC. See chapter 5, pp. 166–171.

[23] Although nationality movements played a small part in the revolution that ousted the Shah, demands for regional autonomy were raised soon afterwards by Kurds, Arabs, Turcomans and Baluch. This led to serious clashes with the central government, especially in Kurdistan. The revolutionary government in Afghanistan

Pakistan, Zaire and Nigeria – had also faced this problem: only Pakistan, divided by geography, was forced to accept secession. Certain characteristics of post-revolutionary situations militate against central governments making concessions to centrifugal demands. Some of these are political: their own precarious political situations make serious territorial concessions difficult; a degree of nationalism and at times chauvinism recurs in the tempests of social revolutions and may provide central governments with a mobilizing ideology; and the inevitable attempts by counter-revolution to undermine the new regimes lead, with varying degrees of justification, to a tendency to assimilate the separatist to the counter-revolutionary forces. In order to mobilize popular support against such challenges, some revolutions draw on the chauvinist political cultures of their countries: the ethnically different and the 'counter-revolutionary' are elided, and a commitment to forms of freedom may coincide with continued belief in nationalist themes that may even, in their new garb, acquire a new force. These political and ideological factors develop in social contexts where other factors enhance this process. In all situations of uncertainty and rapid change, there is a tendency for individuals and groups to fall back onto loyalties of clan, language or race, and to exhibit hostility to those who are different: loyalties to class or unifying political ideology may transcend such divisions, but it is naive to assume that they will always do so. In situations of transition from pre-capitalist to capitalist or socialist society, the very economic and administrative structure of the social formation changes, from one based on fragmentation and self-sufficient units, to one of unification, in a national economic system and under a unified centralizing government. For all these reasons – political, sociological-anthropological, and historical-materialist – periods of re-

---

proclaimed a new equality between nationalities after April 1978: but this was not sufficient to win over previously dominated ethnic groups and aroused opposition in the areas inhabited by Pushtun tribes, who considered concessions to other nationalities as provocative. The Zanzibari revolution of 1963–4, a profound social upheaval, involved direct conflict between the Arab ruling class and the African population.

volutionary change are ones in which ethnic conflicts are likely to increase.

The Eritrean and other ethnic conflicts in Ethiopia are not historically anomalous; they are characteristic of state formation in the modern world. They may also be less irrelevant to the future pattern of conflict in the Third World than consideration of them as the relics of colonialism would indicate. For contradictions of this kind belong as much to the historical time of post-colonial revolutions as to that of arrested pre-capitalist monarchies, or the decolonization of Africa. The explosion of the nationalities issue in post-revolutionary Iran and in Afghanistan suggests that ethnic divisions may well be a major facet of contemporary Third World social upheavals. The linguistic mosaics that underlie India and Pakistan, and many countries of Africa, indicate that the potential for even greater conflicts exists there. Nor is this a form of conflict unique to the developing world: the recent histories of Britain and Spain, or Canada and Belgium, suggest that national and regional issues, often involving language or religion, do not fade away. They may resurface after decades in unexpected but tenacious ways. The ideological presentations of the Ethiopian conflicts espoused by the central government and its regional opponents find their parallels in many countries of the contemporary world.[24]

Misinterpretation of the character of nationalism, at the centre and in the regions, can lead not merely to the misinterpretation of revolutions; it may also lead to the neglect or partisan distortion of one of the central issues of the post-colonial world. For the nationalism of the developing countries is increasingly directed not against the colonial powers of the imperial age but against other countries and ethnic groups within the Third World itself. This is evident

---

[24] As one Kurdish writer, Ismet Sheriff Vanly, has written: 'Within the artificial frontiers inherited from imperialism, many Third World states practise a "poor people's colonialism". It is directed against often sizeable minorities, and is both more ferocious and more harmful than the classical type. The effects of economic exploitation are aggravated by an almost total absence of local development and by a level of national oppression fuelled by chauvinism and unrestrained by the democratic traditions which in the past usually limited the more extreme forms of injustice under the old colonialism' (Gerard Chaliand, ed., *People Without a Country, The Kurds and Kurdistan*, London 1980, pp. 204–5).

in the growing oppression of minorities in Third World countries, and in the growing number of wars between Third World states, of which that between Ethiopia and Somalia is only one. Yet the increasingly intra–Third World character of contemporary nationalism is also evident from the pattern of political change in the revolutionary states themselves: indeed, it is in this regard that one of the starkest and most negative features of the revolutions of the 1970s can be identified. Far from leading to greater emancipation from oppression or to greater tolerance, some revolutions have instead led to new outbreaks of repression and racism amongst these Third World peoples. It may be argued that such chauvinisms are themselves the relic of the colonial period, or that the rise of conflicts within the Third World is a product of the continued machinations of outside parties. Both claims have some validity: the historical antagonisms of some Third World peoples do owe much to imperial patterns of division and domination, and the intensity of some Third World conflicts has certainly been exacerbated by external forces – the latter is true, for example, of the Ethiopian–Somali conflict. But such attributions are of limited value, especially as they too often serve to reinforce the propensity of Third World nationalists to cast all their opponents as in some way tools of an imperialist agency.

This quite pervasive feature of the political cultures of the Third World has its obvious historical roots: it is a reflection of past domination, which continues to shape modes of thinking beyond the time when it was truly effective. It also reflects some recognition of the enduring influence of the developed world in the Third World. Yet in the overblown form in which it normally arises, it is not an emancipatory perception of foreign control, but an ultimately paralysing and enslaving paranoia. It justifies passivity in the face of internally generated chauvinisms, the repression of legitimate democratic movements amongst national minorities, and the jingoistic mobilization of indigenous populations against fellow Third World peoples. The truth that the intra–Third World wars and the post-colonial revolutions of the 1970s together underline is that, given the passing of colonial domination, nationalism in the Third World may take on an increasingly regressive character. This, rather than the ever-resourceful machinations of imperialism, is the tragic lesson of the Eritrean experience in Ethiopia: it is a phenomenon that the USSR and its allies have done little to mitigate, but have rather chosen to compound with ideological and material support spuriously justified.

International Determinations

The role of external factors in shaping the course and consequences of the Ethiopian revolution, the theme of chapter 6, has been subject to many interpretations, not least because of the many general theories or preconceptions concerning how far revolution in the Third World is internationally determined. Recent theoretical literature on revolutions has, to a greater extent than previously, emphasized the international dimensions of the specific national structural crises from which revolutions emerge. Empirical observation too suggests ways in which external factors take effect: in quite a number of cases, the regime that is overthrown by an internal revolutionary movement has been already seriously weakened by an international confrontation, and such revolutionary movements often draw support, whether moral or material, from outside their own country. Discussion of revolutions in the Third World itself is, for its part, often shaped by the prevailing political culture of 'agency' and 'conspiracy' already alluded to: the Shah of Iran, for example, appears to have sincerely believed that the American and British governments played a major role in his downfall, whilst his opponents continue to see 'the hand of America' in all political events in their country both before and after the 1979 revolution there. As in the analysis of nationalism, so here, the proclivity of Third World political actors to reduce the course of history to the interventions of one or other external power points to a real and visible level of foreign participation, both historical and contemporary; but it may also occlude the workings of internal and local forces by attributing everything to demonologically conceived international factors.

Some analyses of Ethiopia give considerable, and even

primary, importance to external forces: for example, to the role of Soviet and Cuban military aid, or to the encouragement provided by Arab and Western states to the Eritreans and Somalis. Such interpretations derive all too often from preconceived political schemes, whether the reductionism of East–West relations prevalent amongst writers in the developed Western societies, or the reductionism of Third World political cultures; and they elucidate only a part of what has taken place. They often fail to identify the internal conditions that were necessary for the external factors to have their effect. They overstate the degree to which external forces can control local forces. They enable events to be seen in uniquely polemical lights. It is noteworthy, moreover, that the attribution of external agency is always made to those to whom the attributor is opposed, never to those whose cause is considered just. Yet none of the major protagonists in the Horn of Africa conflict of the 1970s was primarily acting at the behest of forces external to the region. Nor were the international dimensions of these conflicts an initiatory factor in the worsening of East–West relations. In both regional and wider terms, the error of overstating external determination occludes the manner in which local forces and conflicts were able to mature, and only then to acquire international support.

At first sight, indeed, it would seem that external forces were remarkably absent from the course of events in the Horn. The very lack of a strong colonial past in Ethiopia, and the low level of foreign investment, were distinguishing features of the *ancien régime*. When the crisis developed in 1973–4, the USA, although allied to Haile Selassie for three decades past, was unable and disinclined to play a significant role in events, either for or against the revolution. Nor, on the other side, did any identifiable external forces play a role in the revolutionary upsurge of 1974 or the subsequent evolution of PMAC disputes. The irredentist proclivities of the Somali government were, for their part, generated by the history and social structure of Somalia itself. Whilst the Somali government sought foreign assistance, there is no direct sense in which Somalia could be seen as having acted at the behest of others, of having done something it would not otherwise have done. The Eritreans too were nobody's clients: whilst deriving military sustenance from outside, their movement was a product of the manner in which Ethiopia itself had subjugated the former Italian colony, and was given a new impetus by the policies of the post-revolutionary Ethiopian regime. It was inevitable that those opposed to one or other of the local actors should seek to deny its indigenous genesis. Yet, whilst each actor sought assistance from outside, and whilst the capacity of these actors was certainly enhanced by the assistance received, each was nonetheless implanted within the social formations and the history of the Horn itself. It was the character of this implantation that primarily determined how these forces were able to advance their respective causes. It is, therefore, a matter of importance, both in elucidating the Ethiopian revolution and in constructing a more general analysis of the role of international factors in specific revolutions, to identify how much external elements did, and did not, influence the course of the Ethiopian revolution.

In certain definite respects, events in the Horn during the 1970s must be seen as having been in part caused, and in part influenced, by external factors. In the first place, there is Skočpol's trans-national dimension, in terms of which every specific revolution must be seen.[25] Skočpol identifies such factors as the global yet uneven incorporation of countries into an international capitalist system, and the transformation of states by the need to compete internationally. These, certainly, underlay the French, Russian and Chinese revolutions. In the Ethiopian case, it is evident that the former played an important, indeed determinant, part in bringing about the structural crisis of the 1970s, as well as in providing some of the specific conjunctural elements, such as the rise in oil prices, that sparked the explosion of February 1974. The spread of capitalist relations and the maturing of the agrarian crisis in Ethiopia in the early 1970s resulted from the manner in which, however belatedly, the country was being incorporated into the world market. The second of Skočpol's considerations, international state competition, is also per-

[25] Skočpol, pp. 19–24.

tinent to Ethiopia. The Italian invasion and, later, competition with Somalia, did stimulate changes in state policy; but trans-national competition worked in another, more important, dimension. Ethiopia was not independent in the same way as absolutist Russia or France: its state structure in the post-war epoch was reliant upon assistance from abroad, on the financial assistance and military aid provided by the USA.[26] While external support enabled it to dispense with transformations of the domestic economy that might have otherwise been necessary, it had two other consequences that were to induce the revolution: as we have seen, it detached the state apparatus increasingly from the society and thereby allowed the agrarian crisis to assume even more acute dimensions; and it led to a conflict within the state apparatus itself between those who were affiliates of the *ancien régime* and those younger, educated people who, in both the civilian and military sector, were increasingly aware of the contrast between Ethiopia's condition and that of the rest of the world.

What was true of Ethiopia was, in different circumstances, also true of the Eritreans and Somalis. The nationalist movements in both countries had arisen in societies that had been affected to a much greater degree than Ethiopia by colonial administration and capitalist transformation. Their political experiences also were influenced to a great extent by colonialism and by Arab nationalism, to which both were exposed. They were particularly affected by the issues of post-colonial border delimitation, since what both were in essence disputing were the frontier delimitations bequeathed to the Horn by the retreating colonial powers and the UN. In the Ethiopian case, therefore, the trans-national political impact was most clearly seen in the crises that erupted in 1974 within the state apparatus and, more generally, within the social formation; in Somalia and Eritrea it was a combination of socio-economic transformation with the particular historical formation and grievances inherited from colonial-

---

[26] US support for the absolutist state in Ethiopia was motivated by global considerations of rivalry with the USSR: this aid involved the transposition of this international rivalry between states, which is one of the elements identified by Skočpol, into a particular regional context, where a rivalry of a different kind already existed.

ism that laid the basis for their respective challenges to Addis Ababa.

A second and more immediate form of foreign participation was in the realm of military assistance. This is, of its very nature, a product of industrial societies that can most easily be transferred to other societies, despite great differences in social and political organization. It is a resource that impoverished Third World societies like those in the Horn are unable to produce for themselves. It is a direct and often very influential acquisition which can have a decisive impact upon a local situation by introducing a rapidly assimilable new material and political element. The availability of European military equipment was an important factor in enabling Menelik to establish his rule in the 1880s. In the more recent events in the Horn it is evident that the local forces would not have been able to wage conflicts on anything like the same scale had they relied on their own military productive resources. But the impact of foreign military assistance went far beyond the mere provision of arms, to include the role played in these societies by the armed forces themselves. These were administratively as well as logistically the product of foreign aid programmes going back three decades. Both in Ethiopia and in Somalia the elements that were to play such a central role from 1974 and 1969 respectively had been developed and supplied, administratively, financially and militarily, in this way. In the Eritrean case, there was no state-to-state military assistance of the kind seen in Somalia and Ethiopia, but the arms used by the Eritreans were all acquired from outside, and their political and administrative structures owed much to the influence of Arab left-wing groups, if not to the structures of some of the assisting states, such as Syria and Iraq, themselves.[27]

[27] The influence of external military formation is evident in the biographies of some of the main protagonists in the Horn of Africa conflicts. All three chairmen of the PMAC – Aman Andom, Teferi Benti, Mengistu Haile-Mariam – had been on training courses in the USA. Somali President Siad Barre began his career in the service of the fascist carabinieri, went on to work for the British, and ended up as chief inspector of the colonial police. The chairman of the Eritrean Liberation Front, Ahmad Nasser, is a graduate of Baghdad Military Academy, whilst the two leaders of the Eritrean People's Liberation Front, Ramadan Nur and Isais Afeworki, both underwent military training in China.

If it is clear how the introduction of military supplies into the Horn raised the conflict to much more lethal levels, it is a matter of some contention how far the actual levels of military supply led to results that might not otherwise have come about. The most plausible instance of such a reversal is the argument that the Soviet and Cuban aid to Ethiopia in 1977 in some way tipped the balance against Somalia, as it was later to do against the Eritreans. There is no doubt that the provision of Soviet arms and Cuban troops did enable the Ethiopians to achieve a more rapid and more decisive victory than would otherwise have been possible. Yet given its demographic preponderance, and the fact that it felt itself to have been invaded, one may doubt whether even the most debilitated Ethiopian government would ever have accepted a Somali conquest of Ogaden. Moreover, the weakness of the Ethiopian armed forces, which the Somalis were able to exploit in the summer of 1977, was itself not a natural 'given', but to a considerable degree a result of the US decision to suspend arms supplies to Ethiopia earlier in the year. Had these supplies continued and – probably more importantly – had the Somalis expected the USA to resupply Ethiopia to the level that Addis Ababa would have requested, then it is much less likely that the Somali attack would have progressed as it did, or indeed taken place at all. Moreover, the Somali and the Eritrean cases were more symmetrical with the Ethiopian than might at first appear: both the Somalis and the Eritreans were themselves fighting with a military potential derived from outside sources; and whilst the assistance given to the Ethiopians was certainly greatest in quantity, this was a matter of degree rather than of an absolute asymmetry in access to foreign military supplies. The Eritreans were able to take advantage of a disarray that was bound to be temporary. The speed of the Ethiopian rally was in both cases a surprise; but the historical tendency of the Ethiopian state to assert its underlying strategic predominance was not.

Beyond the formative impact of the world economy and the specific contribution of military assistance, there lies politics itself. Twentieth-century revolutions are even less confined than their predecessors to closed political units; they reflect not only the struggles of populations against foreign domination but also attempts by states with a capacity for strong international action to influence their course. The inter-state hierarchy that has determined the system of trans-national economic relations also has its effects on political relations in countries going through revolutionary change: this has been particularly evident in the post-1945 period, when any social upheaval within a specific state has been seen as bearing on the global balance of power between East and West. However local their causes, these revolutions are situated in a broader environment that must inevitably affect their trajectory.

In terms of historical formation, the policies of external powers were extremely important: the USA sustained and shaped the post-war Ethiopian state, and Somalia was similarly taken in hand first by Italian and British colonialism and then, after 1964, by the USSR. Yet what is striking is how, in the maelstrom of the mid-1970s, neither side was able to control its junior ally. The USA was unable to prevent the collapse of the imperial regime and, having maintained minimal contact with the successor state, effected an almost complete rupture with it in 1977. The Russians were unable to prevent their Somali ally from moving further into the Western and conservative Arab camps. Both states demonstrated a significant measure of autonomy from their international patrons. Indeed, it would be possible to say that they were able to act as they did in some measure because of the accumulated resources they had already acquired from the latter. The turn-around in international alliances of 1977–8 was therefore not contingent; it was not one in which the policies of the great powers shifted for reasons of convenience. Rather it reflected important changes within the two countries concerned. Somalia fulfilled its long-nurtured desire and launched an attack upon a weakened Ethiopia with the encouragement of its new allies. Within Ethiopia a revolution that had begun in a politically inchoate form had by 1977 acquired more definite features, and was more firmly established. What was, in retrospect, striking about the shift in alliances was not that it occurred, but that it took so long to come about. Between 1974 and 1977 there subsisted a disjunction between the internal and international dimensions of the Ethiopian revolution that was overcome only with the changes of 1977. On Somalia's side, the gradual move to the right was to provide, via the Ogaden offensive and its consequences, the occasion for it to alter its own international alignments.

These are some of the comparative issues raised by the Ethiopian revolution. The most important question of all, of course, is what the character of the post-revolutionary society and state will be. While it is too early to be able to establish this with certainty, it is possible to specify some of the analytic limits within which this question can be discussed, and to identify some of the trends within post-revolutionary Ethiopian society that can be expected to contribute to the outcome. That issue, condensing many of the questions raised in this introduction with the empirical discussion contained in the following chapters, forms the subject of our conclusion.

2

The Fall of the Ancien Régime

A Legendary Land

Ethiopia has long exercised a special fascination over the world beyond.[1] Alone of the countries of Africa it escaped colonial domination and preserved its highly articulated precolonial social structures and culture throughout the period of imperial dominion in the continent. It was one of the ancient civilizations that survived into the latter half of the twentieth century, and therefore became a symbol of political independence and cultural continuity in Africa as well as for many of African descent living in the Americas. If the Japanese victory over the Russians in the war of 1904 had a catalytic effect upon nationalist movements in Asia, symbolizing as it did the triumph of a non-European power over the Tsarist state, it should not be forgotten how an earlier such victory, that of the Ethiopians over Italy in 1896, played a similar role in parts of Africa. In the 1920s, the West Indian nationalist movement began to identify with Ethiopia both religiously and politically, in a tendency that was to take its name from the ruler of the country, Ras Tafari, later known as Haile Selassie. The Italian invasion in 1935 provoked widespread opposition among young African nationalists: Kwame

---

[1] For a succinct discussion of foreign images of Ethiopia see Donald Levine, *Greater Ethiopia*, Chicago 1974, chapter 1. On the emergence of Ethiopianist cults in the West Indies, see Ken Post, *Arise Ye Starvelings*, London 1978. Throughout this study, we use the term Ethiopia rather than the now somewhat dated Abyssinia. 'Ethiopia' is the ancient Greek name for a land lying south of Egypt: 'Ethiops' means literally 'Black Face'. 'Abyssinia' is derived from the Arabic *al-Habasha*, the name of a tribe who crossed the Red Sea two millenniums ago. 'Etiopia' is the current Amharinya word for the country.

Nkrumah, Leopold Senghor and Jomo Kenyatta were all stimulated to organize support for the Ethiopian cause. In France there was agitation amongst Arab immigrants from North Africa, whilst in the USA there were many demonstrations by the black community, who clashed with the pro-fascist sectors of the Italian immigrant body. Even in the post-war epoch, Ethiopia has retained a special place in African affairs: for this reason it was chosen as the headquarters of the Organization of African Unity in 1963. Its elaborate social system, its survival as an independent state, its religious rituals, its variety of cultures and languages, and the personal prestige of its last monarch all combined to give Ethiopia this special aura.

Yet Ethiopia has also exerted a comparable attraction over the minds of many Europeans, for whom it has long had an almost mythical appeal as a Christian kingdom preserved in isolation over centuries, and as an African society that, with its highly developed social and religious institutions, approximates in many respects to the Europe of the Middle Ages. The reasons for this fascination were legion. The Ethiopian monarchs claimed descent from the union of Solomon and Sheba. Ethiopian Christianity fused orthodox pomp and doctrine with transformed Christian myths and elements of Judaism. Its art remained medieval in European style down to the present. In the later Middle Ages, the legend of Prester John, the Christian king reigning somewhere south of the lands of Islam was, like the tales of El Dorado and the accounts of the court of the Great Khan, part of the mythology of an early modern Europe seeking to push its dominion outwards and, as it organized plunder, to discover the exotic and the majestic in the world beyond. In the earliest account of his fabled kingdom, written in the twelfth century, Prester John is described as ruling over seventy-two kings and over the three Indias. In his realm 'were to be found all the strange beasts recorded in mediaeval bestiaries, including the salamander which dwelt in fire; from its incombustible envelope were made the Prester's own robes, which were washed not with water but with fire. In his dominions were also the Amazons and the Bragmans and the unclean races of men whom Alexander the Great had walled up in the cities of the north to emerge at the last day. His palace was built according to the designs of St Thomas, the apostle of the Indies, and contained a marvellous mirror in which he could see all parts of his dominions. . . . He went to war preceded by thirteen golden crosses, each followed by ten thousand horsemen and a hundred thousand footmen, and it was his great ambition to march to Jerusalem and annihilate the infidels'.[2]

If such was the myth of Prester John, the reality of Ethiopia was first reported to the European world by a Portuguese priest, Francisco Alvarez, who visited the country in the 1520s. Whilst falling short of the Prester John myth, his account was nonetheless one of a strange land, both alien and hauntingly familiar to the European visitor. Alvarez described the shifting royal capital and told how the king moved court, accompanied by four lions 'and a hundred men each carrying a jar of meat and a hundred men carrying a basket of bread'.[3] He describes the system of nobles, the Rases and the Shums, who surrounded the monarch, the elaborate martial structures, and the use of lumps of salt as a system of payment and universal equivalent. Alvarez described one of the most peculiar practices of the Ethiopian monarchy, the imprisonment of all the males in the royal family, apart from the king and his direct male descendants, on *ambas*, flat-topped hills that dot the Ethiopian countryside. He also recounted the peculiar beliefs and customs of Ethiopian Christianity, the multitude of monasteries and clergy, including a special order of canons who administered the royal churches and who were alleged to be descendants of the Old Testament priest Zadok.

In the centuries that followed, other travellers were to visit Ethiopia and bring back their accounts of this strange society. Even in the twentieth century, Ethiopia maintained its fascination, in part because it preserved its ancient political and social system. The European powers did not include it in their colonization of Africa in the late nineteenth century and the Italian assault of 1935 served, if anything, to give Ethiopia a new lease of life – both legendary, since the country and its

---

[2] A.H.M. Jones and Elizabeth Monroe, *A History of Ethiopia*, Oxford 1978, p. 59.
[3] Ibid., p. 68.

ruler were cast as noble victims of attack, and real, since the restoration of Haile Selassie to power in 1941 was accompanied by substantial new external support for his regime. Other countries in the Third World had similarly escaped direct colonial transformation and exerted their own fascinations: Saudi Arabia, North Yemen, Nepal, Afghanistan and Thailand. Tibet, like Ethiopia, combined many of the features which contributed to the Ethiopian legend – a strange, apparently preserved ancient culture, a close combination of religious and political institutions, a mountainous remoteness. Yet few had come to have the international importance that Ethiopia acquired, and none had social, religious and cultural institutions so apparently evocative of the European Middle Ages.

It was against the background of this legend, and in conditions of social upheaval marked by the realities of this enduring *ancien régime*, that the revolution of 1974 occurred. Whilst it had been evident for many years that the Ethiopian polity could not continue without major changes, few could have predicted the depth or the extent of the upheaval that was to occur. In one sense the legend of Ethiopia served to obscure the conditions within which the revolution occurred, since it had distracted attention from the abject misery of the mass of Ethiopia's population and from the conflicts that were developing within the imperial domain. The indulgence shown to Haile Selassie masked the catastrophe of his tenure. But in another sense the legend and the revolution are linked: for it was precisely in the conditions of an archaic and still predominantly pre-capitalist order, and in a society with many characteristics unique in the contemporary Third World, that the Ethiopian revolution occurred.

The Historical Background

Ethiopia is a country of 395,000 square miles, about twice the size of France with, in 1981, a population estimated at 31 million. The centre of the country is formed by a vast block of mountains and plateaux, enjoying a temperate climate and annual rains; 80 per cent of the Ethiopian population are agriculturalists inhabiting this area. To the south-east and south this central region falls away steeply to the arid lowlands of Danakil and Ogaden, bordering the Red Sea and Somalia, while to the west it tapers away more gently to join the plains of southern Sudan. The dominant ethnic group, composed of speakers of Amharinya and Tigrinya, was formed in the first millennium BC when Semitic invaders from the Arabian Peninsula mingled with the aboriginal Hamitic Agau people. The script used by Amhara and Tigreans is an adaptation of the pre-Islamic script of South Arabia. The first identifiable Ethiopian state was formed in the first century AD at Axum, in today's Tigray province. From the conversion by Coptic missionaries in the fourth century, Christianity, in the monophysite version holding that Christ had only one nature, was the dominant religion in the highlands and from the seventh century the Ethiopians were in conflict with the expanding forces of Islam.

The Axumite kingdom fell at some point in the seventh century and it was not until around 1270 that a new powerful Ethiopian monarchy was re-established – based in Welo province, south of Tigray. Over succeeding centuries the centre of this state shifted location, with the capital moving westwards to Gondar in the sixteenth century, to Tigray in the middle nineteenth, and then to Addis Ababa in the 1880s. But although the Christian monarchs were able to fight off attempted Muslim invasions in the sixteenth century, the kingdom was comparatively weak from the middle of the seventeenth onwards, with rival princes competing for influence and the Islamic nomads of Somali and Oromo stock moving steadily across the southern realms of Ethiopian influence. The tide was turned, however, in the nineteenth century under Emperors Tewodros (1855–68) and Yohannes II (1872–89), based in Tigray, and Menelik II (1889–1913), who established Amhara dominance based in Shoa. They were able to develop a strong state covering the area known now as Ethiopia, and to subject the Oromos and part of the Somalis to their rule. On Menelik's death in 1913 the throne passed to his grandson Lij Yasu. But he was ousted three years later by the Shoan nobility for espousing Islam and this opened the way for a young nobleman, Ras Tafari Makonnen, to assume executive power. He became regent in 1916 and, on the death of Queen Zauditu in 1930, had himself crowned as Emperor Haile Selassie I.[4]

The consolidation of the Ethiopian state in the late nineteenth century and its preservation as an independent entity thereafter was both encouraged and hindered by the European powers. The British sent an invading force in 1867–8 to rescue some British subjects, and in so doing provoked the Emperor Tewodros's suicide. The Italians were able, for their part, to annex the port of Assab in 1869 and from there gained control over a wider coastal area along the Red Sea which in 1890 they called 'Eritrea', after the Greek word for red. But the Italians were unable to impose a protectorate on Ethiopia as a whole, losing 8,000 of their own troops and a further 4,000 native soldiers in the battle of Adowa of February 1896. The Italian defeat at Adowa was a result of the same miscalculation that was to delude the French at Dien Bien Phu in 1954: they did not believe that their opponents could move large numbers of troops across hundreds of miles of country to confront them. The Tripartite Treaty of 1906, between France, Italy and Britain, recognized the independence of Ethiopia, minus the Italian province of Eritrea. It was an agreement where the requirements of international equilibrium prevailed over the demands of territorial acquisition, just as in 1907 similar Anglo-Russian treaties preserved the formal independence of Persia and Afghanistan.[5] When the Italians tried to redress the

---

[4] The pattern of conquest in the late nineteenth century has led some writers to treat the Ethiopian system as an empire on the European analogy, and to see Amhara rule as comparable to the imperialism and colonialism of Britain, France and so forth. The fact that the Ethiopian kings referred to themselves as 'Emperor' lent support to this view. However, if the Ethiopian system is to be treated as an empire, it must be seen as a pre-capitalist empire, with different motive forces and forms of integration. Its economic character is quite distinct from that of the European empires. Moreover, as Levine and other scholars have shown, the interaction of the Amhara with the Tigreans, Oromos and other nationalities was a process that had been continuing over centuries. It involved a far higher degree of cultural interaction than was the case with modern capitalist imperialism, and was as such comparable to other cases of ethnic and tribal interaction. The practice of describing Ethiopian governments as 'imperialist' in that European sense, and of drawing analogous political conclusions from this, lacks analytic foundation.

[5] The ideological factor, of Ethiopia as a Christian kingdom, may have played some further role in holding off European intrusion, not so much by restraining Italian policy as by making Ethiopia an African state to which other European powers could

defeat of Adowa by re-invading Ethiopia in 1935 they did not receive international support, and were ejected in a joint Anglo-Ethiopian campaign in 1941. Again, international constraints helped to preserve the imperial regime. In the post-war period, British and later US aid helped the Emperor to re-establish control over his country; although the British held Eritrea until 1952 and part of Ogaden until 1955, these areas were in the end returned to Ethiopian control, against the protests of a significant section of the population in both regions. Ethiopia therefore remained a rather isolated and apparently independent kingdom, until the explosion of 1974.

The history of modern Ethiopia has to a considerable degree been encapsulated in the biography of the man who, for many years, ruled it and represented it to the outside world. Tafari Makonnen, son of Ras Makonnen, a relative and courtier of Menelik's, was born in the town of Harar in 1892. His mother died when he was a few months old, his father when he was fourteen. While receiving the conventional education of a Shoan noble, Tafari was also educated by local French missionaries from whom he learnt to speak their language with ease. In keeping with the conventions of Ethiopian administrative practice, he was appointed, at the age of fourteen, Governor of the town of Gara Huleta in Harar province in 1906, and when, on the death of his father, he acquired the title of Ras, the young Ras Tafari spent some time at court. He became Governor of Sidamo province and in 1910 Governor of Harar. As the person in charge of one of the important urban centres of the empire, he was well placed to exert influence during the crisis that developed upon the accession of Lij Yasu, the Muslim monarch, in 1913, and when Lij Yasu was deposed in 1916, Ras Tafari, supported by the Shoan nobility, brought about a situation in which, aged only twenty-four, he gathered the reins of power in his hand.

---

plausibly extend sympathy and support. The precondition of Ethiopia's independence was, however, not so much a strategic understanding of the great powers as the establishment in the 1880s of a new central government capable of defeating European armies and preventing internal disunity that European states could have taken advantage of. See Sven Rubenson, *The Survival of Ethiopian Independence*, London 1976, pp. 407–10.

He was now Regent and heir apparent, and in 1928 he became king or Negus. In 1930, upon being crowned Emperor, he took the name of Haile Selassie, literally, Power of the Trinity. His official title was now Lion of the Tribe of Judah, the Elect of God, King of the Kings of Ethiopia.

The turning-point in his reign was the Italian invasion of 1935: judging himself unable to prevail over an army that was far superior in strength, Haile Selassie left the country in May 1936, to the anger of many of his followers, who continued a heroic resistance against the occupiers. His appeals to the League of Nations were in vain, and he remained an exile in London until the war broke out. In 1940 he returned to the Sudan and in 1941 accompanied the British troops that invaded Ethiopia and defeated the Italian occupiers. Both before and after the Italian period, Haile Selassie had declared his belief in the need for reforms: in the 1920s he had expanded health and education services, and sought to abolish slavery. In 1931 he announced Ethiopia's first constitution and in the post-war period, encouraged and assisted by his new Western allies, he took these reforms further and began the construction of a new governmental machine and army. But despite his apparent interest in change, Haile Selassie never implemented the reforms necessary for the preservation of his dynasty and for a non-revolutionary transition to capitalism. Following the logic of absolutism, the level of political concentration increased during his reign at the expense of provincial nobles. But the constitutions he promulgated, that of 1931 and the revised version of 1955, entailed no substantive dilution of his autocracy and no encouragement of an alternative social base. He had neither the strength nor the vision to implement the reforms for which there was so much need; in particular he allowed his rural reform measures, modest enough in themselves, to be blocked by provincial opposition. Not only was he unable to grasp the depth of the crisis that was gathering, but he laid the basis for many future difficulties by his systematic and institutionalized imposition of Amhara domination: the arbitrary handling of the Eritrean question and the humiliation of the Oromos and Somalis in the south were to generate profound resentments. His reign ended in a horrendous and eloquent episode: the famine that ravaged the northern provinces in the early 1970s and which he sought for so long to ignore.

For much of his reign, however, he seemed to command the reverence of large numbers of his subjects. The constitution of 1955 insisted that he was directly descended from the marriage of Solomon and Sheba, and that 'by virtue of His Imperial Blood, as well as by the anointing which He has received, the person of the Emperor is sacred'. His long years in office, his survival through the Italian occupation and his quick defeat of the 1960 coup attempt against him, all combined to produce an image of someone invested with special powers of survival. Even in 1973, when he belatedly visited the famine areas, crowds of starving people worked to cover the rocks along the road he would travel with white paint and to comb the hair of their dying children. In the end his opponents were to use his image against him: by carefully discrediting him in the course of 1974, and then successfully deposing him by decree, the young officers of the PMAC won for themselves a symbolic triumph of great potency.

The continuity of Ethiopian society was therefore far more than a myth. In the elaborate rituals of the Orthodox Church as in the ceremonial of the court there was a very real, if often interrupted, connection with an ancient past. The events of 1974 ruptured that continuity. Yet they were marked by nearly two millenniums of Ethiopian history and civilization, in a number of important respects.

1. The imperial state had not, despite appearances, been able successfully to transform itself into a functioning modern administration. The Emperor took all major decisions and his power in the provinces was weak. Aristocratic power remained strong. The newly-inducted state employees were therefore necessary for the preservation of this system yet ultimately unassimilable by it: herein lay the roots of revolution from above.

2. Ethiopia's only access to the outside world was via the ports of the Red Sea coast, and from the seventh century onwards it had faced invasion from that quarter: by Islamic armies in the seventh and sixteenth centuries, from the Egyptians and Italians in the nineteenth century, and again

from Italy in the twentieth. Any attack or separatist movement from that quarter was perceived by the highland Christians within this overall historic pattern of threat and attempted isolation from the Islamic/coastal area.

3. The ethnic diversity of the country was a product of both migration and Shoan expansion, with the Christian Amhara-Tigrean section, representing 35–40 per cent of the population, dominating the more than 80 other linguistic-ethnic groups.[6] Yet if Christians made up an estimated 35–40 per cent of the population, at least the same proportion were Muslims, the rest adhering to animist beliefs. By far the largest of the other nationalities were the Oromos or Gallas, making up around 40 per cent of the total population; the majority of them were Muslims, but there was a Christian minority as well. The hierarchy of administrative power and land-ownership established by the imperial regime greatly favoured the dominant Christians.

4. As a result of the fact that it had remained independent, the transition to capitalism was in a relatively early stage even in the 1970s. In many regions pre-capitalist relations of production were dominant and even commercial contacts with the world market were limited. Ethiopia remained a country where, par excellence, the bourgeoisie of the advanced capitalist countries did not, as the *Communist Manifesto* put it, 'batter down the Chinese walls', or 'force the local ruling classes, on pain of extinction, to adopt the bourgeois mode of production'. The overthrow of the imperial state in 1974 would have been impossible without the impact of outside forces, yet it was a task performed, in the first instance, by indigenous actors. It is in the effects of this belated transition and in the manner whereby it eroded the foundations of the imperial state that the structural causes of the 1974 revolution can be found.

5. As a result of the continued predominance of pre-capitalist

---

[6] No adequate census of the different nationalities in Ethiopia has yet been carried out, but rough figures indicate that there are over 250 different languages and dialects in the country. See Edward Ullendorff, *The Ethiopians*, London 1973, chapter 3 and Levine, chapter 3.

social and political relations, Ethiopia was marked by a very low level of integration at the material, economic and ideological levels. This social fragmentation was functional to the preservation of the monarchy, as it had been in the states of medieval Europe. But it was the very lack of integration that was to provide the basis for some of the greatest difficulties faced by the post-revolutionary regime and which economic development had to overcome. In the most basic material domain, there was an exiguous communications system: 14,000 miles of road, of which only 1,250 miles were asphalted, and about a third all-weather roads. Three-quarters of all farms were more than half a day's walk from the nearest road, and 40 per cent of the population lived more than two days' walk from any educational or government centre. There were only 50,000 trucks and automobiles in the country. This lack of a communications infrastructure pertained directly to the lack of economic integration: while the country was interlaced by trading systems, only a quarter of the agriculture produce was marketed, the great majority of the rural population living in subsistence conditions. In cultural and ideological terms, a similar situation prevailed: with overwhelming illiteracy, the population retained its primary adhesion to local communities of religion, language, and, where operative, clan and tribe. The ethnic stratification of the Amhara regime confirmed this. Even that most pervasive of ideological unifiers, the radio, was limited in its effect: there were at most half a million radio receivers serving 20 per cent of the population. Yet the relationship between objective fragmentation and political response was more complicated than might appear. The area of greatest political opposition, Eritrea, was one where a high degree of integration had occurred. Moreover, beyond the ethnic differences evident throughout the Horn, there lay a definite community of culture, evident to an outsider, that separated its peoples from the Arabs and from black Africa. The conflicts of the 1970s were not fought between strangers, but between the peoples who had been locked in conflict and had inter-related culturally for some centuries.[7]

---

[7] See Levine, pp. 40–86, for an account of the cultural factors unifying the various elements of the Ethiopian whole. The existence of stratification amongst these

Prelude to Revolution

On the eve of the 1974 revolution, therefore, Ethiopia was, albeit slowly and unevenly, experiencing the impact of the earlier phases of the transition to capitalism. In both town and countryside, capitalist relations and small capitalist enclaves were developing and were, to varying extents, corroding the pre-capitalist economy and social relations. Whilst there are reasons for qualifying these attributions, it is possible to describe the social condition from which the transition was being made as in some degree feudal and the state that administered power as being analogous to that of the absolutist states in Europe. The 90 per cent of the population living in the countryside were, in most cases, still subjected to pre-capitalist property relations and to the extraction of rent or tribute from them by a nobility and associated church institutions. Land ownership was extremely uneven with, on one estimation, 2 per cent of the owners owning up to 80 per cent of the land. This was to some extent masked by the official breakdown of households on the basis of their relation to land. According to these official figures there were 1.6 million owned holdings to 1.5 million tenanted ones and a further 447,000 households without any land at all. The real figure for tenanted land was believed to be much higher, rising to 65 per cent or even 80 per cent of households.[8]

The system of land tenure followed two broad patterns, one in the north, the other in the south. The distinction between these two systems was to shape both the manner in

---

various peoples in no way contradicts the claim that they share social and belief systems. The integration of Eritrea was because of, as much as in spite of, its separate experience of Italian rule: Eritrean traders and skilled personnel gained positions of influence throughout the country under Haile Selassie, a reflection of their higher level of commercial and educational qualification.

[8] On the land system see especially Patrick Gilkes, *The Dying Lion*, London 1975, and John Markakis, *Ethiopia: Anatomy of a Traditional Polity*, Oxford 1974. The application of the concept of 'ownership' to Ethiopian land raises many problems that cannot be gone into here. In the eyes of some, including Haile Selassie, all land belonged to the state, i.e. himself, and the grants were conditional and temporary. In practice this did not always apply and temporary grant-holders could in some situations develop into owners, with rights of legacy.

which capitalist social relations began to develop and the impact of the 1975 land reform decree. In the north, where the population was mainly Christian (Amhara and Tigrean), and where the historical seat of an Ethiopian state had lain since the fourth century AD, most land was cultivated under the system of *rist*, that is, by communities belonging to a putative common lineage. They divided cultivation rights among themselves on the basis of their relative influence and power. In theory the land itself was inalienable: no individual member of the community could sell the land or even claim continuous tenurial rights over a particular plot. In practice land-use rights were bequeathed by families or communities. Although *rist* holders enjoyed cultivation rights by virtue of their membership of the lineage and had effective possession of the land, they did not, typically, have legal title to it, and had to pay dues to the agency that did. These took the form of a percentage of the crop, at least one-tenth, corvée labour, or tributes of cattle and honey. This land in the north was held as fiefs or *gult* by nobles or by the church, which held an estimated 25 to 40 per cent of the total cultivated area. Those possessing *gults* did not have hereditary rights over the land, or estates, but they could levy taxes and labour services from the *ristegnas* beneath them. Their rights came with the offices they held; in return they paid a flat fee to the central authority and, when required, levied troops from the local peasantry. Hence, although having permanent rights, the *ristegnas* were in practice tenants. Yet the *ristegnas* as a whole were not necessarily the most deprived in the northern area; stratification existed within the *ristegnas*, and below them was an inferior category of tenants who paid rent to the *ristegnas*, and who in recent times made up around 10 per cent of the total population in these regions.

This northern system dates from the sixteenth century, when the kingdom at Gondar was established. That in the south dates from the nineteenth century, by which time the centre of power had moved to the central province of Shoa, with the capital at Addis Ababa. As the Amhara monarchy extended its power south of Shoa to the Oromo people, it appropriated most of their land. It tried at the same time to assimilate part of the Oromo leadership through forced conversion from Islam to Christianity and by allowing them to retain some landowning rights. The main consequence of the conquest was nonetheless the confiscation by the imperial state of around two-thirds of the land. This was held as *mengist* or state land; it was used by the monarchs as the reserve from which grants of land were given to state officials in return for services performed or on retirement. It is indicative of the continuity of the system that right up until the early 1970s Haile Selassie was giving grants of land to soldiers and other state employees.[9] As would be expected, much of the southern land given originally as *gult* to state functionaries became, over time, effectively private property with almost no corresponding obligations to the state. The church too was able to appropriate a sizeable proportion of these new lands for itself. The indigenous Oromo population suffered more than the Amhara and Tigrean *ristegnas* of the north. The dues they paid were far higher – ranging up to 50 per cent or even 75 per cent of the crop – and they were ruled as subject peoples by a discriminatory Christian regime that garrisoned an alien force among them and imposed an alien culture.

There has been considerable debate about whether or not this system can be termed 'feudal', and the question raises both theoretical and empirical issues.[10] If feudalism as a mode of production is defined by the mode of extraction of the surplus – the payment of 'feudal rent' by the labourers to the 'non-labouring' owner of the land – then it can be said that feudal relations obtained in many parts of the Ethiopian formation. The tributes paid in the north could be seen as in effect a form of feudal rent, paid to the *gultegna*, whilst the higher rates of surplus extraction in the south also derived from the ownership enjoyed by the newly-created landown-

[9] Gilkes, p. 112, shows that after the war 48,000 *gashas* (1 gasha = 40 hectares) of land were given as grants by the emperor, in many cases to civil servants and army officers. After the attempted coup of 1960 land grants more than doubled, 80 per cent of them going to members of the police and the armed forces.
[10] For a good summary of the debate on whether Ethiopia was feudal see Donald Crummey, 'State and Society: Nineteenth Century Ethiopia', in Donald Crummey and C.C. Stewart, ed., *Modes of Production in Africa: The Pre-colonial Era*, London 1981. See also Gene Ellis, 'The Feudal Paradigm as a Hindrance to Understanding Ethiopia', *Journal of Modern African Studies*, vol. 14, no. 2, 1976.

ing class. However, if the concept of feudalism is expanded to include the institutional arrangements associated with European or Japanese feudalism then substantial divergences arise. First, the relationship between *gult* land and *gultegna* was not as permanent as that under feudalism: the nobility did have permanent ownership of some land, but estates as such were not the dominant form. Rather, certain families had a hereditary claim to political offices that carried with them *gult* rights. The system of appointments by the monarch to these offices was not wholly arbitrary, but neither was it automatic. Secondly, the relationship between land and labourer was more transient than that associated with serfdom; although the link survived in the north, the labourers in the south had lost their hereditary claim to cultivate the land. Hence the unity of the labourer with the means of production associated with feudalism had been disrupted by the confiscations of the post-conquest period. Overall, it can be said that the Ethiopian social formation, which exhibited a heterogeneous combination of social relations, was a formation that contained social relations analogous to feudalism: it was parallel in certain of its institutions but diverged in important respects.

Prior to the Second World War, when Ethiopia was invaded by the Italians and then reoccupied by the British forces that installed Haile Selassie in 1941, this pre-capitalist system remained almost untouched, except for Eritrea, where Italian colonialism had since the 1890s been developing capitalist agriculture, and the environs of Addis Ababa, where the demand for food from the urban population had expanded market relations. The first substantial alterations in agrarian production and social relations came in the 1950s when the state encouraged foreign enterprises to introduce mechanization in selected project areas, and when the richer farmers in some areas began to develop cash crops, in particular coffee, for export. Here a landless agricultural labouring class emerged.[11] Even market relations were in a subordinate position. On one very rough estimate for 1970, a

---

[11] David and Marina Ottaway, *Ethiopia, Empire in Revolution*, New York 1978, p. 18, estimate that in the early 1970s there were 5,000 'modern Ethiopian farmers' cultivating 750,000 acres.

fifth of the population, or 4.7 million people, was dependent on the sale of their produce for their livelihood, with the other four-fifths still living in subsistence agriculture.[12]

This partial transformation was certainly too slow and belated to resolve the problems of the Ethiopian economy, and it was the failure to resolve the agrarian question that undermined the imperial state in the end. At the same time, the processes set in train by this development of capitalist relations were themselves such as to pose new problems for the survival of the regime. First, there was already pressure on land in the north. The generation-by-generation subdivision of *rist* land coupled with a natural rise in population inevitably led to the impoverishment of some *ristegnas* and their displacement from the land, along with the sub-*ristegna* peasants. The mechanization programmes introduced in the Awash Valley, south of Addis Ababa, and elsewhere similarly reduced employment and pushed peasants off the land or displaced nomads who had used these lands for herding. This process was intensified by the encroachment of landowners on *rist* land, especially after the attempt to abolish *gult* rights in 1967. A second area of conflict arose from the attempt to increase production in agriculture and to remove obstacles to the development of capitalist relations. When the state tried to abolish *gult* rights and to increase direct taxation of those who owned lands by abolishing the exemptions to which *gult*-holders had traditionally been entitled, many of the latter converted their tributary rights into outright land ownership, thereby dispossessing the peasants who had till then had cultivation rights on the land (as in the north) or customary access to land (as in the south). In the north the landowners were also able to mobilize the *ristegnas* on their land against the attempted reforms, which were presented as a threat by the state to their traditional rights and independence. The measures undertaken by the state – abolition of *gult*, increased agricultural taxation – fell short of the mildest land reform, understood as land redistribution; but even these were successfully resisted by the provincial aristocracy and lower landowners on whose support the state had traditionally relied.

[12] *Area Handbook for Ethiopia*, Washington 1971, p. 403.

Third, the crisis of the agrarian sector was starkly illuminated in the early 1970s by a famine that ravaged seven provinces. It affected three million people and by the end of 1973 up to four hundred thousand people had died.[13] As in pre-revolutionary China, these periodic famines did not in themselves provoke the fall of a government, let alone a social system, especially as those directly affected were, at best, too weak and preoccupied with survival actively to resist the situation in which they found themselves. Moreover, the fact of the famine was concealed from the rest of the country and particularly from the more politically aware sections of the urban population for some time – to which may be added the indifference of many in the city to the plight of the peasantry. Yet once it had become an internationally known issue, in 1973, the famine did contribute to weakening the regime. There was no nation-wide famine; the toll of regional famine emphasized, by its very selectivity, the gross inadequacy of Ethiopia's agrarian and distribution system and the inability of the government to rectify it by basic reallocation measures. The students in Addis Ababa, in particular, adopted this interpretation and advocated appropriate reforms. Moreover, by reducing available food supplies, the famine contributed to the inflation experienced in the capital in 1973–4, which was, on some estimates, as high as 80 per cent in early 1974 (the rise in oil prices was another contributing factor). The international outcry over the famine and the Ethiopian government's attempted concealment of it also contributed to undermining the legitimacy of the regime precisely because it had always used Haile Selassie's evident support abroad as an inducement to compliance at home.[14]

Development of the non-agricultural sectors was comparably restricted. The only significant mining was of gold at Adola in Sidamo province, which the emperor appropriated for his private use. Urbanization was proceeding at about 6.6 per cent per annum and three-quarters of the adult population of the capital were migrants. But in 1974 the total urban population was only around three million, or 11 per cent of

---

[13] Information supplied by Patrick Gilkes.
[14] On the concealment of the famine by the imperial government and international agencies, see Jack Shepherd, *The Politics of Starvation*, Washington 1975.

the total population. A study conducted in 1976 indicates that there were twenty-five centres with a population of 20,000 and over, but only two, Addis Ababa and Asmara, had over 60,000. Close on half the urban population, 1.1 million people, lived in Addis Ababa alone. Industrialization had been proceeding since the early 1960s, at a rate of around 16 per cent per annum in the years prior to the revolution,[15] but it still made up only 4 per cent of GDP in 1975, and was confined almost entirely to import substitution. Food processing and textiles were by far the main employers, accounting for around 70 per cent of the total manufacturing labour force. The latter was estimated at around 58,000 in the early 1970s, concentrated in Addis Ababa (38,000) and Asmara (14,000).[16] We do not have accurate data on the ownership of these plants, but one survey carried out in 1967 indicated that of 489 commercial and industrial enterprises with capital of over $5,000, 385 were foreign-owned, and this pattern certainly continued. 'Foreign' capital, however, was predominantly that of expatriate Italians, Greek, Lebanese and Armenian residents in Ethiopia. Artisanal production was much less developed than might have been expected, in comparison with other countries – such as nineteenth-century Egypt or India – at comparable stages of development. In Addis Ababa itself close on 40 per cent of the labour force was in the more modern sector – commercial or industrial – and another 22 per cent in state employment. Traditional crafts employed under 10 per cent of the labour force, and a large number of the urban population, women as well as men, were in semi-employment on the edges of the expanding urban economy. In the early 1970s over half the labour force of Addis Ababa was reported unemployed.[17] The latter, often dismissed as 'lumpenproletarians' in Ethiopian political discourse, were to play an important role in the conflicts following the outbreak of the revolution.

[15] For the pattern of industrialization, see Gilkes, chapter 5.
[16] *Area Handbook*, p. 380.
[17] John Palen, 'Migration to Addis Ababa', in A. Brown and E. Neuberger, ed., *Internal Migration*, New York 1977. More recent work on the subject of 'marginality' has questioned how far the appearance of unemployment in Third World cities corresponds to reality.

Ethiopia is potentially a very rich country. Up to 65 per cent of its total land surface is suitable for some agricultural purpose, either growing crops or herding, and the World Bank has estimated that it could support a population of 310 million, ten times the present figure. Yet in the decade up to 1974 agricultural output was growing at around 2.5 per cent per annum, equal only to the rise in population. Ultimate responsibility for the failure to develop its productive potential – Ethiopia was the poorest country in Africa in 1974 and one of the half-dozen poorest in the world – must lie with the archaic social system that persisted there. This paralysis was accompanied by a remarkably low level of integration into the international economic system. Total foreign investment in 1974 was estimated to be $300 million, of which two-thirds was Italian and only $22 million American.[18] The most substantial link was via the state itself – a direct subsidy by the US government to the imperial apparatus.[19] Ethiopia had a permanent deficit on its foreign trade, and exports were dominated by primary commodities, in the first place coffee, sales of which accounted for over 60 per cent of total export earnings in 1965–75, most of these from the USA and Italy. It was therefore an economy dependent on one crop, whose price fluctuated widely on the world market and whose production affected only a small part of Ethiopian agriculture. Indeed, the absolute size of Ethiopia's coffee exports was meagre: at $300 million these were no larger than the coffee sales of El Salvador, a country with less than a fifth its population.

The Imperial State

The slow development of capitalism in the economic field was paralleled by a gradual transformation of the state, such that the state apparatus became a partial promoter of capitalist development and, at the same time, the site of a conflict between groups associated with this capitalist development

---

[18] Ottaways, p. 193, n. 36.
[19] Total US military aid was over half the amount given to all of black Africa, at over $270 million from 1952 to 1974. Economic aid for the same period came to over $350 million.

and those associated with the pre-capitalist order. The gulf thus created within the state was to be more than a reflection of the conflicts within the socio-economic formation as a whole: it became the politically most acute contradiction within Ethiopian society, the conflict that was to determine the fall of the *ancien régime* and the nature of the new post-revolutionary system. This conflict within the state would not have taken its fateful course without the other, more fundamental, socio-economic changes: but it was this intra-state contradiction that shaped the course of the 1974 revolution and the process of 'revolution from above' that accompanied it.

Prior to the Second World War, the Ethiopian state was small and decentralized – quite different from the colonial apparatuses that developed elsewhere in Africa. At the centre were the emperor and the institutions associated with him – the Crown Council, drawn from selected members of the nobility, the *Chilot*, or Crown Court, and the all-purpose Ministry of the Pen, the centre of the executive system. This constituted a compact focus of power around the monarch; in the provinces, power lay in the hands of the landowning nobility and the smaller landowners beneath them who collected taxes, administered the law and raised military forces when required. Until after the Second World War Ethiopia had no permanent army. The provincial nobility resisted central government, and the Italians were able to make use of this during their occupation when some provincial landowners, hostile to the domination of the country by the Shoan nobility, allied with the European invaders. After the war a gradual development of more centralized structures began. A substantial standing army was created, side by side with a civilian administration and the corresponding system of ministries. This growing apparatus remained, as was traditional, under the control of the monarch. The supposedly reforming constitution promulgated in 1955 yielded an 'elected' National Assembly that was filled by provincial nobles, whose only liberty was obstructive. At the same time, although the monarch preserved his power, this growth in state employment was accompanied by the establishment of a set of institutions within which effective dissent was slowly to mature. The civil service grew from around 35,000 in 1960 to an estimated 100,000 in 1973, a third of the latter now located in Addis Ababa itself. The armed forces totalled around 45,000, of whom 40,000 were in the army, with a further 20,000 in related para-military organizations.

The creation of an expanded and partially transformed state necessarily involved the expansion of education, even though the record of Haile Selassie's regime was, in this as in other respects, a lamentable one. In the early 1970s illiteracy remained at 90–95 per cent and only 8 per cent of those eligible attended primary school.[20] Yet the growth of education to something above zero produced a new and influential social category whose very existence challenged the traditional aristocrats and landholders who had till then monopolized the state. These new state officials were drawn from the secondary schools (total enrolment in 1970 was 70,000) and from Haile Selassie University in Addis Ababa (founded in 1960 and with 6,000 students in 1974, plus a further 2,000 abroad). Nearly all those so educated went into state employment. These educated people were used to staff not merely the civilian apparatus but also the army: for a number of years after the mid-1960s Haile Selassie drafted the best secondary-school graduates into the military academy at Harar. By the time of the 1974 revolution there were an estimated 20,000 secondary-school graduates in the army and civil service; there were 4,500 university graduates in all, 3,000 of them educated in Ethiopia. This number may have represented a diminutive quantity compared to the population as a whole, but in relative terms they were a substantial and ultimately unbalancing element within Ethiopia's archaic social and political system.

This pattern of expanding state recruitment is relevant to the events following as well as leading up to the 1974 revolution. The children of the most oppressed classes, in city and countryside, did not enter state employment since they had no access to education; yet those coming into the ministries and the armed forces were from a section of the population socially far wider than the traditional nobility, and

[20] Gilkes, p. 266. Markakis, p. 150, n. 3, gives somewhat higher figures.

a substantial number of Oromos (usually Christian, it should be said) had entered the armed forces. These developments meant that at least some of the social and ethnic conflict within Ethiopian society was reflected, in however distorted a way, within the state itself.

The main agents of the 1974 revolution came from within the state sector, yet there are no accurate data on the origins – social, ethnic and regional – of those who were educated and who later took up employment as state functionaries. Fragmentary evidence indicates that recruitment was disproportionately from the Amhara and Tigrean nationalities. Although some schools were located in the southern provinces, they were in towns where the Amhara settlers lived, and Amharinya was the language of instruction. Surveys in the mid-1960s indicated that over 80 per cent of students at university were of the Amhara-Tigrean nationalities.[21] Where Oromos entered the system, they tended to be from the Christian minority of their nationality. By social origin, most appear to have been children of landowners of at least modest holdings, in between the provincial nobility on one side and the mass of *ristegnas* or Oromo tenants on the other, the same category from which the lower ranks of the traditional provincial administration had been drawn. They were, therefore, hostile to the aristocracy. Information on the armed forces suggests that the top officers were mainly Amhara nobility but that the lower ranks of officers and NCOs were drawn from Tigreans, Oromo and, because of their higher level of education, Eritreans. In the early 1970s, Oromos made up 21 per cent of officers of the rank of Lieutenant-Colonel and above, 30 per cent of those below, and 40 per cent of the ordinary soldiers,[22] with Amhara representing 65 per cent of the top officers, and 40 per cent of the ordinary soldiers. Again, the information available, though incomplete and conceptually rather generic, does confirm that the majority of the intake were from families with at least some land of their own.

One further aspect of the Ethiopian state that merits

[21] Markakis, p. 182, n. 1.
[22] Gilkes, pp. 86, 247–8.

attention is its role in economic development. As most analyses of Ethiopia since 1974 have invoked the existence of what is conventionally termed 'bureaucratic capitalism' this point is of especial relevance. It has been shown that many of the first agricultural development projects in the 1950s were initiated by the Ethiopian state, on its own or in conjunction with foreign enterprises, and the state, often acting for the personal interests of the royal family, also played a significant role in ownership of the urban industrial plants. State boards regulated coffee sales, sugar and cereals exports, and held shares in a variety of textile factories; from 1970 the Agricultural and Industrial Development Bank was used to promote projects in both major sectors. These bodies enabled funds to be channelled to projects favoured by the royal family and aristocratic ministers, and also, where profitable, were a convenient source of extra income through various forms of corruption. The funds available for initial investment were, by comparative international standards, rather low; agriculture was not heavily taxed and much of the internal revenue, as of external aid, was used to cover the current expenses of the state machine. But the term 'bureaucratic capitalism' did denote a tangible phenomenon in the following senses: (a) the state played a significant role in promoting certain capitalist enterprises, investing more heavily than any local bourgeoisie, if less than foreign capital; and (b) these enterprises were organized in part to yield extra benefits to those state employees with access to them.

An overview of Ethiopian society on the eve of revolution would therefore suggest a society entering a transition to capitalism but still marked by pre-capitalist relations of production. In the countryside the dominant class remained the large landowners, who combined their access to the rural product with their control of the provincial administration. Below them were, on the one hand, the traditional rural gentry and small landowners with, on the other hand, an expanding class of medium-sized capitalist farmers producing for export and the urban market. Further down lay a much larger category of rural poor – *ristegnas* and sub-tenants in the north, Oromo tenants and landless labourers in the south with, in the areas of capitalist development, a small sector of petty commodity production and a new class of wage-earning agricultural workers. At the upper end of the urban spectrum were, on the one hand, the provincial landowners who invested in urban property and on the other the officials and nobles associated with the court. In between was the new and growing civilian and military bureaucracy that benefited from the expansion of the state machine but still had not achieved primacy over those traditionally holding social and political power. In the towns there also subsisted a traditional urban sector of traders, mainly foreigners, and craftsmen, with a clergy and a considerable group of semi-employed. In the few larger towns the population had been swelled by migration. There was an industrial proletariat, significant in size but small compared to the mass of urban poor. A substantial number of people were employed in modern services. Parallel to these lay the lower reaches of the state bureaucracy both civilian and military, who had not had the access to secondary education that enabled upward social mobility. It was therefore a transitional society, marked by shifting social relations. If we add to this the complex and overlapping rivalries based on ethnic and regional origin, it can be seen that each group in Ethiopian society was subject to multiple pressures for cohesion and dissolution. These rendered any accurate identification of the causes of their action extremely difficult.

Opposition Forces

In such a society, executive authority was, officially, the preserve of the emperor. The nature of the state was such that there was not even an official state political party of the kind other modern monarchs have sought to encourage. There was however substantial opposition, sometimes organized and sometimes not, which can be tabulated under five headings.

1. There remained considerable opposition from sectors of the provincial nobility who had never accepted the domination of the Shoan monarchy. In particular they resisted the attempts made by Haile Selassie after the Second World War to centralize the country and in some measure to alter the agrarian system. This opposition was especially noticeable

during the Italian invasion and during the rebellion in the late 1960s in Gojjam, an Amhara province in the north-west, by large landowners and their *ristegnas* against the attempted reform in agricultural taxation. This conflict persisted into the 1970s. The first cabinet introduced after February 1974, headed by Endalkatchew Makonnen, was to a considerable extent representative of this aristocratic element who took advantage of Haile Selassie's weakness to reassert their own power. Profoundly misinterpreting the challenge to which the monarch had been subjected, they were preoccupied with tactical adjustments to a system that was in fact about to disintegrate.

2. Opposition among the non-Amhara nationalities was the most evident form of political resistance. Although distinct from it, this type of opposition reflected the agrarian crisis: first, because of the coincidence of ethnic with class distinctions in the conquered south; second, because the fragmentation of the country on ethnic lines paralleled the failure to unify the economy. Resistance was most effectively organized in Eritrea. After its reincorporation into Ethiopia in 1952, in a federal arrangement, regional and democractic rights gained prior to the federation were abrogated. With the elimination of the political parties and trade unions that had grown up in the 1940s during the British occupation, new underground nationalist forces developed, first the Eritrean Liberation Movement and then, in 1960, the Eritrean Liberation Front. Armed resistance by the ELF began in 1961 and by the late 1960s was tying down much of Haile Selassie's army. Yet by 1974 the Eritrean struggle was at a rather low ebb: first, the ELF had split in 1970 and a civil war between the ELF and its rival, the EPLF, developed; moreover, in 1972 Haile Selassie was able to reach an agreement with Sudanese President Jaafar Nimeiry under which the border areas so essential to Eritrean logistics were closed.[23] In the south there was

[23] Eritrea is, officially, a province of Ethiopia, but the term 'Eritrean' does not denote a single nationality. See below p. 176. On the early history of the Eritrean movement see G.K.N. Trevaskis, *Eritrea, A Colony in Transition*, Oxford 1960; Fred Halliday, 'The Fighting in Eritrea', *New Left Review*, 67, 1971; and Gilkes, chapter 6. For an account of just how low the tide of rebellion in Eritrea had sunk by the early 1970s, see Mordechai Abir, *Oil, Power and Politics*, London 1974, chapter 4.

resistance on a less organized scale amongst the Somalis of Hararghe and amongst the Oromo of Bale and Arussi provinces. The Somali population in Hararghe had been under separate British administration from 1941 to 1955 and their sense of separate identity was reinforced when neighbouring Somalia gained independence in 1960. In that year a small Western Somalia Liberation Front was established in the Somali capital of Mogadishu. A separate and more active resistance was growing at the same time amongst the Oromo, who were being progressively deprived of their lands by Amhara settlers in Bale province, where from 1963 to 1970 a substantial armed revolt led by small-scale Oromo landowners took place. Although suspicious of the Somali state, the Bale rebels turned to it for assistance and from 1966 to 1970 operated in coordination with the WSLF. In 1970, however, this alliance came to an end, as the main leader of the Bale revolt, Waku Gutu, surrendered to the Ethiopians. At the same time the Somali state, from 1969 under the control of a military regime that was unwilling at that time to provoke Ethiopia, imprisoned the WSLF leadership. The Bale rebels then broke away to establish a new Ethiopian National Liberation Front, which aimed to unite all the oppressed nationalities in Ethiopia in a common movement based on a revolutionary socialist programme. Although they were able to sustain only a low level of military operations after 1970, the ENLF was symptomatic of a much more diverse growth of self-awareness amongst the whole Oromo population, including those resident in Addis Ababa itself, as students and as state employees.[24]

3. The most visible opposition in Addis Ababa itself came from the students – both in higher and in secondary education.[25] The first stirrings of student activity were in

[24] Interview with Hassan Ibrahim, representative of the ENLF, Aden, May 1973.
[25] Legesse Lemma, 'The Ethiopian Student Movement 1960–1974', *Northeast African Studies*, vol. 1, no. 2, 1979. The atmosphere of the student milieu in Addis Ababa at the time of the 1969 movements is summarized in the words of a popular song of that period: '*Fanna Metamara, Ende Ho Chi Minh, Ende Che Guevara*' – 'Patriot [i.e. one who fought the Italians and did not flee like Haile Selassie] Go to the Country, Like Ho Chi Minh, Like Che Guevara'.

1960, in sympathy with an attempted military overthrow of Haile Selassie, and the first significant demonstrations were in 1965, in support of land reform. There were further confrontations in which a number of students were killed in 1969 and 1971, and the students were the most vocal in their denunciation of the handling of the rural situation. They raised the call of *meretle arrashu* – 'land to the tiller' – and in 1973 a number of students from Addis Ababa were killed while trying to organize provincial protests against the famine. This radicalization of the student body inside Ethiopia inter-related with a separate and ultimately very influential radicalization of the students abroad, in the Ethiopian Students Union in Europe (ESUE) and the comparable body in North America, the Ethiopian Students Union in North America (ESUNA). By the late 1960s the whole movement was generically socialist and strongly influenced by the radical political atmosphere of the period. But at the very end of the 1960s a substantial division opened up in the exile student movement, distinguishing an older generation of students who had gone abroad in the early and middle 1960s from a younger generation, who travelled later in the decade and were more immediately influenced by the radicalization of the students in Addis Ababa itself. The leaders of the former group included several leaders of ESUNA, and a group of students in Paris led by Haile Fida. The second group had a following in the USA, but was based in the ESUE. They originated from an incident in 1969 when a group of students had come out of Ethiopia by hijacking a plane to Khartoum, in protest against government policy in Eritrea. These had later been given some training in Algeria and Cuba. Following conferences in Berlin and Los Angeles in 1971, the Ethiopian student movement abroad was irrevocably divided between these two factions, with dispute focusing on three questions. First, there was the nationalities issue: the older students down-played this issue, arguing that the primary struggle in Ethiopia was anti-feudal and anti-imperialist, and that the question of the nationalities could be solved in the context of such a struggle. The newer generation stressed the need for national self-determination, including, in the view of some students, the right to secession. The particular issue of the relationship between the Ethiopian opposition and the ELF was an acute one, compounded by the fact that many of the second-generation students, including those on the plane hijacked in 1969, were of Eritrean or Tigrean origin.[26] Linked to this was the question of the form of student struggle; the older generation emphasized the autonomy of the student movement, and the younger ones called for students to go into the countryside to attempt a politicization of the peasantry. Finally, the issues crystallized around the organizational form of the exile student movement: Haile Fida and his followers favoured a unitary world-wide union, while the younger generation including Birhane Meskel Reda, one of the 1969 hijackers, wanted a more diffuse, federal structure.

By 1974 these two currents abroad had formed the embryos of what were later to be the two main civilian protagonists of the post-revolutionary struggle.[27] The older generation emerged in 1976 as the All-Ethiopian Socialist Movement, or ME'ISON, and for a time cooperated with the Derg. The young generation, whose views were more in accord with the Addis Ababa studentry, came into public view in 1975 as the Ethiopian People's Revolutionary Party, and soon afterwards launched a guerrilla struggle against the Derg. Both groups claim they existed as political parties prior to 1974; ME'ISON since 1968 and EPRP since 1972. Even though these are dubious claims, it is evident that the seeds of later conflict were sown in the disputes of the exile community and were later to assume monstrous form in the tumult following Haile Selassie's fall. Although the students inside Ethiopia were more numerous and more exposed to the realities of Ethiopian political life, it was the fractionalized and smaller exile community that in time imposed its intellectual stamp

[26] For contrasting views of the nationalities issue see *Challenge*, journal of the World-Wide Union of Ethiopian Students in North America, vol. XI, no. 2, July 1971, which advocates granting the right of secession to all nationalities who wish it, and the same magazine, vol. XIII, no. 1, February 1973, which opposes granting this right.

[27] Markakis, p. 155, gives figures for students abroad, totalling over 1,800 in 1968–9, the largest numbers being in the USA (523), France (193), the USSR and Britain.

upon the student movement, because of its greater exposure to revolutionary political ideas. In the absence of any identifiable communist party or any other source for socialist or Marxist ideas within Ethiopia, these exiled nuclei returning from Europe and North America were for a time to play a decisive role in the development of Ethiopian politics.[28]

4. Opposition was also maturing within the middle ranks of the armed forces, although it was only after 1974 that the extent of this became clear. Prior to the revolution itself there had been one revolt, in 1960, when a conspiratorial group within the Imperial Guard attempted a coup whilst Haile Selassie was on a visit to Brazil. The announced aims of the conspirators were moderate – permitting the retention of the monarchy – and no mention was made of land reform. Yet at least one of the conspirators, Germane Neway, was said to have socialist leanings of an ill-defined kind and in the brief period before the revolt was crushed by other units of the armed forces it was, as we have seen, welcomed by some of the students. After suppressing this attempt, Haile Selassie appears to have redoubled his efforts to prevent further conspiracies by dividing the armed units from each other. After 1960 no further public signs of opposition were noted, although one or two conspiracies were rumoured to have been detected.

Nevertheless a number of factors were undermining the loyalty, unity and political isolation of the army and paving the way for the mutinies of 1974. Many of the middle and lower ranks of the armed forces – a higher proportion than of the civilian bureaucracy – came from rural backgrounds. They must have been aware of the deterioration of the agrarian situation and of the inability of the state to remedy this and promote development. Moreover, like the students, an increasing number of Ethiopian officers were travelling abroad for training in the USA: by 1974 the total who had travelled there came to over 3,000. Others were dispatched

---

[28] A similar process of intellectual radicalization from without would seem to have operated amongst the Eritreans, who adopted first a variant of Arab nationalism and later amalgamated this with revolutionary socialist ideas.

abroad on military missions under the United Nations – to Korea and to the Congo. This foreign experience in some measure contradicted the assumed superiority of many Ethiopians; they were proud of being the only people in Africa to avoid colonial subjugation, a distinction symbolized by the presence in Addis Ababa of the headquarters of the Organization of African Unity.[29] Third, differentials in rank and pay were acute and resentment developed amongst junior officers and NCOs at the dominant aristocratic hierarchy and at their superiors. One axis of this rivalry was between those officers who graduated from the elite Harar academy, and those who went to Holeta, which specialized in junior officers. A final ingredient in the dissension within the armed forces was provided by the ethnic revolts, especially that in Eritrea. Because of their higher level of education – an inheritance of Italian and British colonial rule – Eritreans were to some extent over-represented in the armed forces, especially in the technically demanding air force. Yet there is little indication that sympathy based on regional origin or political perception played much role in the armed forces' response to the Eritrean war. Rather, dissent was expressed at the inadequate supplies and remuneration given to those facing the guerrilla enemy, and demoralization for these reasons came into the open in early 1974. Resentment deriving from such factors was therefore prevalent in the years prior to Haile Selassie's downfall. Whilst no definite conspiratorial group comparable to that of 1960 or to Egypt's Free Officers can be identified, informal networks, often based on common membership in graduation classes at military academy, certainly existed and were to appear in the wake of the emperor's retreat of early 1974. What needs to be re-emphasized above all is that the armed forces were not simply the repressive apparatus of the state, privileged by their links to the throne. They were also part of the small sector of Ethiopian society that was located

---

[29] The first proclamation of the 1960 military rebels began: 'It is clear that the fantastic progress achieved by the newly independent African states has placed Ethiopia in an embarrassing situation. The new government will have as its aim to restore Ethiopia to its appropriate place in the world'. Mengistu Haile-Mariam is reported to have said that he was greatly affected by his own period of training in the USA.

in the towns and yet susceptible to pressure from the countryside; at the same time they were exposed to the outside world. They thus introjected many of the conflicts, internal and trans-national, that were seething beneath the apparently tranquil surface of the imperial regime.

5. The part of the urban population employed in the modern sector had also begun to develop its own organizations, most noticeably the Ethiopian Teachers Association, and the trade union body, the Confederation of Ethiopian Labour Unions. As the antecedents of CELU have been a matter of major controversy in disputes since 1974, some analysis of this organization is necessary here. CELU was founded in 1963 and by 1974 it claimed a membership of 80,000, combining over 120 constituent unions. It was not a militant or underground organization, nor was it the creation or instrument of a political party. Equally, it was not simply an instrument of the state; it occupied an ambiguous middle ground, as organizer of part of the urban employed, the white-collar workers. They were too weak to challenge the state effectively and too substantial simply to be ignored. The decision to permit CELU's establishment was based on a number of considerations. In the aftermath of the 1960 coup, with its evident resonance in the urban population, Haile Selassie was concerned to make certain pre-emptive concessions. Moreover, he was being pressed by the US Embassy to modernize his country and this was one of the few successes such pressure enjoyed. Another factor was the regime's desire to set up a compliant structure through which the independent trade unions in Asmara, the Eritrean capital, could be destroyed in the aftermath of the 1962 assimilation of Eritrea into Ethiopia. CELU operated under the general supervision of the Ministry of Labour, many of its leaders were in receipt of salaries from either the government or the companies where they operated, and they were prohibited from recruiting a very large portion of those in the urban sector, namely those employed directly by the state. Moreover, most of its members were white-collar workers in services, a point that must qualify the subsequent characterization of CELU as in some sense a militant organization of

the industrial working class.³⁰ A topic of further contention is the link between CELU and the African-American Labour Centre, a body established in 1964 through which the AFL-CIO, and through them the CIA, maintained an active role in the trade unions of the continent. This CIA link should not be read, as the PMAC later suggested, to prove that CELU was nothing but an appendage of the US presence in Ethiopia. But most CELU leaders did receive training through the Centre and an estimated 1,000 members participated in AALC-backed meetings. The connection certainly had a strong political influence on the organization's overall policies and the International Confederation of Free Trade Unions supported CELU in the 1974 conflicts. CELU policies were limited to the direct demands of its members and in no way adopted the political dimensions associated with other African trade union movements that had been formed in different traditions.³¹

The 1974 Revolution

The archaic structures of the Ethiopian social and political system, which had survived the Italian occupation and several major strains in the three subsequent decades, were by the early 1970s in an advanced stage of decomposition. Yet the very durability of the system, and the absence of any visible and organized opposition capable of challenging the state at the centre, made it impossible to foresee what form the impending crisis would take. As with the French and Russian revolutions, it was a few apparently small and isolated incidents focused in the capital city and its environs that in the end brought down the edifice with surprising rapidity and initial ease, provoking a countrywide revolt in the process.

The causes of the 1974 revolution can be distributed

---

[30] On the background to CELU, see Ottaways, chapters 2 and 3. By 1980 Ethiopian government statements on CELU had become much milder, and it was seen as a precursor of the 1974 movement, later distorted.

[31] The African–American Labour Centre and its role in relation to Ethiopia is discussed in Rodney Larsen and Don Thomson, *Where Were You Brother? An Account of Trade Union Imperialism*, London 1978, pp. 54–8.

amongst three broad categories: the long-term or fundamental, the medium-term or contextual, and the short-term or immediate. The fundamental causes or the first group comprised what has already been termed the 'structural crisis' of the regime. They lie in the failure of the regime to resolve the agrarian crisis, to develop the country's productive forces in such a way as to improve the population's living standards and even, in the provinces ravaged by famine, to maintain previous subsistence levels. As has been indicated, capitalist development had begun in parts of the countryside and in the towns, and had in so doing somewhat weakened the pre-existing system. But the further development of this was obstructed by the character of the state and of the agrarian property relations. The inadequacy of development in Ethiopia was made evident by the international comparisons to which the educated minority, in the state apparatus and in the educational system, were exposed.

The medium-term situation expressed and compounded the agrarian paralysis. The Eritrean and Bale revolts, although contained, had stretched the resources of the state and were engendering a broader *prise de conscience* amongst other Ethiopian nationalities. At the same time, they placed a considerable strain upon the armed forces and thereby on the state's finances. Second, the famine in Welo served both to expose the incapacity of the state at home and abroad and to raise the political temperature in Addis Ababa itself, where it led to student protest and considerable inflation. This certainly weakened the regime's remaining credibility. Third, the very core of the state itself had begun to atrophy. By now over eighty, Haile Selassie was not merely visibly ageing but had no obvious strong support around him: his son Crown Prince Asfa Wossen was an invalid, his grandson Zara Yacob was of no great intelligence and his prime minister for thirteen years, Aklilu Habte Wold, was an ineffective courtier chosen for his docility. There was no element within the ruling group capable of taking perceptive or difficult decisions. Whilst this debility at the very centre, contingent as it was on personality and biology, was not decisive, it certainly played a significant role in the abject collapse of the imperial regime in 1974.

The immediate causes of the revolution were focused within the state apparatus and the capital itself. They involved the grievances of three significant social groups – the lower ranks of the army, students and teachers, and the taxi-drivers of Addis Ababa, an influential group in a society where taxis were a common form of transport for all but the very poorest sections of the population. The first incident has been rightly compared with the mutiny on the battleship Potemkin: soldiers at a garrison in the southern desert at Neghelle mutinied in mid-January 1974 to protest at their living conditions and in particular at the refusal of the officers to allow them to drink from their well when the others had run dry. When the mutineers imprisoned the envoys sent by Haile Selassie to investigate, the weakness of the central government was starkly revealed. A similar revolt over pay then occurred on February 10–13, but this was at the Debre Zeit air force base near the capital. This had a much more immediate political effect; on February 14 the capital was the scene of substantial demonstrations by students and teachers protesting the government's proposed educational reforms. In subsequent days they were joined by the taxidrivers protesting a 50 per cent rise in the price of petrol following the OPEC price increases. After some days of relatively unchallenged tumult in the capital related to these limited sectoral issues, the protest movement was taken a stage further on February 25, when the Second Division, stationed in Asmara, mutinied. Other military units around the capital then followed suit. Their demands were not merely related to their own concerns – a rise in pay and improved conditions – but also included the dismissal of the Aklilu cabinets. Political rather than just sectoral demands now prevailed. Within a few days Haile Selassie was forced to sack Aklilu and replace him by the government of Endalkatchew Makonnen, who was supposedly committed to meeting the demands of the new protest movement.

In one sense, very little had changed as yet. Most of Endalkatchew's government were from the aristocracy, which was in fact more strongly represented than in earlier cabinets. Their main concern was, as we have noted, to gain a tactical advantage vis-à-vis the throne. The army mutinies subsided for a time; their demands on pay and living conditions had been met, the Aklilu government had fallen. No opposition party or organization had lain behind, or emerged from, the February upheaval. Yet a very real transition had occurred. For the first time in Ethiopian history, popular pressure had forced the emperor to make substantial political and economic concessions and prevented him from exacting his traditional punishments. Moreover, in an intangible but universally recognized sense, the spell had been broken; it was impossible for the regime to reimpose political control, and from the end of February until June, Endalkatchew presided over an increasingly unstable situation. First of all, though noticeably absent in the February movement itself, CELU began to emerge as an opposition force, beginning with a general strike on March 12. The most important single demand, apart from pay increases, was for the right of those in government employment to unionize. After this was conceded, CELU's official membership increased by a half to 120,000. In the following weeks the trade unions and the students continued their strikes and protests, and in April a popular protest movement, led by students, deposed the local officials and installed a 'popular committee' in the town of Jimma, south-west of Addis Ababa.[32]

This ferment was, after a lull, reinvigorated by a visibly more permanent politicization of the armed forces. In the months after February a number of conspiratorial groups, with varying programmes and power bases, began to appear. At first the most prominent was the National Security Commission (NSC), based in Addis Ababa. It appeared to ally with the government and was used by it to crush the strike movement, especially that in the services sector. But neither

---

[32] Summaries of the events between February and November are contained in John Markakis and Nega Ayele, *Class and Revolution in Ethiopia*, Nottingham 1978; René Lefort, *Ethiopie, la révolution hérétique*, Paris 1981; and Ottaways, *Ethiopia, Empire in Revolution*. The most detailed account of the inner workings of the military in this period is given by Pliny The Middle-Aged in 'The PMAC: Origins and Structure', *Ethiopianist Notes*, 2, 3 (1978). Other accounts of a less systematic but often illustrative character include: Blair Thomson, *Ethiopia, the Country That Cut Off Its Head*, London 1975; Raul Valdes Vivo, *Ethiopia, the Unknown Revolution*, Havana 1978; Colin Legum, *Ethiopia: the Fall of Haile Selassie's Empire*, London 1975.

Endalkatchew nor the NSC was able capably to handle the most explosive issue of all, namely the growing demand inside the armed forces for the arrest and prosecution of members of the imperial regime guilty of corruption. This, more than pay or conditions, was the key issue raised by the junior officers and NCOs. Although it had a sectoral element, reflecting the junior officers' hostility to the top generals, it also served as a means of indicting the whole of the previously dominant ruling bloc and of symbolizing their determination to oust it altogether. For the politicized population at large in the streets of the capital, it served over a period of months to disenchant them, if this was needed, with the whole regime. In all, it prepared the way for the ultimate act, the deposition of Haile Selassie.

The situation had, by early June, reached a stage of superficial stasis. Endalkatchew had made no substantive reforms and, as a member of former cabinets, he resisted pressures to prosecute other officials. Haile Selassie appeared still to be in control. A commission to investigate corruption was set up only in the middle of June. The NSC had crushed the strike movement; the pay rises had been granted to the army and the teachers had had the educational reform postponed. This calm was, however, broken by the revolt of the junior officers based in the Second and Fourth Divisions at Addis Ababa. At some point in June they formed a new body, the Coordinating Committee of the Armed Forces, the Police and the Territorial Army. This 'Committee' – usually known by its Amharinya word, the *Derg* – was mobilized by Atnafu Abate and Taffera Taclaeb from the Fourth Division. It held its first full meeting on June 28, announcing its programme on July 2. No official account of its origins has been published, but the Derg was supposed to have consisted originally of 126 members, its members elected by each one of the forty separate units in the armed forces or chosen to attend by higher ranking officers. All were below the rank of Lieutenant-Colonel. The first vice-chairmen were Major Atnafu Abate of the Fourth Division, and a young ordnance officer from the Third Division who distinguished himself by a fiery speech at the first Derg conclave, Mengistu Haile-Mariam. It was a classic case of a body elected in a highly democratic, even haphazard manner becoming a permanent and irrevocable self-perpetuating group.³³

The period from June to September has been called 'the creeping coup'; effective power had been appropriated by this new military Committee, yet this was not at first evident to outsiders and may not even have been clear to the members of the Derg itself. The Derg insisted that a new constitution be put into operation and that officials responsible for concealing the famine be prosecuted. But they continued to arrest aristocrats, including the emperor's grandson. They forced the Endalkatchew government to resign, to be replaced by one headed by Prince Michael Imru, the one aristocrat long known for his opposition to the monarch and his sympathy for some kind of socialist ideas. The Derg's programme itself was not at that time in any way socialist, and focused instead on the generic phrase that was even then attributed to Major Mengistu, *Etiopia Tikdem*, normally translated as 'Ethiopia First'.³⁴ Yet although they initially claimed to want a new constitution that would allow a civilian government to emerge, the Derg gave evidence of a new orientation in mid-August, when they seem to have decided that they, rather than the civilians, should assume effective and visible political power. Simultaneously, they orchestrated a crescendo of accusations against the emperor that in a space of weeks made it possible for the call for his dismissal to be voiced openly. Finally, on September 12, a group of junior officers went to his palace, read a proclamation of deposition and after arresting him, drove the Lion of Judah away in the back seat of a Volkswagen car. In his place, the Derg announced that all governmental power would for the time being be in the hands of the new Provisional Military Administrative Council.

At first, the PMAC was divided in its policy towards governmental responsibility, some of the Derg members favouring a return to civilian rule. This was a demand quickly made by the students and CELU, who objected to the PMAC's alleged usurpation. By late October, however, the Derg

---

³³ Pliny; and Ottaways, chapter 4.

³⁴ In fact, the phrase *Etiopia Tikdem* was used much earlier, in February, by the pro-government Amharinya press – Thomson, p. 35.

majority had decided definitely to remain in office for a substantial period and it pressed ahead with the arrest of those it considered guilty of misdemeanours under the *ancien régime*. In the meantime, and in part to increase its national and international credibility, the Derg had chosen as its spokesman, though not as a member, General Aman Andom. Aman had led the victorious Ethiopian forces against Somalia in a war in 1964 and was known to have opposed the emperor. Aman did not, however, accept the dictates of the Derg and he resisted the call for the execution of the imprisoned aristocrats made by some of its members. He also favoured a conciliatory policy in Eritrea (from where his family originated) and made two visits there as part of a personal campaign of reconciliation. He never accepted independence but sought to negotiate with the two guerrilla groups. Towards the end of the following month, the Derg decided to dismiss Aman, and on November 23 he was killed while allegedly resisting arrest. Soon afterwards fifty-seven officials of the *ancien régime* were shot without trial, as were two members of the PMAC who supported Aman and twelve other military personnel. These executions were possibly a warning to other potential opponents, and put an end to the hope voiced even by the Derg in its first weeks that Ethiopia would have a 'revolution without bloodshed'. A month later, the PMAC issued its first policy proclamation in which it introduced the new concept of 'Ethiopian socialism'. This, it claimed, 'means equality, self-reliance, the dignity of labour, the supremacy of the common good, and the indivisibility of Ethiopian unity'.[35] Though the implications of the last phrase can have been lost on few, coming as it did in the wake of Aman's death, the rapid course of events over the next months must have taken almost everyone by surprise. Before proceeding to analyse these developments, we shall summarily review the main features of the 1974 political revolution.

Main Characteristics of the Revolutionary Movement

1. The revolutionary movement met remarkably little resist-

[35] Ottaways, p. 63.

ance from the *ancien régime*. This was the case both in the capital, where the emperor abandoned his throne of six decades without any obvious response beyond procrastination, and in the provinces, where it was universally expected that the provincial lords would raise peasant armies and march to punish the insurgent capital. There were no serious attempted counter-coups, and no significant fighting took place in the provinces at this time. The executions of November 23 were virtually the first deaths in a process that had been unfolding since February. The executions seem to have shocked much of the urban population, even if the victims were generally unpopular, and in the cold-blooded and secret manner in which they were carried out they presaged the carnage that was to occur later.[36] The reasons for the lack of determined resistance may lie in an apparent disjunction of objective and subjective conditions. Objectively, the bases of the old regime had atrophied and could not be drawn upon to preserve the imperial system. The lack of any decisive leadership from within the royal family or the aristocracy compounded this. But subjectively there persisted a widespread belief that in some way or other the emperor and the Rases would restore themselves, that the current dissidence was transitory. In the end, by inducing a fantastic confidence, this belief in the continuing strength of the *ancien régime* was to prove a weakness, of advantage to its opponents.[37]

2. The initial movement was confined to the two largest cities, Addis Ababa and Asmara and in the latter as in the former it was those employed within the state apparatus or who were candidates for such employment who led the movement. For the first few months the countryside was

---

[36] On the popular response in Addis Ababa to the shootings see Thomson, p. 121.
[37] The lack of resistance by the *ancien régime* in the 1974 period was, however, in contrast to the counter-revolutionary activity of the later years. This took two quite different forms. One was resistance by rural property-owners, tribal chiefs and disaffected peasants. It was very widespread and was a reaction to the reforms and the attempted imposition of control from the centre. It was, however, fragmented and hence not a mortal challenge to the regime. The other form was the organized attempt by outside governments to use conflicts internal to Ethiopia as a means of bringing down the regime: on which, see chapter 6 below.

quiet: it was only in the middle of the year that peasants in the southern provinces began, sporadically, to occupy estates. Apart from the April events in Jimma there seem to have been no popular upsurges in the provincial towns, and the call for land reform was, as it had been since the late 1960s, articulated primarily by urban protesters.[38]. Elsewhere, as in Harar, it was the military who deposed the local officialdom.

3. The movement in Addis Ababa, though generally popular, took a disparate and spontaneous form. It is apparent, but requires emphasizing, that no coherent political organizations existed underground at that time – in this sense Ethiopia in February 1974 was different from Russia in February 1917; in the latter case, there existed organized underground political groups even if they did not at that point control the course of events. There is no evidence to support the later, retrospective claims by either ME'ISON or the EPRP that they acted as organized political groups in 1974 and in any significant degree directed the revolutionary process.[39] Nor, despite the final outcome, would it be correct to see the urban protests of February and March as inherently revolutionary. Rather, they were protests by individual professional and trade union forces on issues directly related to their own economic position, protests made possible by the decomposition of government authority, of which these bodies took advantage. The attack on the nobility and ultimately on the emperor came not from the civilian bodies but from the radical junior officers in the armed forces. Nor should the degree of activity among the protesting civilian groups be exaggerated: to do so can only distort the level of political consciousness among these groups. Only a minority of the Addis Ababa studentry took part in the protests relating to education, and on the available evidence it appears that virtually all the strikes between early March and May

---

[38] There is considerable disagreement about the extent of the rural response; for contrasting views see Ottaways, p. 64 and Markakis and Nega, p. 96. The former write: '. . . by and large, there was no mass uprising'. The latter that '. . . spontaneous uprisings were changing the situation overnight'.

[39] ME'ISON was later to claim that it had been the 'inspirer' of the 1974 movement (*Le Monde*, September 3, 1977).

were by white-collar workers (in the post office, airlines, telecommunications, and so on). The industrial workers of the capital and its environs were, as noted, excluded from CELU.

4. The role of the radical military has therefore to be taken into account without accepting their own subsequent representation of themselves as 'the people in uniform' or as the sole instigators of the revolution. If it was they who sustained the pressure on the throne and the post-Aklilu cabinets, it was also true that their capacity to do so had been greatly enhanced by the student and union protests in February and March. Their initial protests through mutiny were also to a considerable extent sectoral. Indeed some of the civilian demonstrators in March were publicly criticizing the armed forces for docilely going back to barracks after receiving substantial pay increases. Yet the fact remains that from June onwards it was that group of radical military in the Derg who coordinated and ultimately carried out the deposition of Haile Selassie and the effective dismissal of the aristocratic group that had long surrounded the throne. Even earlier, in some isolated incidents in March, some rebellious members of the military were calling for land reform and other radical measures.[40] The radical sections of the armed forces were present in the movement from the beginning (the January–February mutinies) and it was they who pressed the issue to its resolution on September 12. The record and political influence of the civilian forces – the students, CELU, and so on – were such that it may be doubted whether they possessed the organization or any comparable determination to depose the emperor. Such an evaluation does not provide a characterization of the Derg's role subsequent to September 1974; but it must necessarily qualify the Thermidorian perspective within which its role in 1974 is frequently viewed. The evidence available does not sustain the commonly voiced thesis that the army entered the political arena at some stage

---

[40] For an example of a leaflet distributed in early March by the armed forces calling for land reform see Ottaways, p. 48.

subsequent to the revolution itself and either captured or pre-emptively stemmed this process.[41]

5. Rivalry between civilians (students, trade unions, reforming officials, teachers) and military was inscribed in this course of events and allows, as we have seen, of no simple interpretation. If the civilians criticized the military in early March for going back to their barracks, part of the military was then used, through the NSC, to crush strikes in April and May. Then in June the incipient Derg allied with CELU in opposition to the Endalkatchew government and the NSC. Once the Derg had gained the initiative in August their paths again diverged, and one of the PMAC's first measures on September 12 was to prohibit all strikes and unauthorized demonstrations. Yet even after September 12 the response on both sides was not as clear as subsequent vindicatory accounts would suggest. Whilst CELU and the more vocal students called for an immediate popular government to replace the PMAC, the Teachers Association for its part welcomed the establishment of the military government.[42] Conversely, there was a section within the Derg that for some weeks urged a transfer of power to the civilians. However, the rift between the two sides quickly widened: on September 24 the Derg arrested three top leaders of CELU, and in the following weeks the military acted to suppress protest strikes. The stage was being set for a bloody conflict between the PMAC and its civilian opponents that was to last into the early part of 1978.

6. Of equal importance was the imminent conflict between the PMAC and the rebellious nationalities. The largest demonstration of all in Addis Ababa had been in April, when an estimated 100,000 people had called for equality for Muslims and the ending of religious discrimination as institutionalized

---

[41] The EPRP political programme makes this claim in an appeal to 'the broad masses': 'The fruits of your labour, your creation – the revolution – has been snatched from you by a dictatorial stepfather, under the guise of being the guardian of the revolution'. The work by Markakis and Nega contains a measured statement of a similar argument.
[42] Ottaways, p. 107.

by the imperial state. Non-Amhara were represented in the protest movements – among the students, in the white-collar unions, and in the Derg. There were at least five Eritreans in the initial Derg, and also a number of Oromos, including Teferi Benti, the chairman from 1974 to 1977. Aman also was Eritrean by origin. Moreover, the fall of Haile Selassie was seen as a blow to Amhara predominance, by Amhara and non-Amhara alike.[43] Many of the statements made in the early months, by civilians and military, stressed the need for all Ethiopians to be equal. The call for *Etiopia Tikdem* was in part an attempt to inculcate a sense of a national and common Ethiopian identity beyond that of particular regions or nationalities. Even more than in France in 1789, the invocation of a single '*nation*' beyond existing particularities was both an anti-monarchical appeal and an attempt to knit a popular unity to replace a discriminatory one that had been shattered by the revolution. Yet no substantive policy measures were announced or taken vis-à-vis Eritrea, and Aman's individual initiatives for reconciliation were not supported by the Derg as a whole.

Even while Aman was still alive, on November 16, the Derg passed a penal code that applied the death penalty to a number of offences, among them any action challenging the territorial integrity of Ethiopia.[44] The Derg's stress on the 'indivisibility of Ethiopian unity' was indicative of an underlying position; they called for the end of discrimination on a 'religious or tribal basis', but their phrase significantly omitted any recognition of discrimination on grounds of nationality as such. Religion and tribe were part, but by no means the constituent core, of the problem. On the other hand, it must be emphasized that no identifiable group prominent in the 1974 movement is on record as taking a clear stand on this issue – neither the trade unions, nor the students. The Derg did continue negotiations with a committee of elders in Eritrea, and full-scale fighting began only with

[43] Pliny The Middle-Aged, 'The PMAC: Origins and Structure', Part Two, *Northeast African Studies*, 1, 1 (1979), pp. 17–18.
[44] Andrzej Bartnicki and Joanna Manual-Nieko, *Geschichte Äthiopiens*, Berlin 1978, vol. 2, p. 606.

the Eritrean offensive of late January. For their part, the Eritreans played down the significance of the events in Addis Ababa as being beyond their concern.

This neglect on the part of the political forces in Addis Ababa cannot be because the issue had never been raised: it had played a part in the divisions among the exile student community and in the February mutinies. Rather, the silence reflected a deeper resistance amongst those active in the 1974 movement vis-à-vis Eritrea and contradicted the hope of many Eritreans who collaborated with the government up to the November crisis that a conciliatory solution short of complete independence could be found.[45] These hopes proved unfounded, with the result that a new and even more violent conflict was restarted in Eritrea, with profound consequences for the other nationalities throughout Ethiopia.

7. The complexity of events in 1974 and their unresolved character should not obscure the enormous changes that had taken place in the space of a few months. First, an imperial regime that had lasted continuously for a century and, with some variations, for several centuries, had been overcome. The royal family and nobility were in prison or in flight, and within a few months the monarchy itself was to be formally abolished. The state personnel had not been completely changed and those now in power were drawn almost exclusively from the previous administration. Yet the upper layer of aristocrats had been displaced, and the institutions and higher echelons of the state had experienced cleavages along social and ethnic lines that to some degree mirrored those in the society as a whole. Second, an extraordinary change in the political climate of the country had occurred, a transformation perhaps hard to substantiate but of indubitable significance. At the beginning of the year the monopoly of public political expression had been controlled by the king and his

---

[45] Pliny, Part Two, p. 13, discusses Aman's efforts and suggests that he hoped to restore the federation. One of Aman's advisers was the Eritrean writer Bereket Habte Selassie, at that time Attorney-General in the revolutionary government. The death of Aman prompted Bereket and others like him to break with the PMAC and support the guerrillas. See the latter's *Conflict and Intervention in the Horn of Africa*, New York 1980.

associates. Ideas of democracy, let alone socialism, were prohibited. No significant underground political organizations, except those related to issues of nationality, existed within the country. By the end of the year tens of thousands of people had been exposed to new political ideas and experiences. A radical press had emerged and virtually all political dialogue now took place within some set of assumptions, however vaguely understood, about the need for socialism. These changes were, it is true, confined to a small proportion of the population. They amounted so far to what can be termed a political revolution, a change in the character of those wielding power and in the level of awareness and participation in political activity. Although out of reach of these new political ideas, the peasantry in parts of the southern regions had begun to occupy the property of Amhara landowners in response to the visible weakening of the imperial state. These changes were, however, precarious and many expected those who had previously monopolized power – the provincial nobles and possibly even the monarch – to return and take their revenge. No social revolution had yet occurred. But it was partly because of the imminence of such a political counter-revolution that the new government felt pressed to take a series of radical measures designed to undermine the economic and social power of those who might have favoured a return to some version of the previous regime. The events of 1975 were to be as unexpectedly rapid and far-reaching in their effects as those of the year just ended.

3
Revolution From Above: (i) Policies and Problems

The Dynamics of Transformation

With hindsight, it is possible to see the course of the Ethiopian revolution as following a definite political and social logic: a process of radicalization and post-revolutionary consolidation, through which the PMAC established a stable new order on the ruins of the old. Even if, like many post-revolutionary regimes, it has used some of the bricks of the old edifice to construct the new, the fact of a new construction is evident. The view from this vantage-point is, however, deceptive: for the direction of political and social change was by no means clear during the first years after 1974, and there were many who must have doubted whether the PMAC would survive at all. The outcome seemed to depend on haphazard factional disputes, on outside interruptions of internal political processes, on the unpredictable course of the post-imperial tumult. More than that: the pattern of revolutionary transformation seemed to involve a deep paradox, namely the conflict between the military leadership at the top and the various radical civilian forces below. At each stage of the revolution, the PMAC, aware of its own political weaknesses, sought to establish alliances with these civilian forces. Indeed it put into practice much of what the civilians were themselves demanding. But no stable alliance between them proved possible, and the result was even greater conflict: the revolutionary transformation effected by the PMAC therefore involved both the implementation of a radical social programme and the destruction or at least submission of other forces that had helped to bring these changes about.

The question that arises is why this military regime did implement a radical programme, internally and internationally. As we have already seen, there is little in the known intentions of the PMAC leadership that would explain this: they were not members of a secret political party, or of some left-wing military conspiratorial group, but were assembled in a random manner. The answer must be sought elsewhere, in the objective factors that shaped this malleable group of officers in the period after September 1974. The first was the pressure from the population: from the peasantry, for land reform, and from the mass of urban poor, wage-earners and semi-employed, for an improvement in their living conditions. Without taking measures to meet these popular demands, the PMAC could never have survived, nor could it have begun that development of the economy upon which the longer-run survival of the regime still rests. Even the mass organizations created by the regime, the peasant associations and the urban *kebeles*, reflected this need: however bureaucratized or manipulated, these organs did provide an elementary system of communication between leadership and population and that essential bond with the civilian population that the small, often beleaguered, group of PMAC officers required.

Another factor was the pressure from the political parties themselves: attacked for not implementing radical reforms, the PMAC took the initiative to put into practice what its critics and rivals were demanding. A clear instance of this was the land reform, where the militant studentry were compounding the pressure from the peasantry for radical action. By the end of 1976, when the war with the EPRP had begun, the Derg was seeking to mobilize the urban population against these left-wing opponents, to challenge the EPRP's monopoly of radicalism and to crush it in a campaign of mobilized terror. The cruel saga of conflict with the civilian groups should not obscure their very important influence on the PMAC. The third factor that radicalized the Derg was the internal evolution of the officers' group itself: both the factionalism that beset it from the beginning, and the social conflicts that were reflected within it. The emergence of Mengistu as undisputed leader of the PMAC reflected the ascent to power of a man who had a clear if autocractic programme of where

Ethiopia should go, who was prepared to use extremes of brutality to implement that programme, and who was able, by the beginning of 1978, to win the support of the other PMAC members.[1] It would be simplistic to see Mengistu as the representative of one particular class or class fraction within Ethiopian society. Even more so, it would be unjustified to accept the designation of the Ethiopian military as 'the people in uniform'. But the conflicts of Ethiopian society did find a reflection, albeit a blurred one, within the armed forces themselves: it was of great importance that the emperor had been ousted not by a conventional coup, a committee of generals, but by a group of junior army officers. They had been drawn from the intermediate sectors of Ethiopian society; their ousting of the top military leadership, as well as their initial political demands, did reflect the conflict that had been maturing within the state apparatus itself for some time. It was therefore a combination of a generic class hostility to the *ancien régime* with the particular radical programme represented by Mengistu that shaped the course of events within the PMAC.

The fourth radicalizing factor was international. While relations with the USSR had been improving slowly up to that point, and Mengistu had been calling for closer links, the threat posed by the military situation to the PMAC accelerated the process of alignment with Moscow. Even the more nationalistic army officers could see the need for closer links with Russia and for new forms of mass mobilization, in such a situation. There had been, till then, a certain asymmetry between the internal and external coordinates of the revolution; but that asymmetry was ended by the events following the Somali attack. The very absence of a pre-existing pro-Soviet faction in Ethiopian politics made this rapprochement all the easier: had there existed a local communist party, embroiled in the conflicts of 1974 onwards, and inevitably contesting the Derg's claim to the monopoly of power, the development of relations with the USSR would have been more,

---

[1] A forceful statement of the view that Mengistu did, from the beginning, have a clear conception of what he wanted is found in Lefort, *Ethiopie: la révolution hérétique*. The most detailed accounts of post-revolutionary developments are given in Lefort and in Ottaways.

not less, difficult, as the examples of Egypt and Iraq, where such communist forces did exist, show. The fifth and final reason was the most important of all: if it was to survive, the PMAC had to destroy the socio-economic foundations of the old regime. This involved expropriation, a measure of mass mobilization, and the extension of state control throughout society.

The Major Enactments

Following upon the proclamation of a rather ill-defined 'Ethiopian socialism' on December 20, 1974, the PMAC moved with unexpected rapidity and concreteness to give effect to this 'socialism' in a set of major reforms that established control of the main areas of the urban economy and destroyed the bases of the old regime in the countryside. On January 1, 1975, all banks and thirteen insurance companies were nationalized. On February 3 seventy-two industrial and commercial companies were fully nationalized, and the state assumed majority control in twenty-nine others. By late 1976 two-thirds of all manufacturing was under the control of the Ministry of Industry. On March 4, 1975, the most important reform of all, a land reform, was announced: all rural land was nationalized, tenancy was prohibited, and the peasantry was to have the right to till plots of only ten hectares maximum. Compensation was to be paid only for movable property and permanent works, not for the land itself. Peasant associations were to be established to administer the reform and up to 60,000 students were dispatched to the countryside in a *zemacha* (campaign) to mobilize the peasantry. On July 26 all urban land and all rentable houses and flats were nationalized; as in the countryside, the expropriated property was to be administered by associations, in this case the neighbourhood bodies known as *kebeles*. These committees drew in part on pre-existing local self-help bodies, the *edirs*: but they were, in their new form, instruments of state policy. There was to be no compensation for the expropriated land, but the owners of houses taken over were compensated. In all, an estimated 409,000 houses or flats were nationalized; of these 390,000 were administered by the *kebeles*, and the rest by the government. At the same time rents below $150 a year were reduced by between 15 per cent and 50 per cent. Two other reforms that tend to be underestimated did nonetheless mark important changes in Ethiopian society. One was the proclamation of a republic, in March 1975, which brought the many centuries of monarchy to an end. The other was the designation of three Islamic holidays as national festivals on a par with their Christian counterparts. Combined with the land reform, these reforms not only destroyed the position of one essential component of the old system, the monarchy, but also disestablished the other essential component, the Coptic Church, by depriving it of both its material base, in land, and its ideological status.[2]

These measures were announced with little preparation and there was considerable opposition to them from both left and right. The PMAC lacked the cadres to administer them adequately, in either an authoritarian or a democratic manner, and they took place against a backdrop of intensifying crisis in Eritrea and later Ogaden. Even in ideological terms the nature of this 'Ethiopian socialism' remained ill-defined at first. By 1976–7, however, the theoretical framework had become somewhat clearer. In April 1976, under the influence partly of civilian political groups but also of the first group of Derg members to return from brief political training courses in the USSR, the PMAC published the text of a new programme, its *National Democratic Revolution*.[3] Its aim was 'to liberate Ethiopia from the yokes of feudalism and imperialism, and to lay the foundations for the transition to socialism'. The Ethiopian revolution was, it stated, under the leadership of the working class, based on a worker-peasant alliance, and backed by the petty bourgeoisie. The pro-

---

[2] To some extent, the Church divided like the army: an upper fraction, symbolized by the Abuna Teophilos, was associated with the *ancien régime* and removed from positions of influence; many of the lower clergy participated in the street demonstrations. According to one account (*Süddeutsche Zeitung*, April 24, 1980) there were 215,000 priests in Ethiopia, attached to about 20,000 churches. On available evidence, it would seem that clerical resistance has been far less than in comparable situations, and many priests have, as tillers of the land, joined the Peasant Associations. Religious institutions associated with foreign missionaries have, however, been involved in serious conflicts with the government.

[3] Text of the *National Democratic Revolution* in Ottaways, pp. 211–16.

gramme laid special stress on the volatile political character of the lumpenproletariat. The goal was to 'establish a people's democratic republic in which the freedom, equality, unity and prosperity of the Ethiopian peoples is ensured, in which self-government at different levels is exercised and which allows for the unconditional exercise of human and democratic rights'. Among its immediate tasks, the programme listed the establishment of 'a true proletarian party' uniting all revolutionary forces. Prior to this party's being formed, a body called the Provisional Office for Mass Organizational Affairs (POMOA) was to be set up. This was to mobilize support and prepare for an assembly uniting revolutionary forces, which would later establish the people's republic of Ethiopia under the leadership of the working-class party.

The implementation of both the economic and political provisions of this programme was delayed for a variety of reasons. First, instead of being able to forge such a common front, the PMAC became locked in a bitter conflict with civilian political forces. It clashed with the *zemacha* students in 1975, with the EPRP and CELU in 1975–6, and later with ME'ISON, and most of the other left parties. Wherever the responsibility for this factionalism lies, a progressive civilian-military alliance was evidently unviable. Second, for most of 1977 and early 1978 the PMAC was preoccupied with the wars in Eritrea and Ogaden, which threatened its survival as a regime and the very territorial unity of Ethiopia. Third, the tumult of the revolution and the wars, combined with the weak administrative capacities of the new government, meant that no coherent economic policy could be put through in this period. Indeed the land reform had the effect of weakening central influence, strengthening the initiative of the individual peasant family and reducing the amount of produce commercialized by local peasants. Fourth, other factors beyond the Ethiopian government's control raised new obstacles in the economic field: the price of coffee, Ethiopia's main export, fell by 40 per cent at the end of the 1970s, rising oil costs used up half of its export earnings, and the drought that had produced famine in the early 1970s returned to cause a new famine in the north, comparable to that which precipitated the revolution. According to some estimates, over four million people were affected by the new famine, and the government had to resettle up to a quarter of a million of its victims.

It was only in the latter part of 1978 that the PMAC gave signs of being able systematically to surmount the many difficulties that it faced. In October 1978, Mengistu returned from a tour of the southern provinces apparently appalled by what he found there: the mismanagement of agriculture, the peasant resistance to state controls, the lack of official initiatives. It was also evident that four years of revolutionary upheaval had caused immense material and ideological damage to the regime. The PMAC's response was to launch a National Revolutionary Economic Development Campaign, under which two one-year plans were implemented, for the years 1978–9 and 1979–80. In 1980 a much more ambitious Ten-Year Plan was announced. Other measures taken towards the end of the decade suggested a similar desire to consolidate the earlier reforms. As part of the Development Campaign, a mass literacy programme was launched in 1979, and this served both to inculcate literacy, and to spread new political ideas among the population.[4] In 1979, control over foreign trade was extended by the nationalization of all shipping. And towards the end of the year a step was taken nearer the establishment of the party with the founding of COPWE, the Commission to Organize the Party of the Working People of Ethiopia. The implementation of the National Democratic Revolution programme was therefore a long-drawn-out process: we shall first examine the economic performance of the regime, and then consider the political difficulties traversed by it.

Overall economic performance in the post-revolutionary

[4] The aim is to abolish illiteracy in the towns by the end of 1981 and in the countryside by the end of 1986. According to Soviet reports, up to six million people had acquired literacy by the second half of 1980 (*New Times*, no. 37, 1980). The problem of literacy was compounded by the diversity of language in Ethiopia and by the need to decide on what script to use for some of the languages. The tendency was to impose Amharinya as the dominant language and its script as the main system of writing. However, such were the problems associated with this that, as under the *ancien régime*, the language of higher education remained English. By 1979–80 over 1.8 million children were in primary schools: at 38 per cent of those in the age-group, this was over double the pre-1974 figure.

period was disappointing and must have done much to alienate the population from the regime. In the years 1973-4 to 1977-8, GDP rose by only 0.4 per cent per annum; in 1977-8 it fell by 1.1 per cent.[5] Since population was growing at 2.5 per cent per annum this reflected a net fall in per capita income. Rates for the first two years of the National Development Campaign were an improvement: in 1978-9 GDP rose by 5.3 per cent and in 1979-80 by 5.6 per cent. In 1978, however, Ethiopia remained an extremely poor country: per capita income was $120, the fifth lowest in the world, and the lowest in Africa, equalled only by Mali.[6] Industry, which had grown at 7.4 per cent in the 1960s, grew at only 0.4 per cent per annum in the period 1970-78. Agriculture, which had grown at 2.2 per cent per annum in the 1960s grew at only 0.5 per cent in the same period. Indeed per capita food production for the 1976-8 period stood at 16 per cent below its level at the beginning of the decade. The two years of higher growth at the end of the 1970s somewhat redressed this picture: but the underlying problems of the Ethiopian economy, particularly a shortage of capital and a shortage of qualified technical and managerial personnel, remained.

The revolution was able to do little to improve Ethiopia's economic relationship with the outside world. Up to 80 per cent of its export earnings were from coffee, the price of which fluctuated considerably on the world market, and the deficit on foreign trade rose from $108 million in 1974-5 to $263 million in 1979-80. This led to a serious reduction in Ethiopia's foreign exchange reserves and to the imposition of tighter controls on imports during an austerity programme for the years 1981 and 1982. Despite its new international political orientation, Ethiopia continued to trade with its prerevolutionary commercial partners, but indebtedness to the

[5] Data taken from PMAC, *Ten-Year Investment Programme 1980/81–1989/90*, submitted to the UN Conference on the Less Developed Countries, Addis Ababa, March 1981.

[6] The World Bank, *World Development Report* 1980. This report gives stark evidence of the health situation in Ethiopia. In 1977 there was one doctor for every 76,320 people, a ratio 50 per cent higher than in any other country in the world; 6 per cent of the population had access to safe water, and the daily calorie supply per capita was 75 per cent of the minimum required. Life expectancy at birth was 39 years, the lowest in the world.

USSR began to impose a major strain on its export earnings. The USSR was in fact helping Ethiopia by providing oil at East European prices, half those charged by OPEC; but with export earnings running at only $429 million in 1979 Ethiopia had little room for manoeuvre in this sector.[7] Faced with the poor performance of the 1970s, the slump in coffee prices and the limited availability of internal funds, the regime launched an appeal for major new funding to cover the 1980–81 to 1989–90 Ten Year Plan. The aims of this plan were to double GDP over the decade, to boost agricultural output by 60 per cent, and to increase industrial output by 250 per cent. At the same time, it was planned to extend basic health facilities to 85 per cent of the rural population, to eradicate illiteracy, and to build 450,000 new housing units. The overall aim of this programme was described as 'laying a strong material and technical foundation for the building of socialism'.

To achieve targets remotely near these, the Ethiopian government would need internal peace, large quantities of foreign aid and considerable good fortune. In the period 1974–8 foreign aid, in both grant and loan forms, had averaged $271 million per year: yet although this helped to finance the government's capital expenditure and to compensate for the imbalance in trade, it was low by comparative standards. In 1978 aid averaged $4.8 per head of population – compared to an average for the less developed countries of $16.9. Ethiopia's ability to obtain such aid was as dependent on its political as on its economic options. But however successful, it did not reduce the urgent need to increase agricultural output: for it was on the land, where the great majority of the Ethiopian population still lived, that the economic destiny of the regime would be decided.

Land Reform

Of all the reforms enacted, the most important was the land

[7] The data on foreign debt are not clear. Official Ethiopian figures, as in note 5 above, give a June 1980 figure of $681 million. This was 80 per cent up on 1974–5. Of this, $389 million was owed to multilateral agencies, and the largest bilateral creditor was the USA ($139 million). But the figure given for the USSR ($9.7 million) is too low and must exclude the very large military debt. Interest payments for 1979 came to $28 million (*Observer Foreign News Service*, August 5, 1980).

reform. Against the advice of Chinese, Yugoslav and Russian embassy officials, the PMAC enacted extremely far-reaching measures. No legal ownership of rural land was henceforth permitted: only a 'possessory' or 'usufructuary' form of tenancy was allowed. No employment of wage-labour by farmers was permitted on this land, which, therefore, had to be cultivated by family labour.[8] The result of this decree was that in the south of the country the subjugated Oromo peasantry seized the lands, ousting and in some cases killing the *neftegna* owners. Since the Oromo peasantry had not perceived themselves prior to the revolution as owning the land they were not threatened by the new system: from the evidence available it appears that Peasant Associations were formed in many areas of the south. In the north, by contrast, where the system of *rist* land had prevailed and provided a form of ownership to the labourers, the results were less favourable. Landowners were able to claim to peasants that the reform threatened the latter's *rist* rights and to present the reform as an Oromo-Muslim threat to the Amharic-Tigrean Christian order. This image of the reform as an anti-Christian measure received additional confirmation from the fact that Church lands not tilled directly by priests were also expropriated. In the Afar areas, the Sultan was also able to mobilize resistance among his people, since in this Muslim area of the north-east, unlike the Oromo south, both landowner and peasant shared a single religious affiliation.

Resistance thus broke out in many parts of the north. Although it never presented the mortal threat that many had anticipated, it effectively subtracted much of the provinces of Tigray, Gojjam and Begemdir, and parts of Welo and Shoa, from government control during this period. Insofar as one can speak of a socially based counter-revolution, as distinct from resistance primarily on grounds of nationality, it was to be found in these provinces. It operated there, to a greater or

---

[8] The question of why the land reform measure was so radical has not been clarified. Factors combining to produce the version enacted included: the presence within the Ministry concerned of radical agrarian specialists, some associated with ME'ISON; the pressure from without by the students who had gone to mobilize in the countryside; support from a particular faction within the PMAC, reputedly including Mengistu; the growing level of peasant militancy; and the need to undermine the provincial nobility.

lesser extent, under the umbrella of the Conservative Ethiopian Democratic Union, a counter-revolutionary group that operated from the Sudan until 1978. The overall consequences of the reform were nonetheless substantial. First and foremost, the implementation of the reform marked the real overthrow of the *ancien régime*: the transference into social relations of what had already been achieved in the political realm by the deposition of the emperor. Production in the peasant sector rose slightly between 1974-5 and 1975-6, in marked contrast to the normal pattern of at least short-term declines in production following land reforms; this outcome reflected both the good weather conditions prevailing, and the popularity of the reform with the peasantry. Rural incomes rose as the peasants were relieved of the landlords' exactions and the absolute amount grown also increased. Despite the lack of government cadres, Peasant Associations spread through much of the countryside: they were established by the new tenants on a minimum area of 800 hectares, with between two and four hundred families as members. They had local judicial functions as well as the role of providing seeds and other inputs. A new phase was marked by a Decree of December 1975, which specified that service cooperatives would be set up, consisting of between three and ten Associations. These were to procure the inputs the latter required and to market the produce.

The initial stages of the process seem to have gone relatively well; by 1978 there were officially said to be 28,583 Peasant Associations in Ethiopia with a total membership of 7.3 million households, backed by a system of peasant defence units encompassing 500,000 armed villagers. The number of service cooperatives had reached 343. Enormous problems did, nonetheless, arise. The level of participation varied enormously between Associations, and there were certainly not enough arms to equip the full complement of villagers in the defence units. Moreover, apart from the activities of the counter-revolutionaries in the north-western provinces, other substantial social problems have arisen. First of all, the *zemacha* campaign had contradictory effects, in town and countryside. Students sent out into the countryside to mobilize the peasantry around the reform soon clashed with the state officials already there – the police and administrators. The latter may also have had land themselves, or may have looked forward to receiving some in the future. Landlords killed some *zemacha* cadres, and the PMAC itself was increasingly wary of this agitational force that lay outside its control. By the end of 1975 most of the students had been recalled to the cities.[9] The Peasant Association Decree of December 1975 was designed to establish a more permanent mobilizing structure in the rural areas, and the *zemacha* students, whose usefulness to the PMAC was now exhausted, brought back to the cities a deep suspicion of the PMAC's policies. This fuelled the conflict that had already broken out there in the summer of 1975 between the Derg and its left opponents. Second, the newly powerful peasantry withheld much of their produce from the urban market: they were no longer forced to sell it by the landlords who had controlled the marketing system and they enjoyed their new freedom to consume more themselves. This, combined with the strains on the country's transport system occasioned by the wars, led to severe shortages and inflation in the towns between 1976 and 1978. Most important of all, the reform fostered the growth of new class relations among the peasantry.[10] The reform had abolished private legal ownership of rural land, but the tenancies now given to peasants did give them effective control over their plots: they were able to exclude other peasants, and defy government instructions. There appear to be no general figures on ownership patterns after the reform: samples taken in the south over the 1975–7 period indicate that at most a quarter of holdings exceeded two hectares. But, beyond establishing an upper limit on tenancies, the decree had not specified in what form the new land would be distributed. The central government was unable to supervise the local redistribution policies, and it

[9] The dispute over the *zemacha* is often cited as an example of the Derg's hostility to spontaneous mass action. But it is probable that had the campaign continued, outright conflicts would have developed between the students and the peasantry. The latter, having acquired their land, were unlikely to have shown enthusiasm for the forms of collective organization that the students would later have proposed: it was not the *zemacha* students' intention to act as trail-blazers for the rich peasantry that benefited from the reform.

[10] Lefort, pp. 337–48; and in *Le Monde*, July 30, 1979.

was those peasants who had been in a somewhat more privileged position prior to the reform who received most land – those who had been tenants on areas above 1.5 hectares and who had had access to a major instrument of production, oxen. In some cases former landlords slaughtered oxen rather than allow them to be used by the newly enfranchised peasants; but as in other land reforms, for example the Iranian, it was possession of means of production other than land that gave the edge to this upper layer of peasants once redistribution took place.

A further problem was that new difficulties arose in the areas of coffee production where up to 25 per cent of the agricultural work force is to be found. Although hiring of labour was henceforward forbidden, the weakness of the state purchasing body, combined with the reliance of the peasantry on their former landlords for their subsistence goods, opened the door to new forms of exploitation of the peasantry by richer peasants and by merchants. Overall, the richer peasants were able not only to gain a disproportionate amount of land and to continue exploiting the poorer ones, but also to ensure that it was they who controlled the new Peasant Associations, their credit, equipment and distribution. At the same time, problems of a different kind arose on the state farms, that is, those on which larger-scale commercial farming had previously been practised. These received the majority of agricultural credits, but the total area under cultivation fell from 108,000 hectares in 1975 to 58,000 hectares in 1976–7. This was partly because land previously under state farms was transferred to Peasant Associations, but also partly because of disruption of the pre-existing management systems, which the PMAC was unable to replace.

As a result of these problems and because of the impact of the wars, the initial benefits of the reform in output terms were reduced. As already noted, food output did not even keep pace with population growth in the 1974–8 period, and between 1977 and 1979 Ethiopia faced severe food shortages, both in the towns and in parts of the countryside, with the re-emergence of famine in the northern provinces. In 1978 grain output at 600,000 tons had fallen by almost 300,000 tons from the 1975–6 level and the country required imports of 240,000 tons as compared to around 100,000 tons in 1976. In Welo and Tigray up to 4.5 million people were in need of grain relief. Of the total coffee production of around 300,000 tons only around 80,000 tons were being exported in 1979.

The regime's response was the Economic Development Campaign. Agricultural output rose 2.4 per cent in 1978-9, and 4.8 per cent in 1979-80. Equally significantly, it initiated what became known as the 'third phase' of the land reform programme, after the initial decree of March 1975 and the proclamation later in that year on Peasant Associations. This new Decree, of June 1979, placed new upper limits on areas of tenancy and laid the basis for the transition to producers' cooperatives. Under the first stage of this process, *malba* cooperatives would be set up: tenancies were given as 2,000 square metres maximum, and the producers were to share their means of production. In the second stage, known as *welba*, tenancies were to be limited to 1,000 square metres, and the means of production were to be owned by the cooperative. The final stage, known as *weland*, involves a *kolkhoz*-type structure: it abolishes private tenancy over land. According to government officials, these *welands* would include about 2,500 individual adult members, and would cover an area of around 4,000 hectares of land. Official statements stressed the dangers of forcing the pace of collectivization: even the experience with service cooperatives had generated considerable resistance in some areas. But the longer-run import of this Decree was not lost on the peasantry and opposition to it appeared: in early September 1979, there were clashes in Sidamo province in which an estimated 150 people were killed. By 1980 there were just forty producer cooperatives in existence, mainly of the initial *malba* variety, and another 130 were under consideration.[11] But state farms and cooperatives combined accounted for only 6 per cent of agricultural output and 20 per cent of marketed production: the Ten Year Plan declared the need for collectivization, but set no targets for it. Herein lay the

---

[11] Hannelore Borgel and others, *Production, Marketing and Consumption of Potatoes in the Ethiopian Highlands*, Institute of Socio-Economics of Agricultural Development, Technical University of Berlin, Berlin 1980, pp. 19-20. For details on the new system of producer cooperatives, see *Ethiopian Herald*, June 28, 1979.

real limit of the land reform programme and the central issue that would determine the future social character of post-revolutionary Ethiopia.

The Ambiguity of the Reforms

The mobilization of rural resources for the Economic Development Campaign, so essential to the success of the regime's whole programme, has encountered substantial resistance from those who benefited most from the 1975 land reform. The problem is, of course, one that revolutionary regimes have had to face before, but none have found a balanced or democratic answer to it. The course of the land reform, beyond its immense material significance for the Ethiopian revolution, is indicative of the general character of the PMAC's interventions. This, by any standards, very radical measure was carried out within six months of the PMAC's coming to power, and just over a year after the first protest demonstrations in Addis Ababa; yet it was decreed by a group of officers that had no political cadres with which to carry out the reform and who lacked even a previous history of support for such social transformations. Their very weakness had a positive consequence: it led them to try to win popular support by enacting such measures and by handing substantive power to the *kebeles* in the towns and the Peasant Associations in the countryside. Yet this very delegation of power produced a new set of conflicts, which the PMAC, lacking the political mediations needed to resolve them in a non-coercive manner, then sought to surmount by administrative fiat and, in many cases, by direct coercion.

The PMAC was not the first body in Ethiopia to call for land reform. Yet it was the military who implemented the reform, in a manner much more radical than most Ethiopians had expected; the results, coinciding with the propitious weather were, as we have seen, initially favourable in output terms. It has been argued that the Derg carried out the reform only in order to overtake its political opponents; but even if this consideration played a role, it is nonetheless the case that the reform was carried out by the military leadership. It went against the mass of existing landowners and against the wishes of the very layer of junior officers from which the Derg had emerged. The latter thereby lost their traditional right to grants of land in return for military service. The subsequent course of events revealed the oscillations of Derg policy in the countryside: the military allowed the *zemacha* and later the Associations considerable freedom of action, but later reined them in, amidst considerable conflict, once the consequences of such decentralizing initiatives were clear and the PMAC at the centre felt strong enough to exert control. Similar problems arose in the context of the urban reforms. These were not, in the first place, as radical as the land reform: compensation was offered for urban housing that was nationalized, and for the insurance companies and industrial plants taken over, although in practice payment on the latter two was delayed for a long time. Moreover, the 'bureaucratic' state already controlled much of the banking sector and parts of industry, and there was no substantial private Ethiopian property to expropriate. On the other hand where a flourishing Ethiopian capitalist class did exist – in the retail trade – it was left relatively unmolested. Despite the existence of a state purchasing board for coffee, the sale of Ethiopia's largest export commodity remained to a considerable extent in the hands of the same powerful merchants who had controlled it in the days of Haile Selassie. The private sector of the economy therefore still included nearly all of the peasant sector as well as the small-scale artisans who were not nationalized with the larger industrial sectors.

The contradictory effects of the PMAC's policies were clearest in the factories: here, despite a relative quiescence compared to white-collar sectors in the upsurges of February to June 1974, there was a growing militancy as a result both of the state's 'socialist' proclamations and of the left groups' influence. By 1976, widespread demands were being raised for shop-floor control over production. These were repelled with the appointment of powerful state managers, and with the imposition of a new trade union structure. Strikes had been illegal since 1974 and were prohibited in the 1975 Labour Code. The housing law also encountered serious difficulties: as so often happens in such cases, the nationalization led to a net subtraction of the number of dwellings available for rental. Owners distributed houses and flats among their relatives. Since many of the urban owners were in origin rural proprietors, the number of such people in the towns greatly increased as they were driven off the land by the 1975 land reform. The *kebeles* did carry out some housing redistribution and welfare programmes, but even in economic terms they were unable to fulfil one of their major functions – providing a sufficiently large set of retail outlets for food to offset the shortages and hoarding that began in 1976. A more important problem, however, was that the *kebeles* became the site of an urban terror campaign – by the EPRP against supporters of the government and by ruthless state officials against their opponents. Each side sought to mobilize semi-employed youth against the other. The decision to establish and arm the *kebeles* – which numbered 1,800 by the end of 1977, nearly 300 of them in the capital – reflected a dilemma similar to that faced in the countryside, namely the weakness of the PMAC and their need to encourage popular action. Yet even more than in the countryside, the *kebeles* were taken over by political forces that the Derg had to disown. The result was that by the end of 1978 the power of the *kebeles* had been greatly reduced. They were much more tightly controlled from above in financial and administrative matters, and they were progressively deprived of their security functions, losing their right to administer local gaols and to carry arms.

The Derg: Division and Consolidation

Following the establishment of the PMAC on September 12, 1974 the military leadership retained executive power. They made variable use of a cabinet of ministers outside the Derg, but ultimate authority rested with the senior members of the PMAC.[12] Apart from their conflicts with the civilian political forces, the Derg officers were themselves rent by serious divisions. The membership and deliberations of the PMAC remained secret and the civilian government acted as an

[12] The following is based on the articles of Pliny The Middle-Aged; see chapter 2, note 43 above.

additional screen until the Derg Standing Committee was appointed in 1977. The PMAC itself met in full on only a handful of occasions; from 1977 onwards it functioned more as a government body, via a system of committees and a hierarchical structure, and at the end of 1979 a new cabinet system was announced in which PMAC members took up some public ministerial positions for the first time. The Derg therefore went through a dual transformation in the years after it assumed power: organizationally a body of 126 junior officers and NCOs developed into a structured executive body, and ideologically, its initially vague espousal of *Etiopia Tikdem* was sharpened into formal advocacy of 'Marxism-Leninism'.

After the deposition of the Emperor, some members of the PMAC appear to have favoured a rapid transition to civilian rule. But they were in a minority, and the subsequent public history of the Derg was dominated by a set of internal conflicts, in most of which the defeated officers were killed. However, the two main issues of dispute seem to have been not the question of handing over to the civilians but rather (a) how to relate to the civilian opposition forces; and (b) how to handle the Eritrean question. In 1979, economic matters became an issue of dissension. Surprisingly, given the drastic change in Ethiopia's international alignment, foreign relations seem to have played a part in only one of these conflicts. The first clash, which has already been described, was that with Aman Andom in November 1974; although Aman was not actually a member of the Derg he seems to have enjoyed some following within it and two PMAC members died with him. The second clash came in July 1976 when a number of PMAC members, the most prominent among them being Major Sisay Habte and Major Kiros Alemayehu, were ousted after opposing the military resolution of the Eritrean question and advocating more emphasis upon a return to civilian government. Following their execution, a formal PMAC structure was elaborated for the first time, with a Congress comprising all members, a Central Committee of forty members and a Standing Committee of seventeen. But it seems that this restructuring was being used by one faction, led by Derg chairman Teferi Benti, to reduce the influence of

Vice-Chairman Mengistu. On February 3, 1977 the most dramatic of all Derg crises broke out with the assassination of Teferi Benti and six other associates, and the emergence of Mengistu as undisputed leader of the PMAC. The central policy issue in the conflict seems to have been Teferi Benti's desire, indicated in a speech on January 30, to reach some reconciliation with the EPRP, even though the latter had by now launched an urban guerrilla campaign against the PMAC. There is some evidence to indicate that Teferi and his associates were hoping to evict Mengistu, but if this is true Mengistu was able to strike first, accusing Teferi of organizing a 'fascist coup'. Later in the year, in November 1977, the number two in the Derg, Vice-Chairman Atnafu Abate, was also ousted and executed. He had used the occasion of the Derg's third general congress to criticize Mengistu's policies, in particular the use of terror to suppress political opponents. But he also questioned the unequivocal nature of the new alliance with the Soviet Union, and the claim that Ethiopia could make a rapid transition to socialism. While the Derg has not undergone any comparable divisions since Atnafu's execution, two PMAC members were dismissed for mistakes in economic policy in June 1979, following another Congress, and two other members of the Standing Committee, Endela Tessema and Tamrat Ferede, were ousted in late 1979 for quarrelling in public. The continuing debate within the regime as a whole over the establishment of a 'proletarian party' has found its reflection within the PMAC itself, with one group strongly advocating a Soviet party model,[13] and another, more Ethiopian nationalist faction, appearing to resist this.

Of the original 126 members of the Derg, between sixty and eighty still remain within it. The great majority of the Derg officers are graduates of the Holeta military academy, the junior of the two such institutions. Almost all those from the senior academy at Harar were eliminated in the July 1976 and February 1977 purges. In ethnic composition, it seems

[13] Pliny, Part Two, p. 15, gives the members of the pro-Soviet group as: Legesse Asfaw, Fikre-Selassie Wogderess, Gesesse Wolde Kidan, Tamrat Ferede and Teka Tulu. All were members of the initial seventeen-man Standing Committee appointed in 1979; Tamrat Ferede was later dismissed.

that Amharas are still in a majority.[14] The minority of Oromos are mainly Christian and therefore representative of that section of Oromo society traditionally associated, albeit in a junior position, with the Ethiopian state. Of the five Eritreans believed to have been members at the beginning, all have either defected or been executed; only one Derg member, the Oromo Ali Musa, is definitely a Muslim, despite the fact that around 40 per cent of Ethiopia's population adheres to Islam.

The structure of power within the PMAC has gradually adapted to the need for efficient government machinery, and to the emergence of new hierarchies of influence within it. The governing body is the ten-member Standing Committee, which is the core of the revolutionary government. Beyond it lies a Central Committee, believed to have thirty-two members. The congress of all the surviving members is believed still to meet on an annual basis: but it would seem that, while it has powers of discussion and ratification of some decisions, it can no longer take major initiatives against the will of the Standing Committee. The dozens of PMAC members not directly involved in the SC are distributed amongst a variety of posts: some have positions in civilian ministries or on the PMAC committees that oversee each ministry. Since 1978 twelve Derg members have been appointed to positions as provincial governors,[15] and since 1980 four have held positions in the Council of Ministers. There has therefore been a process of transformation: as the PMAC itself has ceased to be the major decision-making assembly, its members have become more closely and more regularly integrated into the administration at both national and provincial level. Nevertheless, the uniqueness of this system should not be overlooked. If the original membership came about by a combination of direct election and accident, it was then frozen as the highest revolutionary authority: that prerequisite of popular control, the right of recall and re-election of representatives, has not applied. So far as is known, no Derg member has ever been subjected to new

[14] Pliny, Part Two, pp. 17–18.
[15] *Africa Confidential*, vol. 21, no. 2, January 16, 1980.

elections by the military who chose him, and none of the members who were excluded or who fled has ever been replaced. The surviving members have therefore remained in positions of influence. At the same time, they have preserved both their clandestinity – no full list has ever been published – and their curious relation to the civilian bureaucracy. The Council of Ministers includes both civilians and PMAC members: the appointment in January 1980 of Major Fisseha Desta as chairman of the Council, and of three other PMAC members to ministerial posts, marked a step towards greater integration in this regard. But the separation of PMAC and government apparatus continues, as does the clandestinity with which major decisions are taken.

The February 1977 crisis marked the emergence of one man, Mengistu Haile-Mariam, as unchallenged leader of the PMAC, and by the end of 1979 'the Chairman' was being projected through the official media in a strong authoritarian light.[16] Mengistu's origins are disputed. Born between 1940 and 1942, he is most widely believed to be the son of an Amhara soldier and a mother of *shankala* or *barria* origin, that is, from a caste of blacks who were traditionally slaves. Mengistu has sometimes been held to be partly of Oromo origin, but this seems to be a confusion based on the fact that as a child he lived for some time in an Oromo province, Wollamo. His father was a soldier and later worked as houseguard to a prominent noble, Ras Kebede Tessema, commander of the territorial army in 1960. Kebede Tessema maintained good relations with Mengistu, even after 1974, and it was through him that Mengistu gained access to the Holeta military academy where he was trained as an ordnance officer. He twice visited the USA for training purposes. He was later to claim that what he saw in the USA, faced as he was with resistance to the war in Vietnam and with the black movement, contributed to radicalizing him, but there is no public evidence of his radicalism prior to the constitution of the Derg in 1974. His subsequent espousal of a 'Marxist-

[16] Two conventional features of personality cult regimes were, however, absent: there were no signs that relatives of Mengistu's were being assigned to positions of influence, and, while his speeches were taken as authoritative statements of government policy, there was no special promotion of the Chairman's 'Thoughts'.

Leninist' outlook in the latter part of 1976 was, it would seem, as much a response to the immediate situation as a reflection of long-standing conviction.[17] In revolutionary situations the outlooks of individuals as much as of classes and nations can change more in a few weeks than in the previous years, and this may have occurred with Mengistu; yet some of the brutalist and commandist features of Ethiopian political culture, as well as his military training, appear to have exerted an influence upon him. A more immediate cause of his political development may have been his three-week visit to the USSR in 1975, a voyage that may have focused his attention on the Soviet model. Whatever his precise political orientation, however, there can be little doubt of Mengistu's determination to rule and to do so decisively: many who have met him, either as government officials or foreign visitors, attest to his great calmness, a cool realism that has enabled him to overcome the many problems he has been faced with.

He has derived from his earlier years an exceptional acquaintance with the regional diversity of Ethiopia. Born in an Oromo area, of mixed Amhara and *shankala* origin, he travelled as child to different areas whilst his father was soldiering and then serving as a houseguard. Like Corsicans and Georgians before him, he has found that his atypical ethnic and regional origins have served him well in dominating an explosive multinational domain. Like those earlier rulers, Mengistu believes in the necessity for strong government: he reminded the delegates to the first COPWE conference that the Paris Commune was destroyed after seventy-two days because it lacked firm leadership. If his words and actions are anything to go by, Mengistu Haile-Mariam intends to make sure that the mistakes of the Paris Commune are not repeated in the highlands of the Horn of Africa.

While the other members of the PMAC Standing Committee have seemingly accepted Mengistu's leadership, all are individuals with post-revolutionary political records in their own right.[18] The secretary-general of the PMAC is Lieutenant-

---

[17] Raúl Valdés Vivó, *Ethiopia, The Unknown Revolution*, Havana 1977, p. 31.
[18] The full list is given in *Ethiopian Herald*, June 25, 1980, as part of the COPWE Central Committee.

Colonel Fikre-Selassie Wogderess: in charge of the ideological affairs of the new political structure, COPWE, Fikre-Selassie was a strong supporter of Mengistu's in the 1974–7 period, but later appeared to incline towards the pro-Soviet faction. The leader of this group is believed to be Lieutenant-Colonel Legesse Asfaw: he was one of the PMAC members who underwent political training in the USSR in 1975 and was a keen advocate of the establishment of a political party thereafter. In 1980 he became head of COPWE's organization committee. Lieutenant-Colonel Fisseha Desta, Deputy Chairman of the Council of Ministers, is, by contrast, reputed to be a man of outspoken nationalist views: a Tigrean by origin, and a graduate of the Harar academy, he has resisted the policies of the pro-Soviet group and is believed to want a more independent foreign policy. Brigadier-General Tesfaye Gebre-Kidan is the Minister of National Defence and originates from Hararghe province: he was closely involved in negotiations with the Russians on the provision of military supplies. Berhanu Bayih, another Harar graduate, has been in practice the man responsible for Ethiopia's foreign relations since the revolution and has been closely involved in attempts to win support in the Arab world. Addis Tedlay is an air force officer later placed in charge of the National Revolutionary Development Campaign. Woubshet Dessie served as PMAC representative in Eritrea in 1977–8 but later became head of the PMAC's Security Committee, responsible for, among other things, surveillance of other PMAC members. Teka Tulu, an Oromo and a policeman by profession, has been a long-standing member of the Security Committee. Captain Gesesse Wolde-Kidan has been appointed Commissioner for Children, an office responsible for much of the relief work among refugees. If, for any reason, Chairman Mengistu were to be removed from his position of dominance, it is probable that his successor would be drawn from amongst these other Standing Committee members. The pattern of decision-making within the Derg does not suggest that any new head of state would be chosen by an open mass assembly of what remains Ethiopia's only democratically elected body.

Civilian Opposition

The initial response from civilian forces in Addis Ababa to the deposition of Haile Selassie and the advent of the PMAC was mixed. The PMAC immediately banned strikes and protest demonstrations, and the majority of those involved in the previous months of upheaval certainly resented this. But the PMAC had the credit of having finally toppled the emperor, and it claimed to be only a provisional administration, so that some months were required for the full force of the civilian opposition to gain momentum. Some civilians, notably those in the Teachers Association, even welcomed the coup, and CELU voiced 'total support' in January 1975; the reforms of the following months further divided the civilians. The first major outbreak of opposition was on May Day 1975 when soldiers killed some demonstrators demanding an immediate return to civilian rule. By the latter half of 1975 a clearly militant opposition had emerged, based on CELU and on the EPRP, which proclaimed its existence in August of that year. The EPRP was demanding an elected assembly and the immediate constitution of a people's democratic republic; and the CELU Congress of September 1975 backed this programme with general strikes that lasted for some weeks.

Between the September 1974 seizure of power by the PMAC and the following September there had occurred a significant *évolution des esprits* through which the underground student-based nuclei inspired by returning exiles and the rather conventional leadership of CELU converged to form an alliance militantly opposed to the PMAC. For the former, it marked a much-desired link to the workers' movement; for the latter it signified the acquisition of a new political outlook quite at variance with its past, and in stark opposition to the PMAC. The PMAC did not, of course, accept these demands and it crushed the CELU protests. Aware of growing resistance among students, it also recalled the *zemacha* cadres from the countryside. In December a new restrictive labour law was proclaimed and CELU officially dissolved. But the initial instinct was not simply repressive: for another year the PMAC tried to win over its opponents in the EPRP and CELU. In early

1976 the press was opened to a debate between ME'ISON and the EPRP. The National Democratic Revolution proclaimed in April 1976 was designed to meet some of the demands of the radical left, and for some time in 1976 CELU was permitted to operate again. Indeed most of the EPRP programme was represented in the NDR – with the exception of a commitment to return to civilian rule. Although the EPRP later tried to obscure the facts, POMOA, the umbrella organization uniting different civilian political groups, did initially include an EPRP associate, Eshatu Chole. Even in the late summer of 1976 the official press was appealing for unity around the NDR. But the key issue of difference remained: whilst the NDR promised that civilian government would come at some point in the future, the EPRP demanded the immediate establishment of a civilian regime.

By the end of 1976 the breach was all but final. The main responsibility for this lies with the EPRP, but changes inside the PMAC contributed to the outcome. In July 1976 the group around Sisay Kiros, who favoured some further conciliation with the EPRP, was eliminated from the Derg, and in the same month the death penalty was introduced for certain political crimes. The state of emergency proclaimed in September 1975, during the general strike, was prolonged and there was a significant turning point after an attempt on Mengistu's life on September 23, 1976; this incident was blamed on the EPRP, but was probably carried out by a military faction opposed to him.[19] After September, the EPRP adopted a policy of assassination of PMAC supporters and between late 1976 and mid-1977 they killed several hundred of them, nearly all civilians. In response, the PMAC, which had already executed fifty EPRP members after the first assassinations, now launched a campaign of what later became known as 'red terror', following a number of speeches in 1977, by Mengistu in which this was advocated as an explicit policy in reply to the 'white terror' of his opponents.

The EPRP was active in a few cities – Addis Ababa, Dire Dawa, Jimma – and its military wing, the EPRA (Ethiopian People's Revolutionary Army) carried out actions in Tigray

[19] Ottaways, p. 107; Lefort, p. 185.

province. The EPRP also made public in 1976 something that had probably existed for some time, namely its alliance with the EPLF in Eritrea. Thousands, many of them summarily shot without the semblance of an investigation or trial, died in the 'red terror', and by mid-1978 the EPRP had ceased to operate in Addis Ababa and other towns. In 1979 the EPRA was still able to carry out some military operations in Tigray, but after clashing with the EPLF and its local ally, the TPLF, it was reduced by 1981 to operations in the mountains near Gondar.

The working class opposition was crushed by the Derg simultaneously. After the defeat of the CELU strike, mainly a white-collar protest, in late 1975, there was a rise of blue-collar militancy in 1976, as workers in individual factories demanded control over work-place decisions. A new body, the All-Ethiopian Trade Union, was finally established to replace CELU in late 1976 but its first three presidents were assassinated by the EPRP. By December 1977 it claimed to have a membership of 350,000.[20] Yet even apart from the EPRP's campaign of combined infiltration and assassination, the AETU was rent by conflicts between ME'ISON, which dominated the AETU leadership, and the Derg, with the result that the AETU leadership was dismissed by the PMAC in May 1978.[21] Though this was officially ascribed to the 'corruption' of the leadership, the real reason was the continuing loyalty of AETU cadres to ME'ISON, a sympathy reflected in the motions passed at a conference of workers and peasants in Shoa (the central province) in October 1977, requesting that the PMAC re-open negotiations with ME'ISON. Whilst all the other twenty-five resolutions of the Congress were published, this one was not. And even after the conflict with ME'ISON had been concluded, in 1978, the loyalty of the mass of wage-earners to this new imposed structure was bound to be suspect. After such a confrontation, and the disappointment of so many hopes, great political and economic problems remained.

[20] Authors' interview with AETU officials, Addis Ababa, December 1977.
[21] *The Guardian*, May 29, 1978. Reports of further conflict inside the AETU appeared in *African Confidential*, vol. 22, no. 6, March 11, 1981.

Assassination and Red Terror

The harsh conflict between the EPRP–CELU and the PMAC raises a number of inescapable political questions.[22] The first concerns the question of violence and its use by both parties in the conflict. The EPRP's resort to urban assassination in the period from September 1976 to mid-1978 was a serious error. In slaying leaders of the AETU or political instructors at the Yekatit 66 ideological school, as well as elected *kebele* officials, they were attacking people who, whatever their specific political positions, were trying to advance the Ethiopian revolution. At the same time, the EPRP's decision to launch this campaign involved a fatal underestimation of their opponents' capacity to survive and counter-attack; it encouraged a situation in which the PMAC resorted to a violent counter-offensive in which most of the EPRP and many others were consumed.

The mistaken nature of the EPRP's policies does not, however, justify the actions of the PMAC and their civilian allies. The November 1974 executions were an early use of violence, dictated by the political situation at that time and at least partly intended to instil fear in the population. Repression, that is the use of arrest, torture and execution of civilian opponents, began with the clashes of May Day 1975, but this did not become a central part of PMAC policy until the end of 1976; it is an inescapable conclusion that, however prone to such actions the PMAC may have been, it was the EPRP's terrorist policies that encouraged the new phase of PMAC repression. Mengistu's call in early 1977 for a 'red terror' to combat what he referred to as the counter-revolutionaries, among whom he included the EPRP, was followed by some of the regime's most repugnant acts of violence. Towards the end of April 1977, as the opposition were preparing for another May Day protest, up to 500 students were killed in

---

[22] EPRP policy can be traced through its initial statement issued in 1975, and through the pages of its journal *Abyot* (Revolution). A cogent statement of the EPRP position is given in Nega Ayele and John Markakis, *Class and Revolution in Ethiopia*, Nottingham 1978. It would appear that Markakis later modified his views, to permit greater criticism of the EPRP; see 'Garrison Socialism: The Case of Ethiopia', *MERIP*, no. 79, June 1979.

Addis Ababa, and around the same time twenty-two people in the area of the Berhanu Salem printing works were slain by a sadistic *kebele* leader, Girma Kebede. The campaign of 'red terror' was officially launched in November 1977 and lasted until May 1978. When we visited Addis Ababa in December 1977 and again in February 1978 the walls of the capital and of the provincial towns on the road to the south were plastered with square printed posters, alternately red, blue and green, carrying the unambiguous message: *Kai Shibir Yefafu* – 'Intensify Red Terror'. In February 1978 we attended a conference in the former National Assembly building in Addis Ababa where three anonymous members of POMOA openly justified the use of terror and the carrying out of instantaneous executions without any judicial procedures.[23] We did not see any cases of this, but several reliable reports testify that during this period bodies of slain opponents were left lying in the streets with placards bearing such slogans as 'This was a counter-revolutionary', 'We are tired of burying them' and 'Red terror will flourish'. No precise figures are available, but it seems that in the 1976–8 period up to 30,000 people, mainly left-wingers or suspected left-wingers, were imprisoned, and several thousand killed in these campaigns.[24]

The very real toll of EPRP and other opposition campaigns does not justify such an abandonment of legality. The EPRP's campaign posed a threat to the PMAC and its supporters: but those suspected of involvement in it could, and should, have been dealt with by legal procedures. The fact that the EPRP and the PMAC justified the terror in identical terms – that is, as a response to the prior terror of counter-revolutionaries – gives neither any moral advantage over the other. The EPRP's self-criticism was, as we shall see, superficial. On its side, the

---

[23] One of the POMOA spokesmen made the following point about the summary justice of the red terror: 'The only way to identify a counter-revolutionary is through the consciousness of the masses. The masses know who their friends and enemies are. After long observation they decide where someone belongs. They are not like the police, who have to arrest and then interrogate a person. The masses know who someone is already. They pick him up only after they have identified him'.

[24] For details see Amnesty International, *Human Rights Violations in Ethiopia*, December 1977, and ibid., November 1978. The killings did appear to have ceased by the end of 1978, so much so that Addis Ababa was being described as one of the safest cities in Africa.

PMAC later disciplined *kebele* officials guilty of some of the most horrendous crimes. Yet no proper accounting or self-criticism was made by any PMAC member and the members of the state repressive apparatus – police as well as army – who practised such actions remained in their posts. Getachew Shibeshi, the PMAC member in charge of the terror in Addis Ababa, retained his position on the security committee until his dismissal in 1979, for other reasons. The move to punish *kebele* cadres is not merely a displacement of guilt, but neither is it an adequate adjudication of the responsibility for the terror campaign which, as has been seen, received its encouragement from the very top echelons of the PMAC itself.

The claim made by the PMAC that the EPRP–CELU opposition was counter-revolutionary in nature and reflected links to the USA and to Arab reaction is not sustainable, and the EPRP's links with the Eritreans, who were associated with some counter-revolutionary and Arab forces, does not remedy this deficiency. It is not surprising, but equally without foundation, to find later attacks labelling EPRP as Trotskyist. The EPRP–CELU alliance did reflect the growth of a new consciousness among CELU members, both blue- and white-collar, after the PMAC came to power; this reflected a very real if delayed politicization that gave the EPRP its broader popular following. On the other hand, the EPRP's presentation of itself is rather exaggerated. Its claim to have played a leading role in the February revolution of 1974 is baseless, the more so as the EPRP did not even exist as a public organization until August 1975. Even the paper in which its ideas first appeared, *Democracia*, did not come out until June 1974, by which time the political initiative was with the radical army officers. There is also exaggeration in the self-image of the EPRP as 'the party of the proletariat', an incipient Bolshevik party. Its social base was always the studentry and to a lesser extent intellectuals in state employment; when it recruited militants from outside these sectors, these were very often unemployed urban teenagers. It came increasingly to rely on these in its own terror campaign and to recruit them on a militaristic basis. Its ties with the CELU leadership, formed in 1975, were ties between two distinct organizations, one student-based, the other a trade union body, and this self-proclaimed vanguard ended up in 1977 in a losing battle for survival divorced from the popular following it claimed to have. Its subsequent decision that the urban struggle had been itself an error is an implicit rejection of the claim that it ever was a proletarian party in anything but the most voluntaristic sense.

The difficulties faced by the EPRP from 1976 onwards were reflected in a number of organizational splits. In some cases the EPRP assassinated members of its own organization who had breached the party's militaristic discipline. At some point in 1977 a faction within the EPRP led by a founding member, Berhane Meskel, called for an end to the urban terror campaign and for some collaboration with the PMAC; but they were defeated and the organization divided again in 1980. Berhane Meskel was captured and executed by the Derg. It was only in 1979 that the EPRP carried out an explicit rectification of its line. At the Fourth Plenum of its Central Committee, reportedly held inside Ethiopia, the EPRP prepared what it called a statement of self-criticism.[25] It argued: (a) that it had misinterpreted the question of state power, by appearing to lay too much emphasis on the immediate establishment of a provisional people's government; (b) that it had been mistaken to give priority to the urban over the rural struggle; (c) that it had failed to evolve an adequate form of united-front work with other groups; (d) that in dealing with the national question it had been over-indulgent to 'narrow nationalists' in Eritrea and to right-wing forces in Tigray (the TPLF); (e) that it had taken too long to condemn what it termed 'social-imperialism'.

It is at once evident that this self-criticism did not go to the root of the problem. The EPRP still characterizes the Derg as 'fascist', a term that does not indicate that they have yet comprehended the nature of the state in contemporary Ethiopia and the changes it has instituted: no fascist regime ever carried out a land reform. The consistency of line to which they allude in the Fourth Plenum document, namely that they have called the PMAC fascist from the very beginning, indicates that their use of this term, even in the period of

[25] The main document of this Plenum is printed in *Abyot*, special issue, September 1979. Further details in *Africa Confidential*, vol. 22, no. 2, January 14, 1981.

the first reforms of 1975, had an element of self-fulfilment as far as the Derg's use of repression is concerned. The EPRP's new rural strategy may well be able to survive longer than its urban campaigns did, because it is located in remote areas, but for this reason it will become even more marginal; the deeper problem, of relying on armed struggle as the main tactic deployed against the PMAC, remains unresolved. The EPRP's self-criticism for its indulgence towards the USSR is, unwittingly, indicative of its general evolution. It began as a highly centralized conspiratorial group, given to workerist demagogy. It then became one fully aligned with the policies of Peking, venerating Mao Tse-tung's thoughts and even the memory of Stalin.[26] In 1979, however, it criticized China and transferred its loyalty to Albania. The EPRP's claim that it always had a theory of Soviet social-imperialism may be doubted, and its August 1975 statement stresses that it supports 'struggles against imperialism, particularly US imperialism'. Moreover, it acted understandably but aberrantly in later advancing the argument that Chinese foreign policy was governed by an internationalist line; the EPRP is working in an area of the world where the Chinese have distinguished themselves by their policies of uncritical accommodation: backing the Eritreans in the late 1960s and then abandoning them after establishing relations with Haile Selassie in 1970; supporting Nimeiry's massacre of the Sudanese Communist Party leadership in 1971; and backing the Somalis during their invasion of Ethiopia in 1977 – something even the EPRP criticizes. Prior to this self-criticism, the EPRP had held the view, shared by much of the rest of the Ethiopian left, that the PMAC was still in some way linked to US imperialism, and they even argued that Mengistu was himself part of a pro-American group within the government.

The EPRP's account of its policies on the national question is also somewhat abbreviated. Although they argue in the 1979 statement that they have always held nationalities to have the right of self-determination 'including secession', scrutiny of the August 1975 statement reveals no such

---

[26] For example, 'EPRP's Message to the Eleventh Congress of the Communist Party of China', *Abyot*, July–August 1977, vol. 2, no. 5; *Forward*, Newsletter of the World Wide Federation of Ethiopian Students, October–November 1977.

specification.²⁷ In the Ethiopian context of that time, recognition of the right to secession could not be attributed to a group unless it stated this clearly. Indeed the position of the EPRP on the national question was less outspoken than that of its main rival, ME'ISON, which tried to work with the PMAC, and which did acknowledge the right to secession in its policy statement. This reserve is all the more striking because, on available (albeit impressionistic) evidence, the EPRP had a disproportionately high percentage of Eritreans and Tigreans in its leadership, in contrast to ME'ISON, which was predominantly from the Oromo nationality, where separatist sentiment was very much less developed. The link with the Eritreans may account, to some extent, for the EPRP's continual intransigence vis-à-vis the PMAC, but material and political cooperation seems to have developed fully only in 1976 when the EPLF and EPRP issued a joint statement.

Even then a difference of opinion on the national question subsisted: the EPRP acknowledged the right of the Eritreans to 'secession', but the EPLF, which denied that Eritrea had ever been part of Ethiopia in the first place, refused to admit that it was seceding, and therefore stipulated merely its right to self-determination. The later divergences with the EPLF, the 'narrow nationalists' condemned in the 1979 documents, may have reflected a similar organizational logic: the EPLF had undermined the EPRP's position in Tigray province by supporting the rival TPLF. As with their policies on international issues, and indeed their whole relation to armed struggle, the EPRP's policy on the national question would appear to have altered rather drastically in response to conjunctural factors. The real root of its erroneous approach lay in the kind of militaristic and highly dogmatic leftism its members had inherited from their exile student days. It is this ideological formation, and social base, rather more than their ethnic affinities as such, that accounts for the policy they pursued against the PMAC and which ultimately threatened to destroy them.

---

²⁷ Section IV of the EPRP programme promises 'to give full rights to the nationalities and peoples of Ethiopia to determine their own future' but talks only in terms of 'a voluntary union based on equality and brotherhood' and of 'internally autonomous regions'.

4

Revolution From Above: (ii) The Post-Revolutionary Order

Civilian–Military Alliances

Despite its conflict with the EPRP, the PMAC's ideological evolution was inseparable from its uneasy alliance with a number of other civilian forces. In the aftermath of the February uprising, several distinct political formations came into the open, with whom the PMAC was forced, by its own weakness, to seek an accommodation. They consisted mainly of Addis Ababa students, but were dominated at the leadership level by returning exiles. The EPRP represented the section which had, by the second half of 1976, rejected the Derg outright, but five other groups allied with it for some time, coming together in POMOA. Chief amongst these was the All-Ethiopian Socialist Movement, or ME'ISON.[1] Its leaders were those who had first dominated the Ethiopian students in exile in the 1960s – Haile Fida, Fikre Merid, Negede Gobeze and the less well-known Kebede Menguesha. ME'ISON, like the EPRP, claimed a clandestine pre-history that antedated its public emergence. According to this account, the organization was founded in 1968, and took up public positions with the paper *Voice of the Masses* in 1974, at which time Haile Fida was running a left-wing bookshop near the university. ME'ISON did not proclaim itself publicly until March 1976, seven months after the EPRP, and just prior to the NDR announcement in whose drafting it played a major role. Four other political groups collaborated with ME'ISON in supporting the PMAC. The Oppressed People's Party of

---

[1] The full Amharinya title is Mela Etiopia Sosialist Nekenake.

Ethiopia, or ECHA'AT, led by Baru Tumsa, a POMOA member, was founded in 1976 as a breakaway from ME'ISON, whom it accused of neglecting the cause of the Oromo people. The Was (Labour) League was established by Dr Senaye Likkay, himself a founding member, in his exile student days, of the Communist Labor Party of the USA. MALERED, or the Marxist–Leninist Organization of Ethiopia, was another small splinter from ME'ISON. All four of these appear to have had some supporters or at least sympathetic protectors within the PMAC; they subscribed to the NDR, but they were in origin products of the radical studentry and continued to recruit most of their members from this sector. The fifth group, Abyotawit Seded, or Revolutionary Flame, was formed by army officers at some point in late 1975 and was generally regarded as being the creation of certain PMAC members, among them Mengistu.

These groups operated in a curious limbo that bespoke the uneasy and conspiratorial character of Ethiopian politics at this time: unlike the EPRP, the five entities were legal, but they were not allowed to operate publicly. While all had separate programmes, they subscribed to the National Democratic Revolution proclaimed in April 1976. The names of some leaders were known, but the membership was supposed to be secret; in the case of Seded, even the top elements remained anonymous. Recruited almost exclusively from the intelligentsia, or, in the case of Seded, from the officer corps, the groups were never mass organizations and despite ME'ISON's claim to be more, it never broke away from its limited context. So shadowy and perhaps notional was much of their activity that the policy differences between them remained obscure. It would seem that three groups – ME'ISON, ECHA'AT, MALERED – supported in principle the right of nationalities up to and including secession, although they did not accept the legitimacy of secession in the conditions prevailing in Ethiopia and subscribed to the NDR which denied such a right, even in principle. ME'ISON and ECHA'AT also argued that democratic rights could be enjoyed 'before the proletariat had assumed full power', a euphemism for some form of continued military rule; the other three said that such rights were possible only when the proletariat had already come to power and that in the meantime there should be an alliance of these parties with 'Marxist–Leninist' elements in the PMAC.[2] This question of freedom of political activity became a major issue in 1977.

Despite their differences, these groups all subscribed to the generic proposals of the NDR and to a rather inchoate Marxism that derived from the student milieu of the late 1960s. It was by 1977 increasingly influenced by Soviet and to a lesser extent Chinese political ideas.

The alliance of these groups formed the basis for the establishment in late 1975 of what later became POMOA – the Provisional Office for Mass Organization Affairs. In 1976 the five established an ideological training school, Yekatit 66 (or February 1974 in the Ethiopian calendar), which produced several thousand cadres in the next two years and from which Eastern European instructors were excluded, despite the pressure from the USSR and East Germany to have them included. In July 1977 the five established a common front, known as EMALEDH (Union of Marxist–Leninist Organizations) which was designed as a further step on the way to founding a new party. But the level of factionalism proved to be such that no convergence was possible. What transpired instead was a gradual attrition of the original 1976 alliance, as each of the four civilian groups in turn broke away, leaving remnants of their own organization together with a relatively unscathed Seded. This was itself officially dissolved in order to make way for the establishment in December 1979 of yet another umbrella body, COPWE. The first to break away was ME'ISON, which went into opposition in the summer of 1977. By August of that year, it had gone underground; only a rump faction, Kay Fana (Red Torch), remained for some further period as a remnant, until it too disappeared and its members reportedly joined Seded. In late 1977, ECHA'AT, a predomin-

---

[2] Information on the differences in party programme is drawn from authors' interviews with AETU and *kebele* officials, Addis Ababa, December 1977. The ME'ISON *Programme* recognizes 'the right of all nationalities to self-determination up to and including secession' and stresses that 'the unity of the nationalities in Ethiopia shall be based on their voluntary will to live together in equality, fraternity, and mutual respect, and on the benefits accruing from mutual assistance'. Was's position was one of support for regional autonomy (Senay Likke, *The Ethiopian Revolution: Tasks, Achievements, Problems and Prospects*, n.d.).

antly Oromo organization, also broke with the Derg and its leadership disappeared. In the summer of 1978 a new crisis broke out when over one hundred POMOA supporters, many of them army officers, were arrested and accused of having dual membership of Seded and Was and of being infiltrators from the latter into the former. The campaign against Was was accompanied by a general onslaught on Chinese policies. In July 1979 members of the only civilian group persisting in its alliance with the PMAC, MALERED, were also reported to have been arrested. Although the official rhetoric of the regime had been insisting on the proximate emergence of a 'party' ever since the NDR of April 1976, this recurrent factionalism, the causes and scale of which it was impossible accurately to gauge, meant that the establishment of such a new entity was repeatedly postponed. Since by the end of 1978 the EMALEDH project of a front of parties becoming a single party had failed, plans for a merger of such forces were officially abandoned and instead a new commission formed of individuals was set up. The First Congress of COPWE, in June 1980, marked the transition to this new party-building programme.

The central conflict within this party-building endeavour broke out in 1977 between the PMAC and ME'ISON. This dispute revolved around control of the political institutions established under the programme of the NDR. According to this programme, POMOA had four main functions: to prepare the basis for merging the five groups into a political party; to develop the mass organizations – trade unions, women's organization, *kebeles*, and so on – to run the Yekatit 66 ideological school; and to give ideological training to the militia. By the end of 1976 the fifteen-member Central Council of POMOA was dominated by members of ME'ISON, which had been able to use its position within POMOA to establish wide-ranging influence. This posed a challenge to the PMAC by its pervasive extension through the civilian ministries, and through the *kebeles*, trade unions and parts of the Peasant Associations. ME'ISON also vigorously supported the use of terror against their old foes, the EPRP, and a number of ME'ISON leaders from the student exile days, most prominent among them Fikre Merid of the POMOA Council, were assassinated by the EPRP. Yet the political advance, possibly facilitated by the fact that the military were preoccupied with their own conflicts leading up to the February 1977 shootings, led in time to a breach with the PMAC. By August 1977, ME'ISON had officially severed its links with POMOA in an attempt to return to underground work. This proved to be a disastrous initiative, for like the EPRP before it, the organization miscalculated the possibilities of such opposition political work. Haile Fida and several of his associates were captured and imprisoned, whilst a number of other ME'ISON officials went into exile. Yet although it had, by all appearances, ceased to function in any meaningful way within Ethiopia by the end of 1977 sympathy for ME'ISON continued in much of the state apparatus and mass organizations.

The PMAC claims that ME'ISON took advantage of its influential position in POMOA and of the crisis attendant upon the Somali and Eritrean wars to attempt to seize state power. In particular, the military charge that ME'ISON instructors took control of the Tatek ('Get Armed') militia training camp outside Addis Ababa and were planning to use the forces there to seize power in a capital largely emptied of soldiers because of the demands of the front. The turning point would seem to have been a major militia parade in Addis which for the first time indicated the potential armed support that ME'ISON could rally if it gained control of this body. The other major issue raised by the PMAC was ME'ISON's role in the terror and in particular its support for *kebele* leader Girma Kebede, held responsible for the murder of twenty-two innocent people in 1977. Whilst the PMAC ordered and itself helped to prosecute the terror, and continued to carry it out after ME'ISON had disappeared, it is also apparent that the latter used its positions of influence in government and in the *kebeles* to pursue old political feuds. The Girma Kebede incident was indicative of a more general excess of zeal on the part of ME'ISON from which the PMAC, for a combination of reasons, wished to dissociate itself.

ME'ISON, for its part, made a number of specific charges against the PMAC, starting from the position that the alliance with the latter was always a critical and tactical one and that it felt the moment had come for a revolutionary civilian regime

to replace the military leadership.³ ME'ISON charges that the
PMAC was not carrying out the destruction of the old state
machine but was retaining its 'feudal-bureaucratic' structures. It also charges that the PMAC was blocking a possible
restoration of political freedoms, by which it would appear to
have meant freedoms for independent activity by ME'ISON. It
claimed that the PMAC was departing from the nationalities
policy laid down in the NDR. This did not concern Eritrea:
despite its acceptance, in principle, of the right to secession
ME'ISON did not recognize the legitimacy of the existing
Eritrean leadership. Indeed it argued that, by persisting in its
policies after the 1974 Ethiopian revolution, the Eritrean
movement had become an instrument of Arab reaction. The
real ME'ISON–PMAC division in this matter was over Ogaden:
whilst ME'ISON opposed the Somali invasion, it was an
organization drawn in particular from Oromos and hence
sensitive to the way in which the southern question was being
handled. ME'ISON's complaint was therefore not that the
Somalis were being opposed but that, in the face of the Somali
invasion, the Derg was rearming the old Amhara settlers in
the south, the *neftegnas*. These landowners would then be in a
better position to re-establish the power that the 1975 land
reform had taken from them. They saw this as a retreat on the
nationalities issue, and as a 'rehabilitation of reactionaries'
that cast a slight on the mainly Oromo militia that ME'ISON
had been helping to train up. ME'ISON also justified its break
by reference to international issues. It argued during 1977
that pro-American and even 'reactionary' forces remained
strong within the PMAC and continued to warn of a possible
pro-American coup late into the year. At the same time, and
whilst avoiding characterizations of the Soviet Union as
'social-imperialist', ME'ISON criticized the Soviet Union for
failing to provide adequate assistance. 'The Soviets want to
put a brake upon our revolution', one leader argued.⁴ 'They

---

[3] ME'ISON's analysis of the conflict is given in *Voice of the Masses*, Central Organ of the All-Ethiopia Socialist Movement, August 1977, and in the interview given by Negede Gobeze to *Le Monde*, September 17, 1977. See also *Le Monde*, September 3, 1977. The PMAC's reply is 'The Ethiopian Revolution and the Right Opportunists: Stand of the PMAC', Addis Ababa, May 1978.
[4] *Le Monde*, September 3, 1977.

have forced Mengistu to eliminate us and to rely on the bureaucracy'. Unlike the EPRP, they did not demand an immediate transfer to civilian rule or a break with the USSR, but they did pose an identifiably different political programme for the Ethiopian revolution.

ME'ISON's analysis was less unrealistic than that of the EPRP. Their break with the PMAC cannot justify the cruelty to which ME'ISON members, in common with opponents of all political stripes, were later subjected. Yet ME'ISON's analysis is questionable on a number of scores. It is indicative of the general tendency towards ultra-left abstraction that afflicts many socialist groups in the First and Third World, especially those influenced by the leftist thought modes of the student movement in the advanced capitalist countries. The argument over rearming the *neftegnas* may well have a basis in fact, but as is so often the case it is phrased uniquely in class terms ('reactionaries') and passes over in silence something that was evident to all concerned, namely the national dimension of this issue. Moreover, the criticism fails to take account of the gravity of the overall situation confronting the PMAC in the summer of 1977 in the face of a massive Somali onslaught. Precisely because of the national issues involved, and the possibility of Oromo sympathy for the Somalis, the PMAC knew that the local elements upon whom they could most rely would be the *neftegnas*. ME'ISON's move into clandestinity in the summer of 1977 reveals this underestimation of the gravity of the situation in an even starker form: such a move, in those circumstances, could only have weakened the resistance to the Somali invasion, and, precisely because of the invasion, the regime was gripped by a war fever that made oppositional political activity and the restoration of some political freedoms all the more unlikely. One Arab observer who met the ME'ISON leaders in 1977 remarked to us that, although sincere militants, they appeared, with the exception of Haile Fida, to be still living in an essentially pre-revolutionary atmosphere more redolent of a student meeting than of a situation in which questions of state power were at issue. This disregard for reality would seem to be born out in their documents of this period: in the midst of a foreign invasion, they issued a call for the complete liquidation of the bureaucracy and criticized the Derg for using officers of the former imperial army.

ME'ISON's evaluation of the international dimension has also been disproved by the subsequent course of events. Soon afterwards the USSR provided large-scale aid to the Ethiopian state of a kind inconceivable in mid-1977, and despite ME'ISON's criticisms, the Russians seem to have tried in 1978 to persuade the PMAC to resolve their differences with the organization and reintegrate its cadres. On the other hand, the existence of a pro-American sector within the PMAC was shown to be an illusion since even Atnafu, the PMAC leader who made his bid for power in November 1977, was in favour of a non-aligned stance. But ME'ISON's analysis is most flawed in its evaluation of its own role: far from making self-criticism for its enthusiastic role in the red terror, it seeks to justify it.[5] At the same time, and in terms similar to the EPRP, it overestimated its own ability to lead a clandestine struggle against the Derg: whilst it made more modest demands of the military, it probably had less mass support, at the moment of its break in mid-1977, than the EPRP had when it went on to the offensive in the autumn of 1976. After the break, some of ME'ISON's cadres sided with the Derg and retained influential positions; many others were dead, in prison or in exile. ME'ISON's dramatic break was therefore based on an analysis which, like that of its arch-rival, led many militants to imprisonment or death.

Ideological Innovations

In the course of 1975 and 1976 a significant ideological change took place in the Ethiopian political context. Prior to the 1974 revolution there had been no group active within Ethiopia, including Eritrea, that professed adherence to socialism, such sympathies as there were being restricted to exiled students or individuals like Lij Michael Imru. But by 1976 virtually all the contending groups had come to use a

---

[5] 'The most important thing to realize is that this situation has been deliberately exaggerated in order to poison international opinion', thus Negede Gobeze, *Le Monde*, September 17, 1977.

vocabulary influenced by Marxism and to propound socialist policies. In the PMAC's case this evolution led from the nationalist assertion of *Etiopia Tikdem* through the first general conceptions of 'Ethiopian Socialism' to the more specific policies of the National Democratic Revolution which saw Ethiopia's future in socially revolutionary terms. After Mengistu's accession to full power in February 1977, the ideological orientation became more explicitly Marxist–Leninist. The ultimate goal was now the establishment of a 'proletarian party' that would replace the military council altogether.

It is impossible to know what combination of factors led to this change. A group of officers formed in an aristocratic army, many of them trained for some time in the USA, and who, prior to 1974, had given not the slightest sign of interest in socialism, were now quoting Lenin in their statements. The atmosphere prevailing amongst the civilian left groups certainly played a part and affected the PMAC, and one can assume that some of the officers were at least instinctively anti-monarchical before 1974. Above all, however, it was the course of events in 1974 and 1975 that must account for this change and for a broadening of intellectual horizons: as the histories of other revolutions have shown, sharp changes of political tempo can in weeks produce shifts of political consciousness, after years of apparent stasis. Given the fragility of the Ethiopian state and the dramatic way in which it crumbled, the rapidity of this change does not in itself mean that the ideological shift within the PMAC was mere affectation. On the other hand, convenience and some opportunism must also have played a certain role, and the permanent political shifts involved are far too recent to assess. The regime was committed to carrying through radical reforms, it needed a new legitimating and nationally cohesive ideology, it felt challenged by civilian groups to the left, and it relied for essential support upon the USSR and its allies. However, this pressure to the left was always controlled by the prime concern of the PMAC, the retention of power, and in adapting Marxism–Leninism it selected those themes that served its purposes. If it began to inculcate ideas of class struggle and materialist analysis of society, it also drew on such themes as 'red terror' and the need to fight all secessionists as 'counter-revolutionaries'.

Another source of new ideological influences, and one that first reinforced but later competed with the civilian influence, was Eastern Europe. For although the USSR refused for two years to meet the PMAC's requests for arms, a set of low-level agreements was signed after September 1974, under whose terms some PMAC members and thousands of other Ethiopians went on short training courses in the USSR and Eastern European countries. As a result, there was by 1976 a body of Ethiopians whose political outlook was to some extent formed by the Soviet conception of socialism. At the same time, although some students had been to the USSR before – to Lumumba University, for example – there existed no Ethiopian Communist Party; the influence of the left milieu in North America and Western Europe was much stronger. Until 1977 generically pro-Chinese views were more common than pro-Soviet ones amongst the Ethiopian left. A *Progressive Dictionary* of Marxist terms, issued in late 1976, was rather Maoist in tone.[6]

As late as November 1977 the Amharic press was using quotations from Mao in its theoretical articles, and the Was League was particularly influenced by China. However, the influx of large numbers of Soviet books and periodicals, linked to the strategic alliance with the USSR and to increasing numbers of Soviet-trained cadres, led by 1978 to the predominance of an orthodox Eastern European Marxism at the official level. China's alignment with Somalia and with conservative forces in the Middle East also reduced its appeal. State publications now condemned those whose views they opposed as Trotskyists, anarchists and Maoists, and even 'Anglo-Saxon Marxism', represented by two theoretical journals, one based in Britain, the other in the USA, was anathematized.[7] A visitor to Addis Ababa in 1978 would

[6] See Olga Kapeliuk, 'Marxist–Leninist Terminology in Amharic and Tigrinya', *Northeast African Studies*, vol. 1, no. 2, 1979, p. 28, note 2. According to Kapeliuk, the Dictionary included a section on socialist countries: Albania received eight pages, the USSR only six.

[7] 'One important factor that has inhibited the development of socialist theory in Ethiopia is the pseudo-Marxist Anglo–American literature which had been for a long time the mainstay of political thought for the radical Ethiopian intelligentsia.

have noticed the familiar covers of the Moscow Foreign Languages Press on sale at the airport, and on pavement bookstalls.

This inflow of Marxist ideas, paralleled in the importation of socialist thought by returning intellectuals, required a massive cultural enterprise at both the educational and linguistic levels. Prior to 1974, so far as we can ascertain, not a single Marxist classic had been translated into Amharic or any other major Ethiopian language. Significantly perhaps, Soviet translations of Russian literature into Amharic did exist, but the language of political study was English and, as translation of Marxist texts began, a new vocabulary had to be introduced. In some instances rough terminological approximations were reached: thus *hebratesabawinet*, or socialism, was derived from *hebratesab*, meaning 'society'; *abyot*, or revolution, meant 'refusal'; *corqannat*, 'infantilism', of the left variety, came from *corqa* meaning a child; and *enestawinet* 'feminism', from *enest* meaning a 'woman'. The very word for 'proletarian' became a site of political struggle between EPRP and the PMAC–ME'ISON bloc. The EPRP used a word based on the word for 'sweat' – *lab* – to produce *labader*, whilst ME'ISON used *wezader*, a word derived from *wez* meaning 'moist skin', but with a connotation of beauty and comfort.[8] The *Communist Manifesto* was translated into Amharic in 1975 and into Oromo in 1976, and the *Progressive Dictionary* was designed to assist the reception of Marxist terminology by providing a list of approved Marxist–Leninist terms along with Amharic explanations. At the same time, a small number of original Ethiopian Marxist texts began to appear, mainly by ME'ISON members. But in a few cases English terms were simply incorporated into political discourse so that someone ignorant of Amharic and listening to a political speech in that

---

The theoretical distortion of Marxism à la *Monthly Review*, the so-called *New Left Review* and so on, have contributed their part to arrest the development and crystallization of serious socialist thought in Ethiopia' (Ethiopian Revolution Information Centre, *Tasks, Achievements, Problems and Prospects of the Ethiopian Revolution*, Addis Ababa, September 1977, pp. 27–8).

[8] Kapeliuk; and Alem Mezgebe, 'Ethiopia – The Deadly Game', *Index on Censorship*, vol. 7, no. 4, July–August 1978.

language could easily discern such familiar terms as *feodalizm, yu-es imperializm, bureaucratic-capitalizm* and that familiar object of fulmination, *lumpen*. It is easy to suspect that this all-encompassing Marxist vocabulary was at times uttered with little conviction, and that its use was determined as much by opportunistic or chauvinistic purposes as by more revolutionary concerns. One Ethiopian observer remarked to us that 'socialism is like singing'. But whilst the level of mass 'politicization' must remain suspect, this does not mean that the whole process was without longer-term effects: very large numbers of people have now been mobilized in Ethiopia and thousands of new cadres have been formed as a result. This is especially remarkable because of one surprising absence, namely the application of any particularist limiting phrase about the 'Ethiopian' character of this socialism. The statements of 1974 used such a term; but the NDR and later documents do not. Thus there is no reference to African socialism, of a kind familiar in Tanzania or Ghana, or, with corresponding modification, in many Arab countries. There is no concession to supposed 'third ways' of the Peronist, Libyan, or Iraqi variety. While such a resolutely anti-parochial orientation does run the risk of obscuring the particularities of the local society, as has happened in Afghanistan, it may have prevented the Ethiopian revolution from making some of the cultural and class concessions that such other, qualified, varieties of socialism tend to conceal.

The Elusive 'Proletarian' Party

The revolution of 1974 was, in each of its phases, carried through without parties playing a significant role. Some civilian groups have subsequently enjoyed temporary influence, but none has been able to play a leading role in the post-revolutionary regime. The most important reason for this is the obvious fact that the military holds power and is unwilling to relinquish it. The refusal of the military to share real power, accentuated by the divisions within the PMAC over this question, which prevented any consistent conciliation from being attempted, is the root cause of the political problem. Yet this alone cannot explain the tangled course of events, least of all the long delays involved in establishing a political party: for had the PMAC decided, in the time-honoured style of military dictatorships, to set up a client political apparatus, it should, in theory, have been able to do so. The Derg was, however, pushed along this path precisely by its own weaknesses, and by its inability to rule on its own: it needed civilian allies in the tumultuous post-revolutionary situation, and its uneasy relationship with unions, *kebeles*, Peasant Associations and the Addis studentry reflected the inability of military cadres alone to run the country. This weakness both impelled the PMAC to try to establish a working relationship with the civilian forces and at the same time constrained it from granting substantive independence to them.

The underlying cause of the Derg's weakness was not, however, just a shortage of competent political and administrative personnel, but a reflection of the balance of forces that existed after the revolution, in which politically active civilian forces had emerged and after which, despite the military character of the regime, further politicization took place, in town and country. In other words, the civilian forces had, despite their own often rhetorical and evasive rhetoric, a real political context in which to grow and from which to derive strength to resist the PMAC. This balance of forces had come about because of the way in which the revolution occurred – not through a straightforward military coup, but by a protracted challenge to the old regime, in which both civilians and military had participated. This combination, unplanned and often conflictual, was what made the revolution successful. At the same time it established the terms in which a debilitating post-revolutionary conflict was to take place, with each side claiming to be the true progenitor of the 1974 upheaval. Only in this way could the conflicts involved in revolution from above be settled. A separate ingredient, of considerable significance in the subsequent history of civilian–military relations, was the political culture of the civilian milieu, in particular its factionalism and tendency towards a rhetorical simplification of political reality. Several factors contributed to shaping this. One was certainly the detached status of much of the left, which operated through student activism and underground meetings, and lacked roots in broader social classes, urban or rural. Whilst claiming to speak in the name of the oppressed, these groups were in fact divorced from those social contacts that could have exerted some strategic control upon them. A second factor was the very refusal of the army to allow them to play an autonomous political role, to the point that, although legal, they had to conduct their affairs in a clandestine half-light. A third factor was the pre-revolutionary ideological formation of these groups, which were heavily influenced by the trends prevalent in Europe and North America in the late 1960s and in which a resort to demagogy and an impatience with the demands of careful political preparation were often dominant. Far from correcting this early formation, the 1974 revolution may in some measure have reinforced it: the very advances made by a spontaneous popular upheaval and the apparent absence of political organization will have done little to instil the political sobriety and experience that leaders of other revolutions, in China or Vietnam, have had to acquire to negotiate the long years of pre-revolutionary struggle.

Underlying all these elements, drawn more or less from the recent political history of the Ethiopian intelligentsia, is the influence of other traditions, namely those of Ethiopian society itself, where conspiratorial practices had historically prevailed over forms of collective political activity. The radicalism of the mid-1970s, far from overcoming these older traditions, revitalized them, and gave them an appropriate disguise in the factional language of the international left. The rhetorical orientation of much of the civilian movement affected all factions, ME'ISON as well as EPRP, both in their dealings with other groups and in their internal life. It also reflected the manner in which the Ethiopian left had been formed at home and abroad, the lack of experience of practical mass work, and the failure to combine a socialist intellectual commitment with a concrete appreciation of the specific features of Ethiopian society or the political traditions of the country. Here, of course, the military were at an advantage. They were not just more determined and able to dispose of repressive power when needed, but by virtue of their formation within the imperial state apparatus they were at least conscious of the political forces at work in their country and were endowed with some of the practical experience that would enable them to control a state machine and outmanoeuvre their more vocal but ineffective civilian rivals.

The Soviet Union and its Eastern European allies encouraged the drive for a political party. The NDR commitment to establishing such a party was favourably reported in the Soviet press and, in addition to providing large quantities of English-language texts, the Russians, as we have seen, also tried to provide advisers to the Yekatit 66 ideological school. The main advocates of a new party within the PMAC were in the group led by Legassie Asfaw and Fikre-Selassie Wogderess, who had apparently returned from their training courses in the USSR convinced that the Soviet political model was appropriate to Ethiopia. But for this very reason, it would seem that Mengistu and those loyal to him were resistant to the project of establishing a party, until it could be guaranteed that power within it would not pass into the hands of this pro-Soviet faction.

The establishment of COPWE at the end of 1979 appeared to signal the end of these five years of uneasy civilian–military relations and of dissension within the PMAC itself on the question of the party. Following the announcement that all previous political groups had been dissolved, along with POMOA, it was stressed that COPWE membership was available on an individual basis only. In practice, this gave more opportunity for control by the top leaders. The membership of the Central Committee was kept secret until the First Congress of COPWE, in June 1980, and when published it demonstrated clearly enough what the structures of power within it were.[9] Of the 123 full and candidate members of the CC, seventy-nine were members of the armed forces or the police. The seven members of the Executive Committee of COPWE were all members of the PMAC's Standing Committee. The other three SC members and all the estimated thirty-two members of the PMAC's Central Committee were on the COPWE CC. All fourteen provincial committees were headed

[9] For list of names, see *Ethiopian Herald*, June 25, 1980; for analysis, *African Confidential*, vol. 21, no. 16, July 30, 1980.

by PMAC members. A number of civilians involved in POMOA and Yekatit 66 were also appointed, but the membership was striking for its failure to represent any of the mass organizations established by the regime: there were only two women, and no representatives at all of the peasant and trade union organizations. While the official reason for this was that COPWE was only an organizing committee, not the party itself, this lack of representation indicated how far COPWE was seen as an instrument of the top leadership. To judge by what became known of its workings, COPWE was indeed a hierarchical organization. The provincial congresses that elected the 1,500 delegates to the First Congress were stage-managed affairs at which delegates ratified a prepared list of candidates. In early 1981, following the second meeting of the COPWE CC, seven members were expelled, amongst them Lieutenant Demissie Kassaye, a PMAC member in charge of mobilizing workers.[10] There were unspecified problems involving the peasant and trade union organizations. It would therefore seem that the factionalism of the previous period had not ceased. Even the nominations to the nine committees established by COPWE told their own story, of a certain predominance of Mengistu's more loyal supporters over the pro-Soviet personnel. But the real problem with COPWE lay not so much in the factionalism it reproduced, as in the centralized structure of authority within it, which was bound to be carried over into whatever party was eventually established.

One definite function for any new party structure was bound to be that of coordinating the various mass organizations that had sprung up over the previous years. In contrast to the normal pattern of revolutionary mobilization, where an already existing party creates new mass organizations, the latter came into existence before the party. Whilst there were, as in the peasant and trade union organizations, continual changes at the top, this fluidity of leadership coexisted with continual organizational growth lower down. The AETU, established in 1975 to replace CELU, was an essential component of the regime's drive for greater industrial output.

[10] *Africa Confidential*, vol. 22, no. 6, March 11, 1981.

The *kebele* system continued to have responsibility for urban administration, even after it was deprived of its political autonomy and role in security. The All-Ethiopian Peasant Association was by far the largest of these and, through the vicissitudes of agricultural policy, it retained a central place in the extension of control into the rural areas. The organization of women also had an important, if understated, role. Whilst women, for obvious reasons, played no role in the military apparatuses, they did participate widely in the civilian movement, and one of the more positive political themes that the exiled students brought back from their studies was a special emphasis on the need for the emancipation of women. A Women's Committee operated within POMOA. As late as 1977, official state documents were stressing the double oppression of women, as workers and women. This was in contrast to the more orthodox theory of the Eastern European countries that became official policy in 1978 and which gave primacy to class over gender oppression.[11] In the countryside, moreover, the establishment of Peasant Associations went together with the setting up of local women's associations. Nearly all women had been integrated into these structures by 1980, and women appear to have participated quite widely in the peasant associations. In the towns, the establishment of women's organizations appears to have encountered opposition from the already existing women's organizations associated with the EPRP and ME'ISON.[12] In the countryside the obstacles would have arisen from the tradi-

[11] For an official statement advancing the theory of women's dual oppression, see *Ethiopia in Revolution*, Ethiopian Revolution Information Centre, Addis Ababa, July 1977, pp. 37–9. By 1978, however, this view was being rejected in favour of the view that women faced only class oppression (interview with Terowarq Waqeyhu, Chairwoman of the Women's Committee in POMOA, Addis Ababa, February 1978). For an evaluation of the record of the Communist parties on women see Maxine Molyneux, 'Socialist Societies Old and New: Progress Towards Women's Emancipation?', *Feminist Review*, no. 8, Summer 1981. While the EPRP attacked what it saw as the 'revisionist' official view on women, ME'ISON member Negest Adane published *Women in the Development of Society* (in Amharinya) in 1977, during the period when ME'ISON was represented in POMOA.

[12] One of the main features of female employment in Addis Ababa was the very widespread incidence of prostitution. The Mayor of Addis, Alemu Abebe, told us in December 1977 that there were up to 100,000 women engaged in prostitution in the capital. At that time, some effort had been made to resettle them in rural areas, but prostitution as such had not been prohibited or restricted.

tional structures and suspicions of village life. These different if reinforcing problems may explain why it was only in July 1980 that a national structure, Revolutionary Ethiopia's Women's Association, REWA, was established.

The emergence of a 'proletarian' party will solve only some problems. It will in all likelihood be a highly centralized organization, based on 'proletarian discipline' of a kind all too familiar over the past fifty years. Such a party will provide a structure for consolidating the post-revolutionary regime and for incorporating civilian support in a systematic manner. It will not allow of democratic procedures and expression; changes of line or personnel will be effected through conspiracy and manoeuvre, and the military leadership will maintain firm control of it. Factionalism will, on past evidence, continue, but it will as likely reflect competing factions within the military as a tolerance of divergent civilian views. However, it is important to note that on the evidence of their past history, organizations such as the EPRP or ME'ISON would not allow greater political freedoms to other socialists were *they* to direct the party's affairs. There is no easy democratic alternative in Ethiopia. The history of PMAC–civilian relations, and the difficulties encountered in setting up a party, are indicative of the problems and character of the Ethiopian revolution itself. The creation of a hierarchical body by the top leadership, including only the tamed remnants of the civilian forces, will be an instrument for social and economic mobilization but will only partly resolve the deeper political problems that have subsisted since 1974.

The Post-Revolutionary State

The establishment of a new party structure and of the associated mass organizations formed part of the wider process of constructing a post-revolutionary state directed by the personnel and policies of the new leadership. The state, defined as a set of institutions through which political power is wielded, and as the means through which classes exercise their political domination over society, forms a central part of all social and political analysis. But the state cannot be seen as a mere instrument of class rule: it has a certain element of what is conventionally termed 'autonomy' from classes, and is able to act in some degree independently of, and even contrary to, the interests of those on whose support it rests; and it is itself the forum or site of political conflicts between different social forces. This 'autonomy' exists even in the most settled and developed capitalist societies, but it is all the greater in other situations. This is so in revolutionary contexts, where the normal controls of social class over the state may be attenuated, and where the very conflicts of the revolutionary period are concentrated on the state – either on gaining control of existing apparatuses or on establishing new institutions capable of replacing those through which the social relations of the old order are reproduced.[13] The autonomy of the state may also be greater in situations of transition from one mode of production to another, where social forces associated with both modes may compete for power not just over the state, but within it, in such a way that the institutions are again released from the class controls imposed in situations where one mode and one system of social relations are dominant. Finally, the autonomy of the state may be greater where class relations are themselves less developed, due to the disruption of the social system by external influences or by the predominance of social relations determined by factors other than class, such as ethnic and lineage bonds. This latter form of autonomy is characteristic of the Third World, where the underdeveloped system of class relations, by contrast to the developed capitalist countries, gives additional weight to the potential influence of the state in political and economic affairs. It will be evident that all three forms of 'autonomy' have pertained in the Ethiopian case: Ethiopia is a society undergoing a revolution, its social relations are transitional and heterogeneous and its class forces are still partially developed. The state is therefore both a reflection of the conflicts within society, the object of that conflict, and a means by which those concerned to transform society can hope to achieve their aims. If it is to a

---

[13] Skočpol, chapter 4, elaborates an argument on the particular role of the state in revolutionary situations.

considerable extent limited by the objective structures of Ethiopian society — it cannot arbitrarily remould social relations irrespective of the conditions prevailing — it is nonetheless an active agent in the process of consolidating a post-revolutionary order. It reflects to some degree the interests of class and social forces but it may also play an active role in class formation, in constructing new social relations of which its agents are a part. The discussion that follows will focus on three aspects of the role of the Ethiopian state after 1974: the changes in institution and personnel; the relations between the state, on one side, and the population and economy, on the other; and the conflicts within the state over policy — the state as the site of conflict.

As discussed in chapter 2, the Ethiopian state was the site of the decisive conflict that brought the revolution about, the conflict between supporters of the absolutist state and proponents of a new social order. The administrative expansion of the post-1941 period, combined with the growing agrarian crisis and international pressure, produced a revolution from above. Two other aspects of the imperial state were also important in subsequent events. First, unlike all other state apparatuses in Africa, this was not a post-colonial state, in the sense of one created by colonial rule and bequeathed to the independent country with a connection to international capital: the international links established by the Ethiopian imperial state were of a quite different character, supportive but not constitutive. Hence the conventional option for the personnel of such states, association with the metropolitan countries, was not immediately available in Ethiopia. Linked to this was the role the state already played in the Ethiopian economy, as a result of its absolutist and incipiently 'developmental' character. The survival of a predominantly pre-capitalist order had precluded the emergence of an Ethiopian bourgeoisie capable of playing either the economic or the political role seen elsewhere in the Third World. Hence the state was already an important factor in economic activity, and the normal brake on even the more verbally militant of military regimes, the indigenous bourgeoisie, was lacking. At the same time, the social barriers represented by the classes associated with the old order, the nobility, were themselves swept away in the revolution. The, in African terms, unique character of Ethiopia therefore gave the state a particularly 'autonomous' and potentially radical role.

Information on the institutions and personnel of the state is deficient, but it would appear that two main processes were dominant in the period after 1974. On the one hand, there occurred an expansion in the size and role of the military apparatuses; on the other, there was a relative seclusion of the civilian apparatuses, coupled with their subordination to military control. At the time of the revolution, the Ethiopian armed forces totalled over 44,000 men, 41,000 of whom were in the army. Military expenditure in 1971 was estimated to be $40 million. By 1980 the army had expanded to around 75,000 men but was supplemented by a militia of relatively full-time soldiers totalling 150,000 or ten divisions. If to this is added the other para-military groups and the relatively static navy and air force, personnel as of 1980 total 230,000, and defence expenditure totals $385 million.[14] Even taking account of the qualitative deficiencies of the militia, and the lower value of the dollar, these figures reflect a large quantitative expansion in the military apparatus. This numerical growth went together with an extension of military control over the civilian branches of state, and over the new mass institutions established after 1974. At first, as we have seen, the PMAC directed the government from separate bodies but from 1977 onwards its personnel were increasingly integrated into the ministries and provincial administrations as well as into the new political structures such as COPWE. Even the militia, a body often seen as a rival to the armed forces, was placed under the control of personnel drawn from the military apparatus. When it was raised in 1977, training was handled by the police force, and after the initial militia campaigns in Eritrea in 1978–9, the regular army reestablished its full predominance in military matters.[15]

[14] International Institute for Strategic Studies (London), *The Military Balance 1972–1973*; and ibid., *1980–1981*.

[15] Service in the militia was for up to three years and involved long periods away from the recruit's place of residence during which relatives would have no communication with him. It was therefore more an adjunct of the regular army than a people's defence force.

The degree of transformation within the armed forces themselves is more difficult to establish. While those commanders most closely associated with the *ancien régime* were exiled, imprisoned or retired, a considerable number of higher-ranking officers were retained, and more were recruited again in the face of the Somali attack in 1977.[16] When constituted in 1974, the Derg was drawn from ranks below that of Lieutenant-Colonel, with the result that none of the top commanders in 1976 were members. It was only gradually that these junior officers were promoted to ranks such as Brigadier, on a par with the surviving officers of the old regime. Yet the PMAC itself also embodied class forces. While it would be mistaken to see this as a simple reflection of class processes, it is possible to discern a certain social pattern in the outcome of the conflict within the Derg itself. The more senior officers, drawn from the Harar academy, were gradually ousted, only a few remaining in positions of power. Equally, however, the lowest ranks in the PMAC, the NCOs, were also generally excluded from the highest positions in the committee system that evolved. The group that emerged in control were the middle section of the Derg, the Holeta graduates – those with some chances of promotion under the *ancien régime*, but who were blocked by the nobility and Harar graduates above them. Within the overall process of revolution from above, therefore, there were shifts in the social composition of the ruling group.

The personnel of the civilian apparatuses were reduced by the political turmoil of the revolutionary process. As had happened in the armed forces, many higher-ranking members of the bureaucracy fled the country, either in 1974 or later. Those in the foreign ministry particularly were able to leave, and did so in large numbers.[17] Yet it would seem that the majority of the civil service remained in place, accepting if not welcoming the changes which occurred. The conflict with the EPRP in 1976–8 led to further clashes within the administ-

[16] For example, the Chief of Staff of the Armed Forces in June 1981, Brigadier-General Haile-Giorgis Habte-Mariam, was not a member of the PMAC.

[17] The degree of conflict within the Foreign Ministry was graphically illustrated during a visit to the ministry in December 1977. There were several security checks; armed guards were stationed on each floor of the building; and a poster in the main entrance gave photographs and names of several dozen wanted people.

ration, especially as it was amongst graduates of universities and secondary school (those likely to enter ministries) that the EPRP was able to recruit most successfully. In response, the PMAC imposed its own supervision on the ministries and instituted a process of political education for civil servants. Whole ministries participated in public discussions, work outings to the country and education programmes designed to induce support for the NDR and the regime's goals. Diplomats posted abroad were recalled for training courses at education centres in Addis Ababa. But the success of these initiatives may be doubted. It was often the politically more courageous or aware civilians who were exposed and dismissed in such procedures, those who had favoured the revolution; those who remained were often those who were less politically active and found it easier to accommodate to the new situation. Moreover, what was being attempted was a re-education of existing personnel and structures: there was little attempt to transform the hierarchical organization of the civil administration itself or to bring new personnel into the state machine. The response of the civilian administration was to bow to the inevitable, but to preserve relatively intact its personnel, institutional structure and, it would seem, its political preferences.

What has been said so far pertains to the apparatuses at the centre, and in particular those located in Addis Ababa. But it appears that a much greater degree of transformation had occurred in the provinces. This is for two reasons. First, because the provincial administration had been less modernized under the old regime and relied more on the aristocracy and local land-holders: hence the process of social revolution removed many more of these personnel. Second, because one of the changes associated with the new regime was the imposition of much more control from the centre: there was therefore a need for new systems of administration to be established. Here again, PMAC and other military personnel played a major role but in a context more fluid and more transformed than that in the administrative structures at the centre.

The relationship established between the state and the society as a whole is more difficult to discern. Those wielding state power in the post-revolutionary period were drawn almost exclusively from the lower sections of the imperial apparatus and were thus included in what is conventionally termed the petty bourgeoisie; this term, frequently applied to Third World societies, has limited explanatory value, however, given the variety of social categories it encompasses. More important is the fact that the reforms carried out did objectively benefit the social group from which the military leaders were drawn: the land reform strengthened the position of the richer peasants, while the growth of state control in general, and of the military with it, promoted the interests of those who had occupied intermediate positions under the *ancien régime*. However, given the freedom of decision of the military leadership, and the multiple pressures upon it, it would be mistaken to reduce its policies to mere expressions of class interests. The measures taken by the regime had, initially, contradictory effects and different potential outcomes. These depended both on the conflict within the state over what policies to implement and on the degree of resistance that further measures might encounter from those with greatest social power under the new regime.

The new regime's relation to the population as a whole was marked by a number of distinctive characteristics. First, this was a far more centralized and interventionist state than the old. The provincial power-holders of the imperial state were all swept from power, their place being gradually taken by direct nominees of the centre. The PMAC's ability to impose centralized control was at first restricted, given its limited resources and the incidence of rural dissidence; but over time the process of political change was evolving towards a new administratively stronger state. Any solution to the regional and nationalities problem would have to accommodate this, apparently unavoidable, reality. At the same time, building on the policies of the old regime, the new state took the leading place in the economy, and by the end of the 1970s had erected a system of state controls and centralized planning. Whatever the final outcome, it seems that the state will be the main director of economic activity and investment in the coming period. The second major change was in the relationship to the people. Once the regime was established, few could imagine that Ethiopia was a politically democratic country, in the sense of permitting those at the base to express their views openly or to take autonomous decisions: this was true neither for classes, nor nationalities, nor individuals. But this authoritarian structure should not obscure the fact that a new system of mobilization and communication had been established, through the political organizations of the regime. It was through these mediations that a centralized state was being created, however haltingly. They were not based on the recruiting or operating principles of the *ancien régime*: ethnic particularism and heredity played a much smaller part. The central criterion for recruitment was political loyalty – to the regime in general, and to its chairman in particular. Through these mechanisms, very large numbers of people were incorporated into the state system. Again, recognition of the authoritarian structure of these mechanisms is quite consistent with assertion of their novel, and pervasive, character: over seven million people in the Peasant Associations, up to half a million in the Trade Unions, several million in the Women's Associations, and several hundred thousand at one time or another in the militia. The extension of social services also helped to strengthen the bonds between government and population: the literacy campaign in particular was designed to bring the people into political life. Politics, however much it was directed from above, was being brought to the population in a way not previously seen in Ethiopian history.

The mobilization of such large numbers depended on a variety of mechanisms. One was material interest: however differentiated its effects, the revolution did offer the population the prospect of economic and social development. After years of turmoil in the provinces, it also offered something even more valuable: peace. Indeed it is probable, if unverifiable, that even in Eritrea a growing proportion of the population was willing to accept the regime provided it could guarantee an element of prosperity and security. Ideologically, the regime tried to mobilize support on the basis of a new Ethiopian identity, embodied in the slogan *Etiopia Tikdem*. By 1977 this had been joined by the slogan *Abyotawit*

Etiopia Waim Maut – 'Revolutionary Ethiopia or Death', a reflection both of the increased radicalism of the regime and of the new patriotic note being struck in the face of the Somali attack.[18] How far this new emphasis was convincing in a country still marked by pre-capitalist differentiations and where the regime was itself still disproportionately recruited from Amhara, is the subject of the following chapter. The regime did, however, deploy a third motivation, which it used calculatingly and, it has to be said, with success: coercion, including deliberate terror. The executions of November 1974 were, it seems, designed to instil fear in the minds of those associated with the *ancien régime* or inclined to believe that it could in some measure be restored. The later use of terror against the EPRP was not the product of irrational individuals or of an irrational process: it was used deliberately, as a means of demobilizing an enemy and consolidating obedience to the regime, and Mengistu's statements and practice bear this out.[19] By the same token, the terror had its limits: the process was not one of an ever-increasing spiral of violence, and by the late 1970s it had apparently been decided to pursue less brutal tactics.

A similar reduction of tensions was noted within the PMAC: after the execution of Atnafu in November 1977, no other killings of dismissed PMAC members were reported. Coercion on a wider scale also played a role. Recruitment to the militia involved press-ganging large numbers of peasant youth, mainly Oromos, into military service. All political dissent was prohibited in the towns from 1976 onwards. However, the regime deliberately cultivated an image of itself as being in the tradition of strong Ethiopian rulers: Mengistu was compared to Tewodros, the nineteenth-century ruler who re-established a central state after the disunity of the period of princes. In public appearances he sat on the ornate chair used before him by Haile Selassie and he lived in the Gebbi, the

---

[18] Another common slogan in the late 1970s was *Enashenifalen*, 'We Shall Triumph'. The provenance of these two rallying cries may be related to their Spanish equivalents, *Patria o Muerte* and *Venceremos*.

[19] During one public speech, devoted to a denunciation of the regime's enemies, Mengistu threw bottles filled with a blood-coloured liquid on the ground.

imperial palace where, as late as 1980, the emperor's lions were still maintained.[20]

However, the state was not merely the means of mobilizing support: it was also the site of conflict between competing factions. The conflicts within the PMAC, and more generally within the state apparatuses, were both social, between groups reflecting different class interests, and political, between forces advocating different policies with varying degrees of responsiveness to class forces without. The fragmentary nature of Ethiopian society, in which class forces operated in a diffuse manner upon state personnel, and the turmoil of the revolutionary transition combined to give these conflicts within the state a considerable if temporary autonomy from class forces. Hence, while in the longer run the success of any state policy would depend upon securing the support of class forces in Ethiopian society, the triumph of one particular group within the PMAC, and the evolution of state policy, were determined by other, often intermediate factors.

We have already suggested five reasons why the post-1974 regime moved so rapidly and far to the left, so that within three years it was talking of a transition to socialism. Yet the society over which the PMAC ruled was certainly not socialist: pre-capitalist social relations and ideologies persisted throughout much of the Ethiopian countryside, while in both the rural and urban economies petty commodity production and capitalist relations were expanding. The autonomy of the state was such that there existed a possibility that it could, by implementing policies of transformation, place the country on the path to a socialist transition. But this was by no means a necessary outcome and depended upon three levels of determination. First, it depended on the outcome of the conflict within the state itself, between factions of the PMAC, and between radical and conservative elements in both the military and the civilian sectors. Second, it required that policies aimed at a socialist transition secure sufficient cooperation in Ethio-

---

[20] It is widely believed in Ethiopia that Mengistu is, in fact, the grandson of an illegitimate child of Emperor Menelik. Whilst there is no evidence for this belief, the fact that it is entertained may be an additional reason for his being held in some awe.

pian society to provide the social support for this transformation: while the country was in a state of flux, the residues of the old order, compounded by some of the effects of the reforms, placed serious obstacles in the face of such a transition. Most obviously, the regime faced enormous obstacles in implementing any collectivization of agricultural production. Third, the conditions for attempting a socialist transition were not given within the confines of Ethiopian society alone: they involved trans-national factors, of support (from the USSR and its allies) and of opposition (from the West). Any programme of economic development, a prerequisite for beginning a transition to socialism, involved substantial aid from abroad. Neither the intentions of the major capitalist states, nor the reservations of some of the PMAC leadership about the USSR, were conducive to such an orientation. While there are those in the state who favour a socialist option, the possibility of Ethiopia's attempting a transition to socialism rests upon the fulfilment of all of three conditions: the triumph within the state of those favouring this path; the securing of sufficient support from classes within Ethiopia itself; and supportive trans-national conditions. The prospects for such an outcome will be addressed in our concluding chapter.

5
The Regional and National Questions

A Fragmented Society

The overthrow of the imperial regime was not a direct result of tensions between the Addis Ababa government and the provinces. The Emperor was not ousted by provincial revolts, and the mutinous soldiers who rose in the provinces were, in general, as hostile to these provincial opponents as was Haile Selassie himself. The question of provincial rights appeared secondary, therefore, both in the causation of the revolution and in the priorities of those who made it. Yet the revolts of the preceding years, in Bale and Eritrea, helped to weaken the imperial state and to divide its personnel into rival factions. They also played an important part in radicalizing the student opposition. As with the crisis on the land, the crisis in the provinces made a mediated but powerful contribution to the revolution. The fall of the imperial regime then brought this issue to the very centre of Ethiopian politics: if provincial rebellion was at a relatively low ebb in early 1974, the evolution of events thereafter led to a widespread *prise de conscience* among the nationalities in Ethiopia. The result was that in 1977 the PMAC reported that it was facing revolt in twelve of Ethiopia's fourteen provinces, the most serious being in Eritrea and in the Ogaden region, which covered three provinces. At their respective peaks in late 1977, these two appeared to threaten the very existence of the revolutionary regime, and involved the mobilization of tens of thousands of soldiers. Many thousands died in these conflicts, and over one million people became refugees.[1] The economic costs, in destruction and in diverted resources, were immense. But even if the PMAC was, by 1978, able to regain the initiative in both these disputes, it appeared unable to stem the growing discontent amongst other nationalities, particularly in Tigray province in the north, and amongst the Oromo in the south. At the beginning of the 1980s, therefore, the issue of provincial autonomy and of separation remained an urgent one throughout much of the non-Amhara areas.

As we have already noted, the fact of ethnic conflict and of a central government's denial of autonomy to nationalities does not contradict the claim that a social revolution has occurred. Indeed the record of such revolutions is, if anything, the reverse: comprehensive social upheavals in multinational states provoke national and ethnic conflicts to which the revolutionary governments respond in a centralizing manner. The tendency for social revolutions to be accompanied by such conflicts is well demonstrated by two of the upheavals of the 1970s, those in Ethiopia and Iran.[2] Certain general political reasons for this intransigence are obvious enough: the continuation of pre-revolutionary political cultures of hostility towards all opposition, and in particular towards opposition by previously subject ethnic groups; the fear that counter-revolutionary forces from outside may weaken the revolution through support for secessionist movements; the search for new factors of ideological mobilization in campaigns against those seen as threatening the unity of the revolution itself. Where a revolution from above occurs, it is probable that pre-existing attitudes towards subject groups persist among the state personnel. To identify this intransigent trend is not, however, sufficient: beyond the political factors making for a certain revolutionary inflexibility towards such oppositions lie particular historical and material

---

[1] Official (1980) figures from Somalia and the Sudan spoke of around 1.3 million refugees in the former, and up to 400,000 in the latter. Both governments can be expected to have exaggerated the figures to some extent; but their calculations would not include either the large numbers displaced within Ethiopia itself, or the substantial Eritrean diaspora, in Saudi Arabia and in North America.

[2] See chapter 1, p. 39.

factors present in each country. The discussion that follows aims to chart the development of these conflicts in post-revolutionary Ethiopia, and to suggest why it was that a revolution in which the nationalities issue played apparently so secondary a part should have led to such carnage and ethnic unrest in the succeeding years.

The underlying cause of this development was the low level of integration prevailing under the imperial regime. The physical aspects of this, in terms of the lack of communications and a dispersed economy, have already been mentioned, as has the survival and predominance of local and ethnic allegiances far more powerful than loyalty to a central state or some Ethiopian 'nation'.[3] Yet if the pre-revolutionary state had rested upon the disunity of the country and on the balance of its various separate components, the revolutionary state based itself upon a new centralized system: in that process of transition, from a centrifugal equilibrium to a new fusion, conflict was inevitable. This, a sociological rather than a political factor, was the central reason for the pattern of ethnic conflict in post-imperial Ethiopia: far from making concessions to the nationalities, the new state, reflecting the transition from one mode of production to another, was compelled to integrate and centralize.

The second factor was the discriminatory structure of power – political, economic and religious – on which the imperial state had been built in the nineteenth century. Implementing its revolution from above, the PMAC arose from this state and in part inherited it. The oppressed nationalities retained their hostility to the centre. Whilst the revolution was one that altered the character of the central state, it did so only partially. At the same time it gave new rein to forces that had long regarded that state as an oppressor. A third factor, exaggerated by the PMAC but nonetheless important, was the involvement of outside powers in these conflicts. The Arab states supported the Eritreans and Somalis, with the result that these opponents of the PMAC were enabled to continue their resistance. The Derg saw these revolts as evidence of external intervention reminiscent of earlier attempts by the

---

[3] See chapter 2, p. 61.

Arabs and Muslims to encroach upon the Horn. In blaming all its problems upon the foreign enemies the Derg was guilty of simplification; but its members knew that the base areas and much of the supplies upon which these rebellious forces relied were provided by Arab states. The involvement of the regular army of one neighbouring state, Somalia, in the Ogaden conflict also did much to harden hostility at the centre to any demands by the ethnic and regional forces, even demands for autonomy. Fourth, the very weakness and uncertainty of the central government itself contributed to the problem; rent by revolts in outlying provinces and by political problems in Addis Ababa itself, the PMAC lacked the confidence to seek political solutions to these problems. Finally, both sides in these conflicts found their room for manoeuvre weakened by the factionalism within their own camps. As in republican Iran, the elements within the new regime favouring a measure of conciliation were overridden by those espousing an intransigent position on the national question together with an appeal for a generally more radical politics. The PMAC reacted against the demands raised by ME'ISON, EPRP and ECHA'AT for concessions on the national issue, and those in the Derg favouring negotiation were defeated. The Eritrean groups found it the more difficult to envisage any moderation on their part because of the advantages that such an apparent softening might give to their rivals. The results of this impasse have been tragic: whilst Ethiopia faced probably less overt counter-revolution than any other modern revolution, its post-revolutionary history has been marked by extremes of bloodshed that have cost many lives, destroyed areas of the country, stored up new resentments and made the establishment of a stable and popular regime all the more remote.

PMAC Policies

There is no evidence to indicate that when the PMAC was first constituted in June 1974 its members had given systematic thought to the national and regional question or to the need to correct the mistakes of the previous government. There seems to have been some vague intention to end oppression by the imperial regime; but even here the reluctance of the first PMAC statements to admit the existence of a specifically *national* as distinct from 'tribal' oppression was telling. More importantly, however, the PMAC laid emphasis upon the need to preserve the unity of Ethiopia. This desire was exemplified in the very slogan *Etiopia Tikdem* and illustrated by the way in which Aman Andom, the first Derg Chairman, was accused in November 1974 of having shown weakness in his negotiation with the Eritrean guerrillas. Calls for secession were made punishable by death from that month onwards.

Whilst many of the PMAC's main social reforms were proclaimed in the course of 1975, it was only in 1976 that a detailed policy on the national question was evolved, in the NDR of April and in the Nine Point Statement on Eritrea proclaimed on 16 May. Despite certain gestures in the direction of conciliation, both statements were fundamentally unyielding. The NDR began by declaring that 'the right to self-determination of all nationalities will be recognized and fully respected' and continued: 'No nationality will dominate another one, since the history, culture, language and religion of each nationality will have equal recognition in accordance with the spirit of socialism. The unity of Ethiopia's nationalities will be based on their common struggle against feudalism, imperialism, bureaucratic capitalism and all reactionary forces. This united struggle is based on the desire to construct a new life and a new society based on equality, brotherhood and mutual respect'.[4] The NDR went on to specify what it envisaged as the solution by declaring that 'the problem of nationalities can be resolved if each nationality is accorded full right to self-government. This means that each nationality will have regional autonomy to decide on matters concerning its internal affairs. Within its environs, it has the right to determine the contents of its political, economic and social life, use its own language and elect its own leaders and administrators to head its internal organs'. The Nine Point Statement on Eritrea presented similar ideas and offered the people of Eritrea 'full participation in the political, economic

---

[4] *Basic Documents of the Ethiopian Revolution*, Addis Ababa 1977, pp. 13–14.

and social life of the country'.⁵ Calling on the Eritreans to participate in the NDR, it promised that 'the government will at an appropriate time present to the people the structure of the regions that can exist in the future'. It offered to discuss with 'progressive groups and organizations in Eritrea which are not in collusion with feudalists, reactionary forces in the neighbourhood and imperialists'. It offered to assist the return of refugees, and to assist with the rehabilitation of destroyed property, as well as to declare an amnesty and lift the state of emergency.

The problems involved in these two statements were patent. First, they failed even in principle to acknowledge any right to secession: the 'full respect' for the right to self-determination in one section of the NDR contradicted itself two paragraphs later by limiting this right to one of regional autonomy. The refusal to concede this right even in principle inevitably undermined any appeal that the PMAC's other offers might have had. Second, the powers of these regional governments were left imprecise; it was not clear whether, even if established, they would amount to anything of political substance. Third, the PMAC left indeterminate the territorial basis on which the regional governments would be established and the compass of their 'environs'. A necessary part of any such policy was the recognition of what the entities to have autonomy would be, and what their boundaries would include; since Eritrea contains ten distinct linguistic groups, all of which could be seen as nationalities in their own right, it would be possible to set up distinct regional groups for each. Whilst appearing to go a long way towards meeting demands for self-determination this would in effect negate them by fragmenting the Eritrean population. Underlying all these difficulties was a refusal to admit that, independent of class conflicts, there could also be ethnic and national conflicts with their own force and requiring separate attention: 'progressive' or 'reactionary' positions in the Eritrean context, for example, were determined according to whether those con-

⁵ 'Policy Declaration of the Provisional Military Government to Solve the Problem in the Administrative Region of Eritrea in a Peaceful Way', in *Basic Documents*, p. 154.

cerned accepted the indivisibility of Ethiopia. Hence the continuation of chauvinism at the centre was concealed behind an apparently faultless rhetoric of class conflict. The fact that many of those fighting in Eritrea espoused ideas almost identical to the NDR on all other issues was one to which the PMAC appeared blind, as did, in their own reciprocal way, the Eritrean guerrillas themselves. Yet neither in Ethiopia nor elsewhere has any such simple elision of class with national conflicts proved valid. The ready use of a class vocabulary obscures the persistence of ethnic and national issues.

The tendency towards self-legitimation did not just pervade the account of the post-1974 period, when the PMAC defended its attempts at conciliation, but included the official interpretation of the earlier period, which virtually justified the policies associated with Haile Selassie. Where it did recognize the scale of resistance to the imperial regime, it focused on its social rather than on its ethnic dimensions. The preamble to the statement on Eritrea admitted that some Eritreans had been driven to oppose Haile Selassie because of the 'reactionary' nature of his government, but it also upheld the contentious view that the majority of Eritreans had wanted to be integrated with Ethiopia and asserted, moreover, that the 1952 federation of Eritrea with Ethiopia was an artificial device imposed on the latter by outside pressure. A major speech on Eritrea by Mengistu in June 1978 reiterated this view, which accorded almost wholly with the conventional Amhara chauvinist line dominant before the revolution.[6] It would have been a minimum necessary part of any conciliation by the PMAC for it to have offered to restore the federation, yet even this proved too great a concession to make. The most important limitation on these declarations lay, however, in the field of practice, for as it was issuing them, and calling for a political settlement, the PMAC was

---

[6] 'The National Revolutionary War in the North', Address by Mengistu Haile-Mariam, June 7, 1978, published by the Ministry of Information and National Guidance, Addis Ababa. In this statement Mengistu appeared to make some distinction between the ELF and the more socialist EPLF: but any such nuances were later abandoned and seem to have found no echo within the Fronts. If anything, the ELF proved more conciliatory than the EPLF in the 1979–80 period.

preparing, in June 1976, to launch a major offensive in Eritrea, using a peasant militia. This initiative was not only intrinsically inconsistent with any prospect of conciliation that might have been raised by the NDR and Nine Point proclamations; it was also marked by the revival of themes redolent of the chauvinist campaigns of the imperial past, with the Christian peasants being rallied to fight off Muslim invaders and, it was rumoured, being promised land in the areas they won back.[7]

The peasant march of June 1976 ended in a massacre of the militia by the Eritrean guerrillas but it did not render the PMAC more conciliatory, any more than did repeated appeals from the USSR, Cuba and left-wing Arab parties. The PMAC continued to talk of a political solution, but in fact bided its time until it was in a position, in June 1978, to start a full-scale military offensive using the new, more organized militia and regular troops. Some negotiations did take place between the Eritreans – the EPLF – and the Derg, but they came to nothing and in his major speech on the issue in June 1978, preparatory to the military offensive, Mengistu restated the positions first enunciated in 1976. He repeated the proposals of the NDR, without specifying in any greater detail what the central government was offering, and he characterized the Eritrean movement as a 'counter-revolutionary conspiracy' against which the Ethiopian masses were waging 'a revolutionary war'. In explaining this, he stated: 'The structure of people's revolutionary war is national, but it is progressive and international in its content. Its main objective is to free the oppressed people of Eritrea, who are held captive at gunpoint by the separatist groups that are being used by imperialists and reactionary Arab ruling classes, so that they will be able to share the revolutionary gains with the rest of their Ethiopian class comrades and assert their class rights. . . . The primary objective of the people's revolutionary war is to affirm Ethiopia's historical unity and to safeguard her outlet to the sea, and defend her very existence from being stifled.'[8]

As Mengistu's speech implied, PMAC policy in Eritrea was

[7] Ottaways, p. 159.
[8] 'The National Revolutionary War in the North', p. 30.

influenced not just by the situation in that province, but by the overall ethnic mosaic of Ethiopia. This was partly because policies enforced or concessions made in Eritrea would inevitably set precedents for other areas and nationalities; it was also because the longer the war in Eritrea continued, the less likely it was that the Derg would evolve a general nationalities policy that could accommodate the demands of other claimant national groups. The result was that the hard line in Eritrea served to exacerbate ethnic feelings among the former subject peoples of the country, just as it encouraged the re-emergence of Amhara chauvinism at the centre. It also contributed to the disputes within POMOA and EMALEDH: beyond the formal and somewhat evasive argument that there had to be a party to provide the context for a solution to the nationalities problem, there was the aggravating factor that disputes over this issue played their part in encouraging factionalism at the centre in the 1977–9 period.

The one serious attempt to implement a nationality policy was in the Afar region of the north-east, in an area including parts of Eritrea and Tigray, where a congress of Afar tribal leaders was convened in April 1977. This called for the establishment of an autonomous Afar area. No details are available on precisely what the powers of this area were to be, and it remained a mere proposal since the main force behind it, Lieutenant Neguessie Negassa, an Oromo PMAC member who had studied the nationalities issue in Yugoslavia, was assassinated soon after the conference ended.[9] With the increased conflict in neighbouring Eritrea later in the year, many Afars became involved in fighting against the Derg, under the influence of their traditional leader, Sultan Ali Mirah Anfere. One permanent interest in a separate Afar

---

[9] *Frankfurter Rundschau*, September 7, 1979; Pliny The Middle-Aged, 'The PMAC Origins and Structure', Part II. During 1978 and 1979 various position papers on possible systems of regional autonomy were drawn up by government advisory bodies. Under one such system self-government was to be accorded to six separate areas: an Afar region; Tigray and Eritrea, the latter minus the Afar region around Assab; an Amhara region encompassing Gondar, Gojjam, Wollo and northern Shoa; a separate region for Addis Ababa; an Oromo and a Somali region. (Patrick Gilkes, 'Centralism and the Ethiopian PMAC', in I.M. Lewis, ed., *Self-Determination in the Horn of Africa*, London 1981; *Africa Confidential*, vol. 19, no. 23, November 17, 1978.)

region arose from the fact that it would partition Eritrea and detach Assab from the rest of the province. Indeed, from 1978 onwards, the Assab area was governed separately from Eritrea. The Afar experiment may also have reflected tactical considerations on the part of the PMAC since the congress was held just before the expected independence of Jibuti in June 1977. Since there was a large Afar population in Jibuti, the PMAC was keen to win them over to its cause. The apparent stabilization of Jibuti after independence, combined with the revolt of many Afars, therefore destroyed the context in which this particular tentative advance had been possible.

Inadequate in theory and contradictory in practice as the PMAC's policy was, it would be mistaken to see it simply as a continuation of Amhara chauvinism under a new 'Marxist–Leninist' guise. In the Amhara heartlands of Shoa province it seems that the new regime is regarded as too conciliatory towards the previously oppressed peoples. The land reform was, because of its benefits for the peasantry of the south, regarded as a measure favouring Oromos: Muslim students who participated in the *zemacha* campaign had to wear crosses when working in Christian areas. The mere acknowledgement of nationality rights in the NDR caused further resentments. The presence of Oromos in the PMAC strengthened this perception, despite the fact that all or nearly all of them are from the Christian minority historically linked to the Amhara state.[10] This sense of a besieged Amhara populace is all the greater because of the involvement of Arab countries in the Eritrean and Somalia wars, which has revitalized historic fears of encirclement by Muslims and hardened central government resistance to concessions on the nationalities question. The pattern of post-revolutionary Ethiopian politics is not such as to give democratic rights to any nationality, or equal representation in the new state apparatus to the non-Amhara. But administratively, the previous system of enforced discrimination and the power of an Amhara landowning class in landed property and the state

[10] Pliny, pp. 17–18, discusses the ethnic composition of the PMAC. Analysis of the 123 members of the COPWE central committee (*The Ethiopian Herald*, June 25, 1980) indicates that over one hundred were Amhara: some inaccuracy may arise, however, since Christian Oromo may have Amhara names.

have definitely been destroyed. Thus, even if it fails to meet the requirements of the non-Amhara, the ethnic characteristics of the new state system differ in significant respects from those prevailing under the imperial regime.

The new rulers of Ethiopia have repeatedly stressed that they favour a 'socialist' solution to the nationalities question and they cite the precedent of the USSR as the basis for their own policy. The Soviet Union has, for its part, endorsed the Derg's approach, thereby seeming to lend credence to the view that the Ethiopian revolution is following the path of the Russian in this regard. A number of problems do, however, arise. First of all, there is a significant difference between the policy that the Russians have advocated for the Third World, and that which they have pursued at home. The policy favoured in the Third World since the end of the Second World War has been one of opposition to any fragmentation or secession in independent states. The reasons for this are the conventional, and substantial, arguments about the dangers of Balkanization, the benefits of economic union, and the possibilities of unity within multinational states. Soviet policy towards Eritrea has been criticized, in our view rightly, but the position adopted has been consistent with Soviet policy in other countries of the Third World, even where those fighting for separation have been socialist in orientation: such was the case in Burma, where the local communists supported the Keren rebels in the 1950s and 1960s, and in Iraq, where the left was influential amongst the Kurds. Soviet policy in the Nigerian civil war was one of support for the central government against Biafra. The only exception was Bangladesh: here a combination of geographical separation from Pakistan, Soviet support for the Indian policy of dividing Pakistan, and the fait accompli of December 1971 all contributed to endorsement of the secession. Elsewhere, however, the USSR has not favoured such a solution to the problems of multinational Third World states, and in the light of this general policy its approach to Eritrea has been quite consistent.[11]

[11] Tran-Van-Minh, 'L'Union Soviétique et les conflits de décolonisation d'un type nouveau', in Alain Fenet, Cao-Huy-Thuan, Tran-Van-Minh, *La Question de*

The complication arises when this policy for the Third World is matched against the policy pursued in the USSR itself, and, even more so, against the policy urged by the Bolsheviks immediately after 1917. For the policy that Moscow now advocates is not, despite claims to this effect, a Leninist policy, but is rather that favoured by Lenin's 'centrist' opponents within the Second International, the Austro-Marxists. Within the context of the Austra-Hungarian empire, an entity sometimes compared to the Ethiopian, they advocated cultural autonomy and political unity. The policy that Lenin advocated favoured unity, but on a voluntary basis, and conceded the right of secession to nationalities. Much of what Lenin advocated has remained purely formal; it has not been implemented in practice within the USSR, any more than have other democratic provisions laid down in successive constitutions. In that sense the Soviet Union is not an ideal model for comparison. But the appropriate yardstick for evaluating the policy of the PMAC on the nationalities is still the Bolshevik theory and practice, not the later 'Austro-Marxist' approach advocated by Lenin's successors. The gap between Leninist theory and Soviet practice only underlines the need for vigilance in this matter.[12] In the first place, the constitutions of the USSR have always admitted in principle the right to secession. Article 70 of the new, 1977, constitution of the USSR stresses that the Union is 'formed on the principle of socialist federalism as a

---

l'Érythrée, Paris 1979. A clear statement of the Soviet view is given by the Russian Ethiopianist Georgi Galperin in 'Some Aspects of the Nationalities Question', *Asia and Africa Today*, no. 6, 1979. Galperin documents the Amharification of the old regime, which he contrasts with Ethiopianization, a process giving equality to all nationalities. He states that under the imperial regime Amharas comprised 60 per cent of the government, 75 per cent of the officer corps and 70 per cent of the district governors in the southern regions. But he goes on: 'Historically, the former Italian colony of Eritrea is part of Ethiopia, to which it is linked by thousands of economic, cultural and historical bonds. Claims made by the separatist clique that there exists a separate developed Eritrean nation, which even belongs to the Arab world, are manifestly groundless'. He argues against treating secession as 'a political fetish' and states that 'in circumstances when the emergence of a nation is far from consummated, the autonomy principle would seem to present the best, rational option'. Imperialism, he says, seeks to weaken and fragment large states in the Third World.

[12] Michael Löwy, 'Marxists and the National Question', *New Left Review*, 96, March–April 1976; Tom Nairn, *The Breakup of Britain*, London 1977, pp. 82–91.

result of the free self-determination of nations and the voluntary association of equal Soviet Socialist Republics'. Article 72 states: 'Each Union Republic shall retain the right freely to secede from the USSR'.[13] And, in contrast to the PMAC's vagueness on this issue, the Soviet constitution also names the constituent republics of the Union. A second marked difference is that the promulgation of the new nationalities policy after 1917 was accompanied by a clear denunciation of the wrongs visited upon the minorities by the Romanov Tsars, in terms far more trenchant and specific than any used by the PMAC to signal its break with the practices of the Solomonic emperors. Within weeks of coming to power the Bolsheviks indicated their desire seriously to resolve the nationalities issue by establishing a special body, Narkomnats or the People's Commissariat for Nationalities.[14] By contrast, the PMAC did not even mention the nationalities in their first 1974 statements and never set up an institutional machinery for dealing with the issue: the Self-Administration Department in the Interior Ministry was insignificant. A committee to investigate the Eritrean issue, promised in the May 1976 statement, was never convened, and, as noted, the Afar autonomy programme remained a dead letter. The Bolshevik disposition was by no means purely formal: in one case, that of Finland, the right to secede was granted and an independent country came into existence. Moreover, Lenin continued to press for an even-handed policy on the national question and when it became obvious to him that chauvinist tendencies were growing within the party he openly criticized them. The leadership of the PMAC has repeatedly denounced its rivals for their willingness to make concessions on Eritrea, and there has been no comparable identification, let alone criticism, of the 'great Amhara

[13] *Constitution of the Union of Soviet Socialist Republics*, Moscow 1977, p. 56. It is significant that this is a right which most other constitutions deny, even in principle. The most remarkable multinational socialist experiment, that of Yugoslavia, does not grant this right; multinational capitalist countries also tend to preclude it. India is a striking instance of this: the very call for secession by one of the constituent states is banned. The fate of attempted secessions in such developing capitalist states as Nigeria (1960s) or the USA (1860s) needs no elaboration.

[14] A comprehensive discussion of this question can be found in E.H. Carr, *The Bolshevik Revolution 1917–1923*, vol. 1, London 1966, Part III.

chauvinism' that has prevailed in many parts of the military and civilian apparatus since 1974. The failures of the Bolsheviks' policy lay not in their willingness to accommodate the nationalities but in their inability to implement the principles first enunciated: they suppressed nationality movements that had clear legitimacy, as in Georgia, and created a centralized structure that evacuated much of the content of the federal autonomy initially granted. But this ultimately critical balance-sheet of the Soviet experience merely underscores the need for a greater effort by post-revolutionary governments to resolve this issue in a voluntary and generous spirit, and in this light the experience of the USSR stands more as an indictment of PMAC policy than as a vindication of it.

From the first statement on *Etiopia Tikdem* onwards, the starting point of PMAC policy has been the indivisibility of Ethiopia. It has been unwilling to concede even one Finland. Yet the Eritrean example at least escapes one major restriction placed by Lenin on the granting of secession – where the area in question was relatively backward and the duty of the revolutionary forces in the more advanced sector was to assist it. Eritrea had a more developed proletariat, higher standards of living and education, and more developed productive forces than the rest of Ethiopia. Nor is the other major Bolshevik reservation applicable, namely that the nationalities issue was being fomented by counter-revolutionary forces: such forces certainly existed, within and outside of Ethiopia, but the remarkable feature of very many of the ethnic and regional movements was that their ideologies envisaged social transformation and anti-imperialism; except in the case of the EDU the Derg was not confronted by Denikins and Kolchaks, White generals intent upon exploiting ethnic conflicts; rather the PMAC faced national movements most of which were similar to itself in socio-political orientation. It is certainly possible to doubt how deep the 'socialism' of these nationality groupings went, but it would be difficult to argue that some similar reservations might not also apply to the proponents of the NDR and COPWE themselves.

Apart from the differences in political formation between a

revolutionary socialist government and a radical military regime, there were other differences underlying the experience of the two countries. One was the comparatively more advanced nature of the political culture in Russia, with a higher level of literacy and a cadre at least minimally able to disseminate internationalist ideas. Whatever the restrictions and failures of the Russians, their objective situation was far ahead of that in Ethiopia where pervasive illiteracy, the absence of a party, and a complete lack of a national Ethiopian, let alone internationalist, culture even amongst the leadership combined to foster a new intransigent temper.

This weakness in the political culture was reinforced by differences in ethnic balance: whereas in the Russia of 1917 the previously dominant ethnic groups still constituted a clear numerical majority and were still in an indisputable demographic and geographical situation after the revolution, the Ethiopian transition was far more complex, involving the creation of a new multi-ethnic system, with the attendant danger of dissolution. The Amhara-Tigrean bloc, even if united, constituted only 35–40 per cent of the population, and the Amhara alone only around 25 per cent. The Russians were 52 per cent of the total population; with the White Russians and Ukrainians, the equivalents of the Tigreans, they formed a Slavic bloc that comprised three-quarters of the total post-revolutionary population. The Russian revolution was therefore one within an ethnic context that remained relatively unchanged, in contrast to the Ethiopian case where social upheavals combined with the dissolution of a previous pattern of ethnic domination. The very artificiality of the previous system, with a minority bloc ruling over a divided majority, determined the need for a change, for an end of Amhara-Tigrean domination; yet by the same token the transition was more difficult and likely to encounter greater resistance among both the peoples who felt they were losing dominance and those who were potentially going to be emancipated. In the final analysis, the course of the nationalities issue reflected the broader patterns of the revolution itself: the fact that the upheavals of 1974 had originated in the Amhara heartland and in the state apparatus, and that the form of political dictatorship established by the PMAC precluded democratic norms of any kind, for nationalities as for social and political groups. It was in this domain of nationalities policy as much as in the conflicts of the capital that the limits of revolution from above became most evident. 'Autonomous' as it may have been of the property relations of pre-capitalist Ethiopia, the rebel officer corps and its civilian allies in the state apparatus were not free of the ethnic and administrative preconceptions of centralized rule, and of the values associated with them.

Region in Revolt: Eritrea

The most acute and politically complex of the ethnic-regional issues in post-revolutionary Ethiopia has undoubtedly been that of Eritrea.[15] Here the guerrilla struggle, having begun in 1961 against Haile Selassie, had reached a low ebb by the time of the 1974 revolution, but took on a new vigour after the Derg's accession to power. By 1976 a major military conflict was in train, involving tens of thousands of troops on both sides, pitched battles, and the seizure of towns by the guerrillas. At the height of their control over the province, in late 1977, the Eritreans had captured most of the territory, leaving only Asmara, some smaller towns and the southernmost sector around Assab in government hands. The Ethiopian government lost tens of thousands of its soldiers killed or captured, and around 13 per cent of the Eritrean population, or over 400,000 people, had fled to refugee camps in the Sudan. In addition to its sheer scale, however, this conflict raised immense political problems; the guerrillas enjoyed very widespread and enduring popular support and,

[15] There exists a substantial literature on Eritrea, much of it openly supportive of the independence cause. The following draws upon: Bereket Habte Selassie, *Conflict and Intervention in the Horn of Africa*, New York 1980; Basil Davidson, Lionel Cliffe and Bereket Habte Selassie, *Behind the War in Eritrea*, Nottingham 1980; Richard Sherman, *Eritrea: The Unfinished Revolution*, New York 1980; David Poole *Eritrea: Africa's Longest War*, London 1979; G.K.N. Travaskis, *Eritrea: A Colony in Transition, 1941–1952*, Oxford 1960. We would also like to thank the following who have been kind enough to help us in our research: John Duggan, whose study of Eritrea will be published by Monthly Review Press; Idris Hamadai and Omar Alim of the ELF; Andemichael Kahsai of the EPLF; Osman Saleh Sabbe and Woldeab Wolde-Mariam of the ELF–PLF. Sabbe has also published *The History of Eritrea*, Beirut, no date.

with varying degrees of emphasis, proclaimed themselves in favour of a revolutionary transformation of Eritrean society, whilst the PMAC mobilized its supporters for a 'revolutionary people's war', with the support of the USSR, Cuba and the PDRY. In its dimensions, both human and political, Eritrea has been a tragedy of great proportions, in which no simple attribution of responsibility or of socialist credentials is possible.

In Eritrea itself the lull after the fall of the emperor and Aman's two conciliatory visits gave way in early 1975 to fierce fighting. Although the PMAC continued to make some conciliatory gestures after Aman's fall, and also to negotiate, it showed no willingness to accept the basic legitimacy of the Eritrean case. In this context, the two Eritrean groups, the ELF and EPLF, decided to launch an offensive against Asmara.[16] On January 24–25, 1975, they made their first and last ever attempt to capture the provincial capital; after their offensive was repulsed there was a ferocious response from the Derg's side, leading to the assassination of Eritrean intellectuals inside Asmara and artillery assaults on villages from which the guerrillas had operated. Although the Ethiopians later started judicial proceedings against ninety local officials held responsible for particular acts of brutality,[17] January 1975 marked the moment from which any serious hope of negotiation disappeared. Over the next two years, the guerrillas, despite their own differences, made continuous advances, routing the peasant march of summer 1976 and seizing most of the province in 1977. The disarray of the Ethiopian authorities, the changed mood amongst the Eritrean population following much more intense military activity by the Ethiopians, and Sudan's decision to abrogate the 1972 Khartoum agreement and give more support to the Eritreans, all contributed to this new Eritrean capability. Of these factors the most important, however, was the weakness of the Ethiopian government and this was likely, over time, to be made good.

---

[16] Ottaways, pp. 155–6, attribute the initiative to the Eritreans. Bereket Habte Selassie, p. 67, ascribes the responsibility to the PMAC.
[17] *Le Monde*, February 22, 1975.

By 1978 the apparent near-victory of the guerrillas gave way to a new balance of forces: no provisional Eritrean government was established, the Eritreans remained divided, and the Ethiopians retained Asmara, Assab and a few other towns. Once the Ogaden had been cleared of Somali forces, with Russian and Cuban help, the PMAC turned its attention to Eritrea. Three rounds of negotiation, in East Berlin, with the EPLF failed, and in July 1978 the first of a series of major military offensives began. The Ethiopians were unable to make a clean sweep of the province, and sustained very heavy losses, but each wave of government assault drove the guerrillas further and further back so that by the summer of 1980 they were concentrated in a small and thinly populated area of northern Sahel province around Nakfa. Much of the Eritrean population was under government control, at least by day, and, with the seige lifted, Asmara's economy revived. At the same time the shifting situation in Eritrea itself, combined with the dangers to which he was exposed at home, led the Sudanese President, Nimeiry, to re-establish a dialogue with Addis Ababa. Mengistu visited Sudan in May 1980 and Nimeiry repaid the visit in the following November. As a result of this change, the Sudanese government played down the Eritrean case, as well as reducing the level of Eritrean guerrilla activity along the Sudanese–Eritrean border. Whilst there was no complete reversal of the situation as a result of the Ethiopian advances, the balance of forces had shifted markedly and probably permanently in favour of the Ethiopians by the latter half of 1980.

In summary form, the conflict can be presented as follows. All Eritrean groups are committed to full independence and have appeared unwilling to compromise on that. For its part, the PMAC has refused to countenance separation by Eritrea, for at least three major reasons: Eritrea is seen as an important component of the historic territory of Ethiopia; it provides

[18] *Le Monde*, November 26, 1980. The final communique did not mention Eritrea, but Nimeiry let it be known that he was reducing support for the guerrillas and wanted to mediate between them and the Ethiopian government. In 1979 the Ethiopian government began to allow foreign journalists to visit Eritrea again; they reported a substantial degree of government control and urban prosperity; see Jean-Claude Pomonti, 'Avec l'armée éthiopienne en Erythrée', *Le Monde*, October 4–5, 1979.

Ethiopia with its access to the sea; and the demonstration effect of Eritrean independence on the rest of multinational Ethiopia would be catastrophic. Yet the ferocity and endurance of the Eritrean conflict has no simple explanation, as the following account shows.

1. The pre-colonial (that is, pre-Italian) relationship between Eritrea and Ethiopia is open to interpretation by both parties, and has had potent, but contradictory, ideological consequences. The Ethiopians point out that the highlands of Eritrea were, with the province of Tigray, at the very centre of the first Christian kingdom of Axum, which arose in the first century AD. The Coptic Church and the Tigrinya language retain their dominance there to this day, establishing a close cultural bond, indeed virtual cultural unity, with Tigray itself.[19] In the fifteenth century, during the era of the Gondar Kingdom, the area was ruled by a powerful official known as Baher Negast, the Ruler of the Sea, who was part of the Gondar domain, and whilst the Turks occupied the sea coast from 1557 onwards, they did not detach the highlands from the rest of the Ethiopian realm. In the period just prior to the Italian occupation, the province of Mareb Mallash ('beyond the Mareb', the river separating Eritrea from Tigray) was ruled from Tigray. Both past territorial control and the historic importance of the Eritrean region for Ethiopia therefore combine to give it a special importance, a fact compounded by Eritrea's location as the gateway to the sea. In the minds of rulers based further to the south, it is not a marginal or distant province. Eritrean nationalists, on the other hand, argue that for long periods of recorded history their region was separate from the rest of Ethiopia: this was either because no central government functioned, as during the Age of the Princes (1784–1855), or because all or part of the area was controlled by other powers – Turks, Egyptians, Italians. Thus, in the face of the affective link that Ethiopians maintain with what they see as a component of their historic territory, the Eritreans stress the intermittence of the connec-

---

[19] Ethiopian statements (see notes 4–6 above) emphasize that Eritrea forms part of the 'Cradle of Ethiopian Civilization'.

tion. Both protagonists use their arguments from historic precedent to establish contemporary legitimacy.

Both parties make the conventional nationalist assumption that in previous centuries entities corresponding to either 'Ethiopia' or 'Eritrea' existed. This ignores the fact that all nations are historically formed. In reality, no distinct and united area corresponding to Eritrea was at any time an independent entity in the pre-colonial period. An Ethiopian entity did exist, but the extent and centre of the Christian kingdoms of the interior varied considerably over the centuries. In other words, neither 'Eritrea' nor Ethiopia as presently constituted existed in the pre-colonial period. The ambiguous links between 'Eritrea' and the rest of today's Ethiopia must be seen in the light of this ebb and flow, which, variously interpreted, provides both a precedent and a reserve of retrospective legitimation for the conflicts that were to come.

2. The establishment of 'Eritrea' as a province both separate from Ethiopia proper and itself united under one power was a result of the imposition of Italian rule in the latter part of the nineteenth century. Since all nations are historical contingencies, one can say of Eritrea what is true of so many present-day states of the Third World: that their territorial boundaries and growing 'national' consciousness arose from the period of colonial rule. *What was distinctive about Eritrea was not that colonial boundaries separated it from ethnically contiguous areas, but rather that the areas from which it was divided remained formally independent.* In this fact above all others lies the basis of the later dispute: on the one side a historically-formed separate Eritrean consciousness, on the other side a continuing territorial claim which was not, as elsewhere in Africa, annulled or obliterated by a corresponding period of colonial rule. The Italian influence began with the setting up of a trading company in the port of Assab in 1869; but, as with the British in India, commercial influence was followed by state intervention and in 1889 Emperor Menelik conceded a much wider area of control to the Italians in the Treaty of Ucciali. Menelik needed Italian support in his conflict with the rulers of Tigray province, and he hoped

they would be content with the coastal area that was now recognized as their colony. With the delimitation of the Eritrean area by Ethiopia and Italy in the late nineteenth century, an entity of around 47,000 square miles was defined, which by the 1970s had a population of around three million. Eritrea was itself, however, a multinational entity. About half the inhabitants were Tigrinya-speaking, and adherents of the Coptic religion, the two features similar to the population of the neighbouring province of Tigray; the other half of the population were Muslims, speaking Tigre, Arabic, Saho, Afar and some other tongues.[20] Through the experience of Italian colonialism the region acquired a new name, 'Eritrea', and over the next sixty years it was transformed by Italian and then British rule. It experienced economic development and, under the British, a measure of democratic freedom that marked off its society and polity from the rest of Ethiopia. It was against this background that resistance to control by Ethiopia emerged.

3. The period of colonial rule therefore forged an Eritrean social entity and a distinct Eritrean consciousness of a kind that had not previously existed, and which alone would have created difficulties in any future programme of reunification with Ethiopia. But this was compounded by two other factors that increased the gap between Eritrea and Ethiopia: one was a factor of repulsion, the other of detachment. The first was a result of a change within Ethiopia that coincided with the imposition of Italian rule on Eritrea, namely the shift of power from Tigray to Shoa. Whereas previously the Eritrean highlands had been ruled by members of the same, Tigrinya-speaking, group, they now faced an Ethiopia ruled by the once-subject Amhara. The Ethiopia to which they were now asked to 'return' was not the same one from which they had

[20] S.F. Nadel, *Races and Tribes of Eritrea*, Asmara 1944, p. 9, writes as follows: 'These are the most important linguistic groups in Eritrea: Beja, Tigré (or Khasa), Tigrinya, Saho, and Danakil. Languages spoken by smaller groups are: Belein, Baria, Kunama, Ilit, and Arabic. Beja and Tigré are widespread also in the north-eastern Sudan. Tigrinya, Saho and Danakil spread into Ethiopia. The remaining languages, with the exception of Arabic, are limited to Eritrea'. The Danakil language is that spoken by the Afars. All fronts have established Tigrinya and Arabic as the two official languages of Eritrea.

been detached. It was ruled by arrogant usurpers. The second factor was the rise of Arab nationalism which, from the 1940s onwards, exerted considerable attraction upon the Muslim half of the Eritrean population and also upon some of the Asmara Christian opposition groups. If the main formative influence was therefore that of Italian domination, these two subsidiary factors must also have played their part in creating a sense of alienation from Haile Selassie's state.

4. The establishment of the federation in 1950-2 had as much to do with international politics as with the wishes of the Eritrean population. The UN observers sent to Eritrea to decide on this, as on other Italian colonies in Africa, could not agree on what the majority wanted, and a variety of trends emerged: the Christians tended to favour union with Ethiopia, the Muslims separation, but even here there were cross-currents, as the Christian trade unions of Asmara did not favour life under imperial control. The UN voted for federation in December 1952. Whatever the validity of the federation, subsequent events increased hostility to the centre and produced a situation in which a majority in Eritrea appeared to favour independence. There was first the arbitrary manner in which Haile Selassie abolished the federation in defiance of the UN settlement. Until 1974, however, the guerrillas had only partial support. What altered this was the ferocity of the military repression visited upon the population by the PMAC in 1975 and 1976. It was the latter in particular that mobilized the Christian highlands, till then relatively passive, and formed a movement that enjoyed, by all independent accounts, majority support. Like the formation of Eritrea itself, the desire for Eritrean independence was not an ahistorical given, but the product of contingent historical processes posterior to the 1974 Ethiopian revolution.

While it cannot be explained in simple class terms, the guerrilla movement has benefited from certain physical and social characteristics of Eritrean society. Much of the province is rugged terrain, and only 3 per cent of it is cultivable. Neither the Italians nor the Ethiopians after 1952 exerted direct control over much of the countryside, so that the term 'liberated area', applied to guerrilla regions, must be taken in a qualified sense. The Tigrinya-speaking Christians have concentrated in the three highland provinces of Hamassien, which includes Asmara, Serae and Akele Guzai. Here the land-holding system included the *rist* arrangement found elsewhere in northern Ethiopia, known in Eritrea as *tsilmi*. Members of a clan or *enda* enjoy hereditary rights to a particular piece of land, with a less privileged layer of tenants below them. An alternative, more pervasive arrangement was for all those in the village, whether members of an *enda* or not, to enjoy common rights as members of a *diessa* or village community: in practice, considerable inequalities operated here too.[21] Over the period of Italian occupation a system of village chiefs nominated by the colonial authorities was created, but these chiefs did not have special land holdings and there was no great social differentiation in the highland areas. Whereas agriculture was an important source of livelihood in the highlands, livestock rearing was more important in the Barca lowlands to the west, bordering Sudan, and in the coastal areas of Sahel, Semhar and Denakil. Here the population tended to be Muslims and to be organized in tribal federations. The majority of the population therefore composed relatively undifferentiated rural social entities. There were some plantations left over from the Italian period and an artisanal and industrial sector in Asmara.

The guerrilla movement arose among the nomads of the western lowlands, where feuding and raiding by *shiftas* or bandits was historically endemic, with all the ambiguity of banditry in other marginal areas. Drawing upon military traditions present in the population and recruiting from tribal families that had led *shifta* forces in the past, the movement was also supported by the most politically advanced sectors of Eritrean society, those whose sense of lost democratic freedoms was the greatest, the intellectuals and trade unionists of

---

[21] 'Agriculture in the Eritrean Revolution', Tony Barnett, *Behind the War in Eritrea*, p. 112. Information on the class character of Eritrean society remains scanty; even more so is any persuasive evidence on how social factors interact with the independence movement. The literature on Eritrea, both pro and con, is replete with assertions about the class character of the movement, but these seem to lack empirical substantiation.

Asmara. If in the 1960s, however, the movement was an alliance of urban intellectuals and Beni Amer tribal chiefs, it broadened its scope greatly in the 1970s, as the highlands were drawn into the guerrilla fronts. Whilst some leadership positions remained in the hands of the more traditional Beni Amer forces, it was young men from the highlands and from the urban milieu who increasingly came to dominate the fronts. By the mid-70s, therefore, the movement was able to recruit from all three social domains – from the urban milieu, where modern nationalist ideas had developed most, from the nomadic lowlands, where traditional tribal warfare survived, and from the agricultural highlands, where, once antagonized, the village communities were also mobilized in support of the guerrilla forces.

The growth of the Eritrean movement in the period after 1974 is of particular interest, since it was only then that it came to mobilize the majority of the population and in particular the Christian areas. One factor in this process was certainly the popular response to the Ethiopian attacks on the region around Asmara in early 1975. Another was the inevitable sense that if the Eritreans were to achieve independence, this was the time to act: when the Ethiopian state was weak. But there was another strand in the growth of Eritrean opposition, namely hostility to the Ethiopian revolution itself. As noted, Eritrea was comparatively integrated into the Ethiopian economy, through trade and recruitment to the administration and army. Up to one hundred thousand Eritreans lived in Addis Ababa. The class interests of the Eritrean merchants and landowners were, in fact, threatened by the revolution and in particular by the nationalizations of 1975. If, therefore, class conflict played a minor role in stimulating the conflict within Eritrea, it played a larger, negative, role in stimulating the Eritreans living in the rest of Ethiopia.

5. In common with all enduring guerrilla movements, the Eritreans had the essential requirement of external assistance. The most important source of support was that provided by Sudan, namely an open frontier and the sanctuary of military and refugee camps, as well as transit

facilities, in and around the town of Kassala. The level of Sudanese support varied, but even in the aftermath of the 1972 Khartoum agreement the border was not completely closed. Sudan did not provide the main financial or logistical support; this came from sources in the Arab world, most notably Syria, Iraq, Saudi Arabia and Kuwait, and, until 1976, Libya and South Yemen. Prior to 1974 some training and arms were provided also by Cuba, China and Bulgaria, and both before and after the revolution the substantial Eritrean diaspora in the oil states and in North America was a source of funding. Although much Eritrean equipment was taken from supplies captured in the 1976–7 period, the scope of the movement would have been impossible without the very substantial support from the Arab world, which went beyond mere material backing. For the Arab states Eritrea was an 'Arab' cause and, whilst this was an exaggeration, it provided a means by which Arab states could justify their involvement. This Arab commitment exerted a strong influence upon the Eritrean movement itself. Historically Eritrea had had ties to the Arab world: the coastal area had been occupied by the Turks in the sixteenth to nineteenth centuries and by the Egyptians in the 1860s, and both on the eastern sea coast with its links to Red Sea shipping, and on the western frontier with the Sudan, there was long-standing social interaction with the Arab world. The Muslim half of the Eritrean population also felt bonds of cultural attraction to the Arab world, and some of the younger Muslim intellectuals went to universities and military academies in Egypt or Iraq in the 1950s, where they were influenced by Arab nationalism. The language issue is more complex. Certainly the official Arab claim that Eritreans are 'Arabs' in the sense of Arabic-speakers is a distortion. Probably the proportion of Eritreans whose first language is Arabic is under 5 per cent, many of them being in the Rushaida tribe in the east and the Shkria in the west, who migrated to Eritrea from Sudan in the nineteenth century. But amongst the Muslims a combination of religious culture and the underdevelopment of the vocabulary in their own unwritten tongues has led to Arabic becoming widespread as a language of commerce and education, a lingua franca that has taken

The Regional and National Questions 181

Arabic far beyond the small minority for whom it is a mother tongue. The cultural and historical bonds between Eritrea and the Arab world are therefore of an influential kind; they provide the background against which more recent, directly political involvement has become possible. It is for this cultural reason more than for reasons of Arab nationalism that the Eritreans have made Arabic the official language of Eritrea, along with Tigrinya.

6. The Eritrean guerrilla movement was not a spontaneous one, any more than others in Africa, or in Indo-China. It was built up on the basis of an effective system of political organization, which borrowed from forms common in the Arab world, and, in certain respects, from the Leninist model. By the early 1970s the two main fronts, the ELF and the EPLF, were controlled by secret political parties, the former by the Labour Party, the latter by the Popular Revolution Party, centralized and clandestine cadre organizations which ran the affairs of each front. Not only the fronts themselves, but also the armed units, the security bodies, and the mass organizations were ultimately responsible to the leaders of these secret parties. Whilst drawing upon more traditional forms of organization and solidarity, and at times manipulating sectarian tribal and religious sentiments in Eritrean society, both parties also developed programmes and organizational structures reminiscent of other guerrilla movements in the Third World, and the systems of control developed in the Arab world, in the Baath parties or amongst the Palestinians, were reproduced in the fronts. Both the main groups claimed to represent the oppressed peasants and workers and called for cultural and social transformation. Both carried out mass literacy and other social welfare programmes and maintained a visible egalitarianism of living conditions in their own ranks. But both also maintained strong political discipline amongst their followers and dealt mercilessly with those who, for whatever reason, opposed the leadership policies. The success of the fronts therefore lay in their combination of at least three levels of political appeal – one based on local, often sectarian, interests; one based on a developing sense of a shared Eritrean identity; and one based upon a socialist

ideology that emphasized liberation from class oppression and what was termed 'Ethiopian colonialism'.

The Political Character of the Eritrean Guerrillas

Despite its military successes, and its apparent support in much of the population, the Eritrean movement was at the same time beset by divisions that weakened both its ability to resist the Ethiopian forces and its capacity to envisage a political solution to the problems it faced. The Eritrean Liberation Front, established in 1960, was itself set up in apparent opposition to another earlier and less militant lowland group, the Eritrean Liberation Movement or *harakat*,[22] and in 1970 the ELF was rent by a split out of which emerged two groupings: the ELF-Revolutionary Command, comprising the original ELF leadership, and what was then called the ELF-Popular Liberation Forces, comprising a younger leadership with some older members.[23] The ELF–PLF changed its name in 1971 to the Eritrean Popular Liberation Forces, or EPLF. It divided again in 1976, when the external representatives under veteran leader Osman Saleh Sabbe broke away to constitute a group that itself adopted the title ELF–PLF. The EPLF then changed its name to the Eritrean Popular Liberation Front. From 1976 onwards therefore there were three major fronts fighting in Eritrea: ELF, EPLF, ELF–PLF. At least two organizations emerged from other divisions to pose a political challenge to the main guerrilla groups, one named the Eritrean Democratic Movement, breaking from the EPLF in 1975, the other leaving the ELF–PLF in 1980 to form the ELF–PLF 'Revolutionary Committee', under Ali Mohammed Said Berhatu. As is conventional in such disputes, each group has tended to repeat the same accusations against the other, and to stress the weaknesses of its rivals. In this case, there are normally three kinds of such accusation: first, that the rival groups have a religious bias;

---

[22] Bereket Habte Selassie, pp. 58–63, charts the earlier history of the movement. See also Sherman and Pliny The Middle-Aged, 'Eclectic Notes on the Eritrean Liberation Movement', *Ethiopianist Notes*, vol. 2, no. 1, 1978.

[23] For the early history of the split, see Fred Halliday 'The Fighting in Eritrea', *New Left Review*, 67, May–June 1971.

secondly, that the rivals are being manipulated by conservative Arab forces; and thirdly, that their programmes are incorrect ones for mobilizing popular support in Eritrea. To these has, on occasion, been added a fourth charge, namely that the other groups are trying to reach an accommodation with the Ethiopians. Yet Eritrea is not a situation comparable to that in Angola, where one guerrilla force was clearly demarcated from the other in political terms, and many of the issues and events in the Eritrean conflict are obscure. All the groups share a common commitment to Eritrean independence, and despite the accusations of their rivals, all had a considerable level of popular support in the 1977-8 period. Despite this set of common characteristics, certain clear distinctions of following and policy can be identified.

In early 1978, at the height of the Eritrean movement's strength, each group controlled some territory.[24] The EPLF, with upwards of 30,000 people under arms, had its main military bases in the northern coastal province of Sahel: it was active in the predominantly Muslim coastal province of Semhar, and was besieging the port of Massawa; it also had a substantial political following in the mainly Muslim province of Senhit, with its capital at Keren, as well as in the three Christian highland provinces. The majority of its guerrillas were Christian Tigrinya speakers, but it also had following amongst the Muslims of Semhar and Sahel. Its secretary general was a Muslim, Ramadan Nur, who had attended Koranic school in Massawa and later studied in Cairo, but the most influential member of the leadership was Isais Afeworki, a Christian and son of an Asmara small trader. Both received training in China in the late 1960s. The ELF had around 20,000 guerrillas, based in the Barca lowlands of the

---

[24] Our information on the respective strengths and policies of the three major fronts draws heavily on the researches of John Duggan, who spent six months inside Eritrea in 1978. In contrast to most visitors, Duggan spent time with all three fronts, and avoided identification with one at the expense of the other two. We also draw on material provided in interviews with the representatives of the three fronts mentioned above (note 15), and on the publications of the different groups, *Eritrea Information* and *Vanguard* (EPLF), *Eritrean Revolution* and *The Eritrean Newsletter* (ELF), and *The Eritrean Review* (ELF-PLF). EPLF material was also reproduced, until late 1978, in *Eritrea in Struggle*, published by Eritreans for Liberation in North America. For different force evaluations see International Institute for Strategic Studies, *Strategic Survey*, 1977, p. 22.

west, but it also enjoyed following in Senhit and in one of the Christian highland provinces, Serae. Its chairman, Ahmad Mohammad Nasser, was the grandson of Nasser Pasha, a local leader ennobled by the Egyptians during their occupation of the area in the nineteenth century and later imprisoned by the Italians. Born in eastern Akele Guzai, a Saho speaker, Ahmad Nasser had his secondary education in Eritrea and was one of five Eritreans who attended Baghdad military academy in the 1950s. A key political leader and head of the clandestine political structure inside the ELF, Ibrahim Idris Totil, comes from a very different background: the son of a nomad family, he had no formal education and worked as a labourer in the Sudan. Like many of the original ELF leaders he comes from the Beni Amer tribal confederation of the Barca area. He too had received military training in Iraq. In the same period, early 1978, the ELF–PLF had a much smaller following, of about 5,000 guerrillas, based almost exclusively amongst the Muslims of the Barca lowlands around the town of Agordat; but it had some supporters among the Christians of Akele-Guzai, and among former members of the Asmara trade union movement who stayed with Osman Saleh Sabbe when he broke from each of the other two fronts. Sabbe himself, the best known of the Eritrean leaders and a man often criticized by other Eritreans for his ties to conservative Arab countries, is half Saho and half Tigré, a school teacher from the village of Hirjijo, north of Massawa.

The relative strengths and distribution of the three groups indicate that whilst the claims of all three about their own following must be discounted, none was an insignificant force at that time, and none could be categorized as just being the expression of one confessional-geographical bloc. The cross-currents of Eritrean society were reflected both in their leaderships and in the composition of their guerrilla forces. The political programmes of the three indicate further differences but, again, these are less significant than their own controversies suggest. The ELF–PLF has not, so far as is known, produced a political programme: its main appeals have been for independence and Eritrean unity. Its leader Osman Saleh Sabbe explicitly repudiates Marxism, which he regards as inappropriate to a society of Eritrea's level of development and political consciousness.[25] Sabbe does maintain the good relations he is accused of with such countries as Saudi Arabia and Kuwait; but he defends this on the grounds that the Eritreans, like the Palestinians, have to seek aid where they can, and that the other fronts have sought support from similar sources. Yet despite Sabbe's own orientation there is in practice much less difference between his followers at the base level and those of the other groups: during 1978, at least, socialist literature and popular social programmes were present in the ELF–PLF areas, as in those of the other two fronts.

The political differences between the ELF and EPLF are easier to delineate, since they both had programmes, the former's elaborated at its second congress in May 1975, and the latter's at its first congress, in January 1977.[26] Although both call for independence, and use a generally radical and at times socialist vocabulary, it is possible to note some differences (even though the ELF's policies and the composition of its leadership and fighting force evolved considerably in the 1970s so that it included Christians and Muslims other than those in the Barca area, and thereby lessened the strongly confessional character of the 1970 split). The overall aim of the EPLF programme is a 'national democratic revolution' that would establish 'a people's democratic state' and 'safeguard the interests of the masses of workers, peasants and other democratic forces'. The ELF programme also looks to 'a national democratic revolution' and denies the Eritrean bourgeoisie any role in it: the vanguard role is given to the working class, whilst the peasantry is classified as 'the dominant element of the revolution's base in the semi-liberated areas'. Both programmes advocate nationalization of industry and commerce, but whilst the EPLF calls for the abolition of 'feudal land relations' and for an equitable distribution of land leading to the formation of cooperatives, the ELF programme merely calls for land to be 'democratized and organized for the realization of social justice and greater

---

[25] Osman Saleh Sabbe, interview with the authors, London, August 1978.
[26] The EPLF's National Democratic Programme is printed in *Behind the War in Eritrea*, pp. 143–50. The ELF programme is published by the Front as a separate pamphlet, Beirut 1977.

productivity'. Both advocate the settlement of nomads, but on two other indicative internal issues their policies seem to diverge: women and the nationalities within Eritrea itself. The EPLF commits itself to full rights of equality for women and to the promulgation of progressive marriage and family laws; the ELF is much less specific, merely stating that the state 'shall protect the rights of women workers' and 'guarantee equal opportunities'. The EPLF programme devotes considerable space to guaranteeing the unity and equality of all ten Eritrean nationalities. On this subject the ELF is silent.[27] On foreign policy the differences are perhaps clearest of all: the EPLF advocates a policy of self-reliance and restricts itself to propounding a non-aligned foreign policy and to supporting revolutionary movements elsewhere; the ELF, by contrast, specifies a number of resolutions passed at its congress saluting various countries in the Arab world. These include one on Iraq, welcoming what is termed 'the settlement of the Kurdish question within the framework of a democratic solution' concluded in March 1975. That the ELF, representing a movement for independence against a central government, should have saluted the suppression of a similar movement by Iraq, suggests the importance of Iraqi aid to its campaign at that time.

On the basis of written documents alone, it would appear that the EPLF had a somewhat more radical programme than the ELF; but how far these programmes corresponded to reality, and how far there were differences between the policies of the two groups on the ground, is open to question. Given the demands of the war, much of the social programme must have remained a paper prospect, and some of the egalitarian and reforming measures taken by the fronts were as much the levelling effects of wartime necessity as elements of a deliberate policy of social transformation. Some lands belonging to collaborators were certainly redistributed, and a more egalitarian holding system instituted in the areas where considerable differentiation existed; a programme of educat-

[27] This is a significant issue because of the Ethiopian claim that it is rescuing the oppressed minorities of Eritrea from oppression. This applies particularly to the Kunama and Baria, formerly enslaved groups, who tend to sympathize with the Ethiopians against Tigrinya- and Tigré-speakers.

ing and arming women seems to have occurred in the EPLF areas, and to a lesser extent amongst the ELF; literacy and health programmes were common to all three. Some form of political education was also carried out by the ELF and EPLF, but a radicalization at the base was also noted in the ELF–PLF regions. As for the differential sources of foreign funds, it would seem probable that the EPLF received relatively less from the conservative Arab states, given its Christian composition and radical reputation. But it is doubtful if the varying pattern of foreign support inflected the policies of these groups, whose differences had more to do with their internal recruitment and combat areas than with the manipulations of Arab states.

The confrontations with the Ethiopian army took an enormous toll on the Eritreans, both in 1972–4, when the Khartoum agreement gave the initiative to Haile Selassie, and from 1978 onwards, when the Ethiopian army launched its counter-offensive. The Eritreans fought bravely and skilfully, but could not prevail over the superior firepower and numbers of the Ethiopian forces. Yet beyond the costs of the military campaign itself, the Eritreans suffered from other problems that over time severely qualified their successes.

1. The factionalism that produced the split into three fronts did not cease at that point; the kind of cooperation that existed, for example, in Zimbabwe or even among the Palestinians was not attained in Eritrea. Rather there developed murderous competition and factional conflict. Between 1972 and 1974 the ELF and EPLF fought a civil war in which hundreds of Eritreans died, as each side devoted itself to eliminating what it termed 'Eritrean reaction'. The ELF had a special Liquidation Committee (in Arabic, *Lajnat al-Tasfia*) that specialized in this task. Although a certain modus vivendi evolved after the fall of the imperial regime, fighting recurred in 1977 when there were reports of clashes between the fronts or of local agreements on military cooperation being abandoned at the last minute in the face of an Ethiopian attack. An initial agreement on cooperation was signed in October 1977, but despite considerable pressure from the rank and file of the movement and from the Arab

states, the main fronts were not able to cooperate effectively. If the prospect of victory did not concentrate the minds of the leaderships, neither did the setbacks of 1978–9. In the summer of 1980, by which time the Eritrean movement as a whole was in a far less advantageous position than it had been three years before, new clashes between the ELF and EPLF were reported.[28] In March 1981 a new agreement was reached but it seemed that neither the pressure of friendly Arab states, nor the need for a common front to realize the prospect of victory, nor the exigencies of retreat were sufficient, even then, to overcome the deep-seated hostilities within the movement, in which religious, local and organizational rivalries all appeared to play a part. Whether this 1981 agreement would produce results remained to be seen.

2. This costly factionalism between the fronts went together with considerable conflict and repression within the ranks of the organizations themselves. After the 1970 split a Christian minority remained within the ELF, but in 1974 this Tigrinya-speaking trend broke away, under the leadership of Herui Tedle Bairu, son of one of the first ELF leaders. Whilst part of this breakaway group went to the EPLF, others formed their own Eritrean Democratic Movement, a tendency often called by the Tigrinya word *Fallul*, meaning rebel. Around the same time an oppositional group emerged within the EPLF, known by the word *Mankha*, or bat. Both groups protested at the lack of democratic discussion within their fronts. They argued that the leadership put their sectarian interests as leaders of their organizations above the requirements of unity within the Eritrean movement as a whole. They were denounced by their leaderships and many were killed. Although veiled from the observations of others, and passed over by most observers who have been struck by the level of apparently enthusiastic unanimity amongst the guerrillas they visited, the guerrilla groups have operated strong security networks. The EPLF Security Committee, *Halewa*

---

[28] *The Guardian* October 28, 1980; Dan Connell in *New Statesman* November 7, 1980. The EPLF charged the ELF with harrassing its lines of communication and dealing secretly with the Derg, via Moscow; the ELF accused the EPLF of bringing in 'foreigners', i.e. members of the TPLF, to fight them.

Sewra, and its ELF equivalent were designed not only to detect agents of the Ethiopian government, but also to quell political dissent in their own ranks. This reflects the model of enforcement common in Arab guerrilla groups. Indeed the factionalism between fronts, the mutual anathemas, are merely the public face of feuding that continues invisibly within the fronts themselves and which has periodically to be purged by expulsions, excommunications and liquidations. For it is only by casting all critics and rivals as agents of reaction, tribalists or religious sectarians, as all the Eritrean fronts tend to do, that the semblance of voluntary unity within the ranks of each front itself can be maintained. That this internal factionalism and the rigid controls imposed by the leaders have contributed to the movement's failure to consolidate its gains is self-evident; so too is the fact that in this regard the Eritreans share many of the features of the political culture that has caused so much havoc on the Ethiopian side as well.[29]

3. A central reason for the factionalism within the Eritrean movement has been the fact that the groups involved have been competing for foreign support, and have allowed differences within the Arab world to be reflected in their own ranks. The competition between the Syrian and Iraqi Baath parties, for example, was one of the causes of the ELF's division in 1970 and for its continuation; later, both Iraqis and Syrians supported factions inside the ELF. At the same time, by appealing to the Arab world, and identifying more or less openly with its causes, the Eritreans confirmed the Ethiopian sense that secessionism was primarily the product of external intervention, a replay of a historic Arab and Muslim drive to separate Ethiopia from the sea. The fact that many Arab states and not a few Eritreans claimed that they were themselves Arabs confirmed this Ethiopian suspicion.

[29] For Eritrean discussion of the factionalism within their own ranks see Pliny, note 22 above, 'Dibattito sulla Rivoluzione Eritrea', *Altrafrica*, Rome, nos. 4–5, September 1977, and the forthcoming work by John Duggan. This factionalism also reproduced itself in exile, when, in 1978, sections of the EPLF support groups in North America denounced the movement in the field for its failure to attack the Soviet Union; see *Against the Capitulationist Line of the 'Leaders' of the Eritrean Revolution*, Eritreans for Liberation in North America, New York 1978.

There has never been much of a likelihood that the conservative Arab states would be able to use their influence amongst the Eritreans to turn the sea-coast into a base area for advancing their interests in the Horn; indeed the Arab states have had no more ability to control the Eritreans than they have the Palestinians. Their officials have often complained about their inability either to foster practical unity between the fronts or to mitigate the, for them, ominously radical nature of their political and social programmes. Hence whilst the appearance of an Arab connection has made the Ethiopians more intransigent, the reality of reliance upon the Arab states has caused its own difficulties. Reliance upon the Sudan, in particular, has introduced a variable that has no guarantee of permanence.

4. The Eritrean movement's enthusiastic adoption of Arab causes has contrasted with its almost complete neglect of revolutionary movements in a region nearer home, namely Ethiopia itself. The period prior to 1974 was one in which the fronts disdained to support the opposition inside Ethiopia, and neither organization evinced much enthusiasm at the fall of the emperor. Whilst this in part reflected caution about what the new regime would decide for Eritrea, it was also diplomatically short-sighted and politically mistaken, since it confirmed the Ethiopian belief that the Eritrean movement was directed against Ethiopians on a national basis alone. Neither the ELF programme of 1975 nor the EPLF's of 1977 registered the extent of the social and political changes that had taken place in Ethiopia and until 1978 both seemed to regard the regime simply as 'fascist'. The contacts that did exist were uniquely with groups that supported the Eritrean movement and they showed no other political discrimination. Thus in 1976 the EPRP and the EPLF signed a joint declaration, pledging themselves to support each other, despite the fact that the EPRP's original programme of August 1975 does not mention the right to secession; in 1977 the ELF, which in its programme called for a national democratic revolution, was collaborating with the conservative Ethiopian Democratic Union. When, in 1978, the ELF did begin to acknowledge the existence of an 'Ethiopian revolution', it was attacked by the

other fronts for this concession. Yet the failure to register the changes in Ethiopia, and the opportunistic alliance with groups that were themselves of little long-term substance certainly strengthened the PMAC's suspicions that the Eritrean movement was part of a wider counter-revolutionary drive against it. This blinkered hostility was evident in one other secondary but illustrative issue, namely the question of Ethiopian access to the sea. The need for such access was one of the central reasons given by the PMAC for retaining Eritrea, and formed part of the Ethiopians' underlying anxiety. It would have been quite possible for the Eritreans to allay these suspicions by offering to cede part of their territory, around Assab, to provide Ethiopia with a corridor to the Red Sea, in return for PMAC acceptance of Eritrea's right to independence. Yet it seems that no such offer was made, because of the need felt by the Eritreans to maintain their territorial integrity: similar nationalistic stubbornness was also operating on the Ethiopian side as a reason for fighting the Eritreans as a whole. In sum, whilst the prime responsibility for such intransigence must lie with the oppressor group, the Ethiopians, the short-sighted policies of the Eritreans compounded this inflexibility in Addis Ababa.

The optimal solution for the Eritrean question, as for other nationality issues inside Ethiopia, would have been a voluntary union within which Eritrea would have been granted a substantial measure of autonomy. A revival of the 1952 federation, provided it was accepted by both sides, would have constituted such a solution. It would have guaranteed Ethiopian concerns – territorial integrity and access to the sea. It would at the same time have given substantial autonomy to the Eritreans and have enabled the revolutionary movements on both sides of the Mareb river to collaborate in building a new society. Yet the sharp deterioration in relations between Eritreans and Ethiopians after 1974 meant that there seemed no possibility of a voluntary union. In such circumstances there remained only two possibilities: forced reunification of Eritrea with Ethiopia, or independence through military victory. The weight of the Eritrean case, based on separate historical formation and a popular will for independence, is such that the Eritreans do have a right to self-determination, including secession. The conventional reasons for denying such a right are not such as to preclude it here. The Eritreans are not, in internal politics, reactionaries; their authoritarian and factional failings are shared by the PMAC. They are not a 'backward' area towards whom the more 'advanced' Ethiopians have an internationalist obligation. Their international links and subservience to Arab interests are exaggerated. The question of Ethiopian access to the sea can be resolved by Eritrean concessions. The implications for the rest of Ethiopia are not self-evident, since no other province shares the Eritrean experience of separate rule by European colonialism or a history of two decades of armed resistance. It is on this basis that the case for a separate Eritrean case has to rest; as in other such cases, it would be preferable if that right were voluntarily renounced. But the possibility of voluntary federation was precluded by the PMAC, which failed even in principle to accept the legitimacy of the Eritrean movement and to offer it the right to secession, and compounded this refusal by opting for a military solution from 1976 onwards.

On the other hand, whilst justified in principle, the Eritrean case is undermined in practice by the fact that from 1978 onwards there was no real prospect that the movement, or any part of it, could establish an independent state. The opportunity for that, provided by the unique combination of strong Arab support and a weak Ethiopian government, had come and gone in 1977–8. It is extremely unlikely ever to repeat itself. The brief occasion that the Eritreans had for consolidating their independence, or of negotiating from strength for autonomy with the Ethiopians, was thrown away by their own excessive confidence and factionalism. Therefore, the choice facing the Eritreans in the period after 1978 was not whether to exercise the right to secession but whether to continue to fight the Ethiopians indefinitely, with no realistic expectation of victory, or to negotiate for whatever measure of autonomy the PMAC was willing to concede. Under the pressure of the Ethiopian offensives from June 1978 onwards, both major fronts did seem to make some public concessions: the ELF recognized that an Ethiopian revolution had occurred, while in November 1980 the EPLF said it would abide by the result of a referendum on independence, federation or local autonomy.[30] However, it was not clear whether either front could carry the rest of the Eritrean movement with it in its concessions, nor that the PMAC would itself yield ground, given its much stronger position. The continued cost of the war, in human and financial terms, placed heavy burdens upon Addis Ababa. In late 1980 there were reports of considerable unrest within the army over the failure to finish the war. The USSR and Cuba as well as some Arab states also urged conciliation on the PMAC.[31] Were some ultimately negotiated solution to be possible it would be a long way from the voluntary and enthusiastic union of two radical components, but it might spare both sides a continued conflict that could only bring further harm to their own peoples.

Nationalities in Movement: Oromo, Somali, Tigrean

Although, as we have seen, preceded by resistance to Amhara rule, the dissolution of the imperial regime led to much wider regional and ethnic contestation in the areas that had been under continuous Ethiopian domination. This was in some measure a result of the hopes raised amongst the non-Amhara by the 1974 revolution, to some extent too a result of the failure of the PMAC to respond adequately to these hopes and of its exacerbation of nationality issues. But this spread of ethnic consciousness was also a reflection of the fact that the central government remained weak. It was unable to prevent the emergence of rebel forces in provinces where the writ of Addis Ababa had never been fully established and where the destruction of the imperial order, with its attendant provincial nobilities and military sanctions, allowed a vacuum in which nationalist groups gained ground. The continuing war in Eritrea also served to promote this process, by illustrating the limits of PMAC power, and by acting as an inspiration to the young nationalists and more traditional leaders elsewhere to press their particular demands. The relationship between events in Addis Ababa and the provinces remained an

[30] *The Guardian*, November 25, 1980.
[31] See below, chapter 6, pp. 249, 253–6.

indirect, often contrary and tortured one, but the revolution there did, in a variety of ways, promote a general restiveness amongst the nationalities of Ethiopia, the consequences of which it would take a long time to gauge. Whilst it was unlikely that a post-revolutionary order would meet the full demands of these nationalities, or usher in a dissolution of the Ethiopian state, it appeared to be equally improbable that the previous system of domination, based upon the ethnic-religious particularism of the pre-1974 period, could be restored.

Whilst the most substantial endogenous challenge to the PMAC came from Eritrea, and whilst this conflict had a definite catalytic effect, the other conflicts differed in certain significant characteristics from the conflict in the north-east. First, the Eritrean movement was a multi-national one, mobilizing several linguistic groups, whilst the others were based upon single nationalities, identified on the basis of language. Second, the Eritrean movement was defined both in historical formation and geographical boundaries by its separation from Ethiopia during the colonial era; the rebellious nationalities were ones that had experienced subjugation by Menelik in the late nineteenth century and direct Amhara domination since then. Whilst each followed the nationalist proclivity of harking back to a past distinctness with correspondingly 'historical' boundaries, they were in fact more inchoate movements, responding to the 1974 revolution by predicating self-determination for much more loosely defined geographical areas. The Tigreans proposed an area that include all Tigrinya-speakers – and hence implicitly claimed much of Eritrea; the Somalis claimed a region called Ogaden after the tribe which lived there – which covered the three Ethiopian provinces of Bale, Hararghe and Sidamo and included many Oromo speakers; the Oromos talked of an area called Oromia which could, on linguistic grounds, have covered up to twelve provinces and included many other nationalities. A third difference was the relatively underdeveloped socio-economic structure of these areas: whereas Eritrea had been more urbanized and developed than Ethiopia, and had a democratic political tradition, these were comparatively poor regions, ranging from the agricultural lands of Tigray to the nomads of Hararghe. Fourth, the movements were formed in different contexts: the Eritreans continued their campaign before and after 1974 under the control of the same guerrilla groups; the other nationalities lacked such organizational continuity: even in the Somali case, where the WSLF had pre-dated the 1974 revolution, its emergence in 1977 was to a considerable extent a second birth and the continuity with earlier Oromo dissent was far more attenuated. In Tigray the new organization was formed later, as a direct result of the 1974 revolution, and had then to establish and justify a leading position over its constituency. Defined as they were in contrast to the Eritreans, these contestatory nationalities were, in other respects, a heteroclite collection. In the case of the Somalis, adherence to Islam and the religious subjection they had endured as Muslims played a part in their new resentment, whilst the Tigreans were Coptic Christians who resented the Amhara of Shoa for having displaced them in the mid nineteenth century from their previous dominance of the highland empires. Oromo dissidence seemed to include both Christians and Muslims. In terms of external affiliations, the Somalis were distinct from all the others, including the Eritreans, in being for all practical purposes the allies of another state, whilst the Oromo and Tigrean fronts were self-reliant. Politically, the TPLF was the most outspoken of these nationality groups, explicitly espousing a Maoist version of 'Marxism–Leninism' and purporting to criticize the land reform from a left-wing position; the Oromos and even more the Somalis restricted themselves to more generic combinations of socialist and nationalist aims. All three shared the goal of independence for their specific nationality; indeed the only regional or ethnic group not to call for full secession was the Afar National Liberation Movement, a small unrepresentative body that seemed to have less following amongst the Afars than the conservative Afar Liberation Front led by Sultan Ali Mirah.[32]

---

[32] Texts of the TPLF, OLF and ANLM programmes are given in *Brennpunkt Nordostafrika*, Reihe Internationalismus Informationen no. 4, Giessen 1979.

The largest linguistic-ethnic group in Ethiopia are the Oromos, who make up around 40 per cent of the Ethiopian population and include around twelve million people.[33] They were initially seen as the main beneficiaries of the 1974 revolution. Oromo officers played an active part in the PMAC and Mengistu himself was believed by some to be of part Oromo descent. The land reform was especially beneficial in the southern region. The political factions that dominated POMOA in 1976 and 1977 included many Oromo intellectuals. Perhaps 60 per cent of the army, and 80 per cent of the militia raised in 1977, were Oromos. The establishment of Muslim holidays on a par with Christian ones, and the use of Orominya in official broadcasts and publications, were symbolic of what, in the eyes of the Amhara and Tigreans, appeared to be an 'Oromo revolution'. Yet by 1977 there were indications that many Oromos, far from identifying with the revolution, saw it rather as an opportunity to press their interests further and to pose a new challenge to the central government. One factor contributing to this was the Somali invasion of 1977: it not only led to the rearming of the Christian landowners in the South, the *neftegnas*, but it also hardened the persistent suspicions of the Addis Ababa authorities towards all nationalities, especially in the Muslim regions of the south. Whilst neither the Somalis nor, for different reasons, the Ethiopians admitted it, much of the fighting in the Oromo areas involved Oromos who were not supported by Mogadishu and merely took advantage of the confused conditions occasioned by the Somali onslaught.

After the war with Somalia the Oromo influence within the central government seems to have waned. Personnel of Oromo origin may in part have placed their bureaucratic above their ethnic affiliations by siding with the central government: there were repeated purges of their ranks, and many of those who remained were in fact from the Christian sub-section who had long been affiliated to the state. The successive leadership purges of the regime followed a const-

---

[33] On the Oromos, see Bereket Habte Selassie, pp. 77–86; P.T.W. Baxter, 'Ethiopia's Unacknowledged Problem: the Oromo', The Royal African Society, *African Affairs*, no. 308, vol. 77, July 1978; and *Horn of Africa*, vol. III, no. 3, for background documentation.

ant pattern as one supposed representative of the Oromo after another was removed: Teferi Benti in February 1977, ME'ISON in August 1977, ECHA'AT in the summer of 1978, and two PMAC members who were tried in July 1980. The coercive recruitment of the militia and attendant casualities were resented by Oromos. Even the land reform may over time have become a cause of contention between the centre and the Oromo, since the regime's desire to extract the surplus from the countryside and carry through the 'second' land reform against the interests of richer peasants, appeared by 1979 to be provoking resistance in the southern provinces, as did, after 1978, the settlement of Amharas and Tigreans under the 'revolutionary' development programmes. Similarly, the mass literacy campaign, another social measure intrinsically positive for the Oromos, had its antagonizing side-effects: the central authorities enforced an Amharinya script for the language, in contrast to the Latin script favoured by many Oromo intellectuals.

The political complexion of the resistance amongst the Oromos was extremely varied. This was partly because of the diffuse character of those speaking Orominya, spread across twelve provinces, with no cohesive social or political institutions of any kind, and with a high degree of sub-division into clans and dialects. Some resistance was of a conservative nature, by landlords or *balabbats* opposed to the land reform; other resistance was by elements who called themselves socialist. In Bale province, scene of the pre-revolutionary guerrilla resistance, the old partisan leader Waku Gutu restarted operations in 1978 with Somali assistance; instead of using the word Oromo he called his front by the neologistic term 'Somali-Abo'.[34] In the eastern mountains around Harar, guerrilla forces led by a local chieftain, Sheikh Jarra, played a significant role in the 1977 fighting. Sheikh Jarra, who had received some training in Syria and Cuba, had later

---

[34] The Somali government declined to admit the existence of a distinct Oromo nationality and referred to it by the term 'Somali-Abo. *Abo* has been interpreted as a distinctive Oromo word for 'Hello'. For some years after 1974 a Somali-Abo Liberation Front operated from Somalia, and included former members of the ENLF (see chapter 2). By 1980, however, it seemed that this circumlocution had been abandoned, and the OLF was able to open an office in its own name in Mogadishu.

been imprisoned in Mogadishu, and escaped back to this area in 1975. There he raised new forces amongst the Harari and Qotto Oromos, who participated in fighting the Ethiopians after the Somali attacks in 1977. Both Waku Gutu and Sheikh Jarra were wary of the Somalis, but neither presented alternative programmes and neither was in a position to continue independent of Somali government assistance. This was in contrast to a new organization, the Oromo Liberation Front, which was established among left-wing intellectuals, mainly Christians from Welega province, in October 1974. At first they seem to have hoped the PMAC would provide a solution to the nationalities issue, whilst abstaining from the policy adopted by Oromos in ME'ISON and ECHA'AT of actively working with the military government. In July 1976, however, after the PMAC's terms had become clear, in the NDR and Nine Point Statement on Eritrea, the OLF members decided to oppose the government and launch guerrilla operations. The OLF programme, which supports the right of Eritrea to a separate state, calls for the establishment of a 'People's Democratic Republic of Oromia', and for the carrying out of a 'new democratic revolution' not only against the Amhara colonizers, but also against the Oromos allied with them.[35] Beyond its appeal to some Oromos in Ethiopia and abroad, it is not clear how much wider following the OLF has enjoyed. OLF guerrilla elements were reported in action in Arussi province in 1978 and 1979 and, in alliance with Waku Gutu, further south in Bale, but the geographical extension and fragmentation of the Oromo areas seem to preclude any wider mobilizations. It can only be expected, however, that the longer the central government fails to meet the aspirations voiced by more politically articulate Oromos for some measure of autonomy, the greater the potential for further resistance in the Oromo regions. The emergence of a unified and organized opposition amongst the Oromos may appear unlikely, but failure to conciliate the largest and initially most supportive of the country's ethnic groups could have dire consequences, political as well as economic, for the cohesion of post-revolutionary Ethiopia.

[35] OLF programme, in *Brennpunkt Nordostafrika*, p. 59. An OLF viewpoint is found in Gadaa Melbaa, *Oromia*, 'Finfine, Oromia', 1980.

The issue of the Somalis in Ethiopia has two aspects: one intra-Ethiopian, concerning their place within the multi-national state, the other international, concerning the role that the Ogaden Somalis played in the conflict between Ethiopia and Somalia, and more generally in the international crisis that unfolded in the Horn in 1977–8. In terms of its overall effects, it has probably been the most important of all the nationality issues inside Ethiopia; yet this has been because of the internationalization, regional and global, of the issue. In intra-Ethiopian terms it has been a less significant issue, involving one of the numerically smaller dissident nationalities who inhabit an area that is of secondary importance to Ethiopia as a whole: the region called 'Ogaden' may comprise up to a third of the geographical area of Ethiopia, but it has never had the importance, historical, strategic, material or affective, of Eritrea, Tigray or the Oromo regions. The analysis here will focus upon the first of the two aspects of the problem: the intra-Ethiopian. The international dimensions will be explored more fully in the following chapter.

The Somalis are a linguistically homogeneous ethnic group who have inhabited large parts of the lowland Horn for several centuries.[36] So far as is known, no identifiable Somali state ever existed in the past, uniting the main Somali regions, and tribal divisions served to fragment the nomads into rival confederacies. In the late nineteenth century the coastal areas inhabited by Somalis were divided up between European powers – France, Britain, Italy – whilst the Ethiopian state was able, under Menelik, to subjugate parts of the grazing land in the interior. The Somali population of south-east Ethiopia shares certain characteristics with the Oromos, with which it overlaps in northern Hararghe and in Bale. It is Muslim, having first come into contact with the Christian highlands when it expanded from the coastal areas, in the sixteenth century – it was subjected to Amhara domination by Menelik's conquests in the nineteenth. In other respects, however, these

---

[36] For a good general account see Tom Farer, *War Clouds in the Horn of Africa*, second edition, Washington 1979, pp. 69–110; I.M. Lewis, *Somali Culture, History and Social Institutions*, London 1981; Volker Matthies, *Der Grenzkonflikt Somalias mit Äthiopien und Kenya*, Hamburg 1977. The best introduction to Somalia is I.M. Lewis, *A Modern History of Somalia*, London 1980.

Somalis bear more relation to the semi-nomadic Sahos and Tigre-speakers of Eritrea, and to the black inhabitants of the south-west. For the nomadic Somalis, who number between half and one million, have been only tenuously integrated into the highland economic and social system. Unlike the Oromos they have not been partially converted to Christianity or locked into the highland system by colonization. Moreover, just as the inhabitants of Barca and Sahel in Eritrea have historic and economic contacts with the inhabitants of Sudan, so the Somalis of Ogaden have looked for contact as much to the Somalis across the border as to the Ethiopian heartlands. The lands of Ogaden are suitable for grazing during six months of the year, and link into the Somali economy. The trans-frontier grazing patterns of the nomadic herds mean that a substantial part of the Somali population have grazed their flocks on both sides of the frontier defined in the Anglo-Ethiopian treaty of 1897 and the Italo-Ethiopian of 1908.

The fate of the Somali population under the republican government might have been similar to that of other southern nationalities, with a gradual increase in national sentiment following the fall of the emperor. The PMAC made clear its intention to extend the provisions of the NDR to Ogaden, and in 1976 began some small-scale development projects in the provinces concerned. But the dominant factor in the development of the Somali issue was neither local sentiment, nor the meagre initiative of the PMAC, but the policy of the Mogadishu government, which decided in 1977 to take advantage of Ethiopia's disarray and launch a military offensive to reclaim its 'lost lands' in Ogaden. This had been a claim of the Somali nationalist movement that arose in the 1940s in what were then the two colonies of British and Italian Somaliland: following the defeat of the Italians in 1941, the British had retained all of Ogaden until 1948 and a part of it until 1955 before handing it back to Haile Selassie. Somali nationalists claimed the Ogaden as *terra irredenta*, along with Jibuti and part of Kenya. When the British returned the territories there was no substantial political organization in Ogaden nor was there even the kind of controversial consultation practised by the UN in Eritrea: in British eyes these areas were recognized as part of Ethiopia and were accordingly handed back. The cause of Ogaden remained alive, however, and soon after Somali independence in 1960 a Western Somali Liberation Front was established in Mogadishu, claiming to represent the inhabitants of Ogaden. But the WSLF, however resentfully, was able to act only at the pleasure of Mogadishu. The periods in which it could operate against the Ethiopian government were chosen not by the WSLF itself but by the Somali authorities.

Beyond the ideological appeals of irredentism found in all such cases, it is possible to identify three particular factors behind the Somali claim to Ogaden.[37] The first is economic: Ogaden affords grazing during the six months of the rainy season, and reports during the 1960s of oil deposits added a further attraction. Second, the claim to Ogaden serves a function within Somali society as a whole, binding what is a highly fragmented collection of tribes together in the cause of fighting a common enemy: Somalia is still rent by the conflicts between its formerly British and Italian parts, as well as by tribal disputes, and a cause such as the 'liberation' of Ogaden can be used to supersede these internal divisions. But there is a third reason, namely that the claim to Ogaden advances the interests of one of the four tribal confederacies inside Somalia, the Darod, to whom the Ogaden tribes belong. The Darod have dominated post-independence Somalia and have encouraged Ogaden tribesmen to integrate themselves into the state: up to 30 per cent of the armed forces are Ogadeni men; Siad Barre had an Ogadeni mother and hence close ties with these tribes. However, these enduring concerns have not prevented considerable variation in the intensity with which the Somalis have pressed their claim. The civilian government attempted one military campaign, in 1963, but it was rebuffed. When the military came to power, they downplayed the issue. Some WSLF officials were

---

[37] For an account of the tribal structure of Somalia see Lewis, and *The Guardian*, April 24, 1981. According to this latter report, Ogadenis armed by the central government were using their weapons to raid northern Somali tribes, their traditional rivals.

even imprisoned. In the ensuing years Siad Barre and his associates negotiated with Haile Selassie, who visited Mogadishu in 1971, and stressed their desire to settle the issue peacefully. Time and again the Somali government stated that it would not resort to force to regain Ogaden.[38] But, at some point after the fall of the imperial regime in Ethiopia, there was a change of policy in Mogadishu and plans were laid for a military solution to the problem. In early 1977 both the USSR and Cuba tried to negotiate between Somalia and Ethiopia and, in particular, to forestall a Somali attack. But in June 1977 WSLF guerrillas began operating in Ogaden, and in July the Somali regular army crossed the frontier too. For several months it appeared that the Somalis had conquered the territories they claimed and it was only in early 1978 that a combined Ethiopian and Cuban force, with substantial supplies of Soviet arms, counter-attacked and drove the Somali army across the frontier. For two years afterwards the Ogaden was comparatively tranquil, with an estimated 15,000 Cubans helping to garrison the region; but despite their defeat the Somalis refused to abandon their claim and in the spring of 1980 the WSLF began to carry out substantial operations once again. These were no more successful, and, coincident with the revival of fighting, the number of Somali refugees crossing into Somalia greatly increased, rising from 100,000 to nearly 750,000 in a few months. Whilst the Somalis attributed this to a deliberate policy of expulsion on the part of the Ethiopian authorities, others pointed to the disruption of the nomadic economy consequent upon the earlier fighting, exacerbated in 1980 by a drought, and to the WSLF's deliberate encouragement of mass flight into Somalia.

The issue of the Ogaden Somalis is in certain respects distinct from that of other nationalities inside Ethiopia. Whilst they have the same nationality entitlements as other ethnic groups, and have not been offered a reasonable measure of autonomy by the central government, the form in which the question of their self-determination has been posed is one determined by another state. The WSLF is not simply an

---

[38] Luigi Pestalozza, *The Somalian Revolution*, Paris 1974, p. 282, quoting a statement by Siad Barre to this effect in 1972.

instrument of Mogadishu's policy: indeed the tensions within the WSLF on the issue of how to relate to the Somali government have been such that in early 1981 the whole leadership was replaced by a new central committee headed by Mohammad Dirye Urdoh, that was less under the control of Mogadishu. One reason why the WSLF was for so long unwilling to publish a political programme was that this was seen as something that might prejudice its future choice on the matter of joining Somalia. But these internal conflicts are secondary: there is no way in which the WSLF can operate as a serious force without the support of the Somalia government. The campaigns fought in Ogaden have been initiated, sustained and then halted by the Somali authorities. The determining principle has therefore not been the rights of an ethnic minority so much as the rationale of a military regime which, despite its invocations of socialism and many positive socio-economic reforms, has continued to use the Ogaden issue for its own state purposes. In this perspective the Somali initiative in Ogaden is questionable.

First, it was a decision by a supposedly progressive state to settle a border dispute by force against the urgings of many of its former allies. Second, in so doing, it in fact caused immense harm to its own population, and to the Somalis in Ogaden, and it confirmed the chauvinist trend within Ethiopia which declined to make any concessions on the nationality issue. It was for this reason that the Eritreans tried to persuade Siad Barre *not* to attack.[39] Third, the WSLF itself, when allowed to speak, never stated that it wanted to become part of Somalia: the ultimate goal was left open, not as a matter of diplomatic caution, but because it was wary of the Somali government's designs; yet Mogadishu turned the matter into one of territorial transfer. Fourth, the course pursued by the Somali authorities was one they had not taken during the reign of Haile Selassie. When he was in power they talked emolliently, but when a regime which, whatever its failings and crimes, was far more progressive than the emperor's came to power in Addis Ababa, the Somali regime

---

[39] This was confirmed to us by ELF representative Omar Alim. Similar warnings were sent to Siad Barre in 1977 by the Sudanese opposition leader Sadiq al-Mahdi (interview, London, February 1979).

saw fit to attack it. Finally, as will be shown in the following chapter, the timing and direction of the Somali offensive owed much to Siad Barre's attempts to get financial help from the Saudi Arabians and Americans who, he believed, would support him in an offensive against revolutionary Ethiopia. If in the end they disappointed him, it is nonetheless not possible to separate the Somali offensive of 1977 from the wider context of Arab and Western antipathy to the new Ethiopian regime. Deferential towards the imperial regime, and disdainful of the wider political consequences in Ethiopia, the Somali regime brought catastrophe upon its fellow Somalis in Ethiopia and laid enormous additional burdens upon its own impoverished people as a result of the manner in which it purported to champion the (in themselves) legitimate rights of the Ogaden Somalis.

The issue of the Somali minority within Ethiopia is, as we have seen, distinct in one essential respect from that of the other nationalities: whatever the precise views of the WSLF on the matter, the issue is whether the Ogaden area should be part of Ethiopian or Somali territory. An independent Ogaden is not a viable proposition. In this sense, comparisons should be made not with other nationalities within Ethiopia, but with other cases where such a separation exists, where an identifiable ethnic group is divided into an independent state on the one side, and a minority within another state on the other. The issue of self-determination for the ethnic group in general is not in question: its right to self-determination is internationally recognized and it has its own state. What is in question is how much territory that independent state should have and which of the available solutions should be implemented where there is such a separation: boundary redefinition, population movement, or acceptance of the division into independent state and minority region. The implications of the Somali case have been that only the first of these is conceivable: yet many analogous cases exist, in which this solution has not been chosen. The division into Outer Mongolia, an independent state, and the Chinese province of Inner Mongolia, or between Bangladesh and the Indian state of West Bengal, or between Hungary and the Transylvanian region of Romania, are cases in point. These are areas where accommodation has taken place on the basis of a mutual recognition of rights: the independent state waives its irredentist claims, whilst the neighbouring multinational state grants a measure of autonomy to the nationality in question. The question of the Somali minority in Ethiopia bears at least as much comparison with these cases, as it does with the issue of, say, Eritrea, which enjoys no such partial self-determination outside the boundaries of Ethiopia itself.

With the benefit of hindsight, it is possible to see just how rash and ultimately disastrous the Somali attack was. In many ways, it was reminiscent of the attempted invasion of northern Ethiopia by the Egyptian Khediv Ismail in 1875–6. On both occasions, the invading forces misjudged the degree of disunity and weakness inside Ethiopia and imagined that their conquest would be easy. The expulsion of the Somalis in 1977 was carried out with Cuban and Russian support, but this came only after the Ethiopians had themselves stemmed the Somali forces. In the words of one Sudanese observer, 'Siad Barre lost the war when he had not won it in the first two weeks'. Both assaults revived the militant patriotism of the Ethiopian highlands against what were seen as attacks from the Muslim lowlands and strengthened the determination of Ethiopia's rulers to centralize their domain. The international consequences also bear some comparison. While the European powers were sympathetic to Khediv Ismail, they were for a time discouraged by his failures from attempting similar assaults themselves; it would seem that, despite all the protests about the Cuban role in Ogaden, the West drew the lesson from the events of 1977–8 that the new Ethiopian regime was a permanent arrangement. The fate of the invading powers may also contain its own lesson: six years after being routed by the Ethiopians, Egypt itself fell under colonial domination, in the Anglo–French occupation of 1882. The immediate effect of Siad Barre's failure in Ogaden was to render his regime perilously reliant on Saudi and American support.

The province of Tigray has a Coptic Christian population of around five million, and lies between Shoa and Eritrea. As in the Oromo areas, the resistance in Tigray began in a conservative form when the former governor Ras Mengesha Seyoum organized a Tigray Liberation Front in 1974 to oppose the military government. But the TLF later merged with the conservative EDU and in 1976 a new, more left-wing faction recruited from younger intellectuals emerged, the Tigray People's Liberation Front.[40] The TPLF claimed to represent all who spoke Tigrinya and called for an armed struggle, based on the thought of Mao Tse-tung, to establish an independent Tigray province. In common with most other political formations in Ethiopia, it called for a 'new democratic revolution' that would overthrow local feudalists and what it termed the 'colonial' domination established by Menelik; despite an implicit territorial inconsistency, the TPLF voiced its support for the Eritreans. It is probably here that the key to its success lies, for from 1976 onwards the TPLF was receiving logistical support from the EPLF inside Eritrea; in 1980 it intervened to help the EPLF fight the ELF. Whereas it had a few hundred guerrillas operating in the countryside in 1976, its strength later grew to several thousand and it was able to carry out what, from the Eritrean point of view, was the most important function: harrassment of the Ethiopian military lines running through Tigray province, up to the capital at Makele and then on to the Eritrean capital at Asmara. Claims made in mid-1980 that 70 per cent of the province had been 'liberated' were exaggerated, especially given the ambiguity of the term 'liberated', but it did seem that the guerrilla movement had gathered force in the late 1970s in contrast to the overall trend elsewhere in the country, where the central government seemed to be increasing its level of control. In the autumn of 1980 the Ethiopian army launched a substantial counter-insurgency campaign in the province in an attempt to disrupt the rural bases and supply systems of the TPLF guerrillas.[41]

The factors underlying the resistance were not in the first instance nationality-based, nor did the movement reflect a

---

[40] On the TPLF see Bereket Habte Selassie, pp. 86–96, and Ottaways, pp. 85–7. Bereket implies that the TPLF does not seek full independence from Ethiopia, but this is not confirmed by their programme, as printed in *Brennpunkt*, p. 65.

[41] Dan Connell in *The Guardian*, October 17, 1980. Reports of later TPLF actions were published in *The Guardian*, March 31, 1981.

widespread devotion on the part of the population to the ideas of a Maoist youth group. Apart from underlying resentment at Shoans, there was the more immediate issue of what the Tigreans saw as an 'Oromo revolution' that threatened to disestablish the previously dominant Christian bloc. The land reform, which benefited the south and hence the despised Oromos, had relatively little impact on the north with its more homogeneous ethnic and social structures and was seen in some areas as a form of interference by the central government in village affairs. Ras Mengesha's revolt was a classic Vendée, a movement by a rural population under conservative leadership against a revolutionary central government, and in this respect bore some similarities to the risings in Gojjam in 1967, which blocked Haile Selassie's attempts at rural reform. The issue of Eritrea also played its part, not because of widespread sympathy for the EPLF or its rivals, but because the peasant militia of Oromos sent against Eritrea in 1976 was allowed to live off the land whilst traversing Tigray, in the time-honoured fashion of Ethiopian armies. These difficulties in the countryside were exacerbated in the late 1970s by the return of famine, which had so devastated the province in 1973 and had been one of the objective factors precipitating the revolution itself. In the combination of elements that produced it, Tigray illustrated the differential tempo and the many cross-currents of the Ethiopian revolution: beginning as an aristocratic reaction, it ended up under the influence of Maoist intellectuals. Situated in one of the provinces most favoured under the *ancien régime*, it found new sources of resentment in the course of the revolution itself, and posed new difficulties for the PMAC just at a time when the conflicts in Eritrea and Ogaden had to some degree subsided. It was an ironic component of the wider *prise de conscience* of the Ethiopian nationalities occasioned by the fall of the imperial system. Faced with these challenges, the PMAC appeared to have few answers, beyond throttled 'socialist solutions' and a mailed fist.

The Responsibility of the Centre: Past and Future

The level of contestation in the provinces was therefore due to a variety of factors – the transition from one mode of production to another, the breakdown of the complex pyramid of imperial ethnic control, the level of foreign interference, the weaknesses of the central government, the overlap of economic with nationality issues, the differential and asynchronic impact of the 1974 revolution. The most significant political factor, however, without which the others would have lost some of their impact, was the lack of a sufficiently coherent policy at the centre, the lack of that farsightedness, generosity and executive persistence required to allay the plethora of resentments, old and new, that emerge in a multinational country traversing a revolution. Above all else, therefore, the responsibility for the course of events after 1974 must be laid at the door of the PMAC itself. The Somalis and their Arab instigators, and the intransigent elements within the nationality groups, must bear considerable responsibility too, as must the imperial regime that bequeathed these political time-bombs to its successors. The PMAC did try on several occasions between 1974 and 1978 to negotiate with the Eritreans and it did not simply deny that the problem existed. It could also rightly claim that the Eritrean attack of 1975 and the Somali of 1977 had undermined possibilities for conciliation. But what it offered was too little and too vague.

Had the PMAC taken a more cogent, conciliatory line from the beginning or taken stock of the position in 1976, then it is unlikely that the nationality issue would have acquired the menacing force that it was later to do. Since neither the partial restitution of Amhara domination nor the supposed panaceas of socialism could on their own resolve the tensions, it appeared as if the PMAC or its successors would for a long time be faced with that issue which, in the immediate aftermath of the 1974 revolution, they had imagined they could circumvent altogether. The tragedy was that, whatever justice attached to their causes, the solution offered by the various fronts was itself a rather limited one, since it promised to break Ethiopia up into several separate states. This would have had obvious negative economic consequences – evident from the fact that Ethiopia as a whole was so poor. It would no doubt have laid the basis for centuries of irredentism and conflict, since the boundaries of the new states would be contested. It would offer no solution to the nationalities problem: with over eighty identifiable ethnic groups in Ethiopia, there would still be room for further minority struggles inside the new states. Nor, from what could be judged of their internal political systems, would any of these organizations be more lenient towards opponents than the Derg. In practice, no such eventuality seemed likely; but by its intransigence the PMAC was encouraging precisely that nationalistic fervour amongst the formerly subject peoples which would guarantee insecurity and resentment for a long time to come.

Leaving on one side all the theoretical ambiguities in the socialist literature on the subject, and the divergences of theory and practice, the lesson of past ethnic conflicts of this kind is clear: that within multinational states, the preservation of unity is preferable, provided this is done on a voluntary basis, and provided meaningful autonomy is given to the nationalities in question. The arguments adduced by the PMAC and the Russians for preserving the unity of Ethiopia are, in the main, substantial ones. There is no doubt that a multinational Ethiopia would do more to advance the material and, in the long run, political interests of the component nationalities than would a process of fragmentation. Yet the key condition for this solution, one systematically avoided by the Derg and Soviet writers alike, is that this union be voluntary: for, apart from political objections to any forced maintenance of the union as such, there are strong practical reasons for doubting how far involuntary union can be imposed. Those who favour a solution within federal bounds, like many Eritreans before 1974 or like the Kurds in Iraq and Iran, may be driven by the intransigence of central governments to demand independence. For this reason, the conclusion of one Ethiopian writer is unavoidable: that the question of the nationalities in Ethiopia is closely linked to the question of political democracy.[42] If the nationalities can feel that they have some stake in the new regime, that it is in some measure responsive to their demands, then the possibilities of reaping the benefits of a multinational state will be increased.

[42] Addis Hiwet, *The Nationalities Question in Ethiopia and the Horn*, 1978, p. 37.

If, on the other hand, the centre combines a refusal of regional autonomy with a generalized denial of political democracy, then these advantages will be lost to it.

6

The International Dimensions

The Horn in International Politics

No aspect of the Ethiopian revolution is more difficult to elucidate than the international involvement in the events following upon the fall of the emperor. In chapter 1 we discussed the general character of this relationship: whilst avoiding the temptation to reduce events in the Horn as a whole to mere effects of external forces, we analysed how these exterior pressures influenced the region, exacerbating some conflicts, and lending support to particular local actors at moments of need. The impact of external actors upon the Horn was a major one and it meant that the Horn itself became, via this intertwining with world politics, an issue of major international dispute. Ethiopia was an important chapter in the worsening of East–West relations that was to shift geographical focus from Angola in 1976 to the Horn and Zaire in 1978, to North Yemen and Indo-China in 1979, to the plateau of Central Asia in 1980, and to Central America in 1981. As such, it was part of the prelude to the Second Cold War. For right-wing commentators across the globe, Soviet and Cuban policies acquired an exemplary character: they were repeatedly cited as an instance of Soviet 'opportunism' and perfidy in the Third World, and as a 'violation' of the rules of détente. Yet this exemplary function existed not only in the eyes of the right; it was equally vivid in the eyes of much of the international socialist movement, which deplored Soviet and Cuban policies in the Horn. For the Russians and Cubans on the other hand, and for their Ethiopian allies, the root of the conflicts in the Horn lay in interference by other external elements, Arab and Western, intent on undermining the Ethiopian state and re-establishing the regional hegemony that the 1974 revolution had taken from them.

The Horn of Africa has been at the centre of international political conflict on three occasions in modern history. The first occasion was in the 1890s, when the Italian attempt to conquer the whole of Ethiopia was blocked by a combination of Ethiopian military success and rival imperialist diplomacy. The second occasion was when the Italian fascists successfully invaded Ethiopia in 1935–6. The third was in the mid-1970s, as a consequence primarily of the Somali attempt to wrest Ogaden from Ethiopian control. The initiating force in the first two instances was Italian colonialism; in the latter it was the regional reaction to the revolution in Ethiopia itself.

The international dimensions of the conflict were set by certain general features that can be resumed as follows[1]

1. The Horn has never been a region noted primarily for its raw materials, or for the potential markets within it. Italian colonialism did offer Italian settlers the prospect of colonization on the fertile uplands of central Eritrea and Ethiopia, but the major importance of the area in world politics has been its geographical position: aside the lower part of the Red Sea, a source of the waters of the Nile, bordering the Arab world and black Africa, and with good access to the Indian Ocean. Its attraction to US and Soviet military strategists in the post-1945 period has reflected primarily its proximity to the Indian Ocean rather than any continental (that is, African) advantages.

2. The Horn has a special political relationship to both the Middle East and black Africa. Historically its closest ties have always been with the world to the north and east: Christianity came southwards in the fourth century and it is from here that later Muslim threats have also come. Ethiopia has been invaded many times from the north-east and east, never from the south and west. Under Haile Selassie, Ethiopia was

---

[1] A good survey of international dimensions of the crisis can be found in Tom Farer, *War Clouds on the Horn of Africa: The Widening Storm*, Carnegie Endowment for International Peace, New York and Washington, 1979.

valued by the US as an ally of Israel. The greatest single cause of Western alarm about the increased Soviet–Cuban presence in Ethiopia in 1977 was its implication, real or imagined, for the oil-producing states across the Red Sea. Ethiopia's relation to Africa is of more recent development. But as headquarters of the OAU, and as the third most populous state in Africa, after Nigeria and Egypt, Ethiopia has established a position of diplomatic and political influence that outside powers must take into account.

3. The nature of the military conflicts in the Horn has been such as to draw in outside powers. As in the Arab–Israeli case, though to a lesser extent than in that context, the confrontation is between states as well as between a state and a rebel movement: this has raised the level of local demand for military supplies and the consequent commitment of the great-power suppliers. Outside involvement has been brought about not merely through the use by local forces of material supplied from outside, but also because of the ongoing political commitments to the local states that such supplies have engendered. The presence in Somalia and Ethiopia, at different times, of American, Cuban and Soviet personnel deemed necessary to assist local forces has been one clear index of this.

4. The influence of the Horn's neighbours upon the region has played a major role in sharpening the ethnic conflicts within it. It has aroused Ethiopian suspicions of renewed Arab–Muslim hostility, and encouraged those fighting the Addis Ababa government, in Somalia and Eritrea, to believe that this external support will in the end enable them to prevail.

5. Whilst most commentators on the recent history of the Horn adopt an approach that tends to be reductionist in overstating the external causes, the course of events before and after 1974 has underlined the opposite: the continuing autonomy of local events and the primacy of endogenous factors in the determination of particular conflicts. The 1974 revolution was one that the USA was unable to prevent, even

though it took place in a country long subject to US protection. It was an upheaval in which no outside powers played any role. Because a certain amount of US aid continued until 1977, it was frequently stated that the Derg or part of it was 'pro-American': in fact, all significant ties between the Ethiopian state and the USA were broken when the emperor was deposed. For its part, the USSR had no influence over the events of 1974 and there was not even the semblance of a pro-Soviet communist party in Ethiopia at that time. Since 1977 the Ethiopians have had an active relationship with the USSR, and this has enabled them to reassert themselves against the Somalis and Eritreans. But, on available evidence, this has not given the Russians substantial control over Ethiopian domestic policies, or even the degree of influence that the USSR had in Egypt during the 1960s. For their part, the Somalis permitted themselves substantial Soviet aid in the 1960s and were duly castigated in the West as instruments of Soviet policy: yet they were quite willing to break their apparently vital ties with Moscow in 1977 and to welcome the Americans instead. The record of events suggests that despite the limited economic power of these two countries, and despite their need for substantial military support from outside, both Ethiopia and Somalia have retained a substantial margin of political manoeuvre. Even the Eritreans, seen by Ethiopia as agents of foreign powers, are responding primarily to forces inside their own region: indeed the failure of the Arab states throughout the 1970s to persuade the Eritreans to create a single united organization is one indication of the limited power of the latter's external supporters.

US Policy: Who Lost Ethiopia?

The linchpin of US policy in the Horn was, until 1977, its relationship with Ethiopia, for many years America's chief ally in black Africa. Policy towards other issues followed from this.[2] Yet the rupture in the Washington–Addis Ababa

---

[2] On the background to US policy see *Ethiopia and the Horn of Africa*, Hearings before the Sub-committee on African Affairs of the US Senate Foreign Relations Committee, Washington 1976; *United States Security Agreements and Commitments Abroad*, Senate Foreign Relations Committee, Washington 1971.

alliances that followed the revolution has not met with a reaction comparable to that following other recent US losses. Washington has seen no 'Who Lost Ethiopia?' debate like the retrospective discussions that have taken place on China and Cuba, Vietnam and Iran. American debate has focused not on the revolution itself, but on one of its consequences: the advent of Cuban forces and Soviet military aid at the end of 1977. This, rather than the revolution itself, has been the issue around which conservative retrospection has occurred. Yet the absence of a 'Who Lost Ethiopia?' debate reveals certain vital aspects of the relationship, and in particular the almost wholly strategic light in which Ethiopia was long viewed. It is, ironically, this US neglect of internal Ethiopian factors that helps to explain why the revolution itself occurred, and why the upheavals of 1974 led, more or less inevitably, to the crisis of 1977–8.

The US relationship with Ethiopia began during the Second World War when Ethiopia qualified for lend-lease aid and granted the USA a communications facility at Asmara. In the post-war decade, it became evident that (a) the US would now play a *global* anti-communist role, taking in Africa and the Middle East; and (b) the British would be unable to continue playing the main role in many of the countries for which they had been assigned primary responsibility during the war itself. The British military mission to the Ethiopian army withdrew in 1952, and in 1953 the USA took over. The instruments of US policy in Ethiopia were two agreements signed on May 23, 1953. The first was a Military Assistance agreement that provided for US aid in equipping and training the Ethiopian forces. Between 1951 and 1976 Ethiopia received over $350 million in economic aid from the USA and a further $279 million in military aid. In the years 1953–75, 3,552 Ethiopian military personnel were trained in the USA itself. This US military programme was by far the largest in Africa. The other agreement signed in 1953 concerned defence installations. In this case the installation was the communications base at Asmara, known as Kagnew. This was ideally situated for the USA's global radio communications network, since it was far from the northern and southern magnetic poles, and in a zone comparatively free of magnetic storms. From 1953 onwards it formed part of a world-wide circuit running from Arlington, Virginia, through the US bases in Morocco to Asmara, and then on to the Philippines.

If the initial rationale for the US–Ethiopian alliance was, therefore, Ethiopia's generally anti-communist position and the Asmara base, a number of further developments deepened the commitment. In 1960 the USA and Ethiopia signed a new military agreement, the terms of which were only partly revealed. This stressed the USA's commitment to the territorial integrity of Ethiopia, without committing the former to send in troops if this integrity were threatened. American aid was increased in response to the attempted coup against Haile Selassie in 1960, and to fears in Addis Ababa of newly independent Somalia. Once Somalia began to receive Soviet military aid, the importance of Ethiopia as an anti-communist ally was supposedly all the greater. This coincided with the increasingly active role that Ethiopia played in Africa, as the colonized states there became independent. Ethiopia sent a military contingent of over 3,000 troops with half an air squadron to support the UN in Zaire in 1960. In 1963 Haile Selassie mediated in the war between Morocco and Algeria. Aid was sent to General Mobutu of Zaire when he was faced with a threat from the left in 1967. In 1963 Addis Ababa was made the site of the headquarters of the Organization of African Unity, a choice that gave Ethiopia a special diplomatic weight. Ethiopia also maintained a close relationship with another US ally, Israel. It therefore seemed to the State Department that support for Ethiopia had a number of benefits vis-à-vis both the Middle East and Africa.

While Ethiopia maintained a generally open policy and tried not to clash with other African states, there were two specific policies on which Haile Selassie was insistent and on which the USA cooperated. These were Somalia and Eritrea. When Somalia became independent in 1960, Haile Selassie seems to have ensured that the USA would refuse to give it any military aid, despite the fact that the Somali government was generally of a pro-Western orientation. Somalia wanted an army of 20,000 but the West would agree only to 5,000. It was after this, in 1963, that Somalia turned towards a state that *was* quite willing to provide the desired arms: the Soviet Union. US policy on Eritrea took some time to form. When negotiations on the former Italian colony's disposal began after 1945, the USA at first supported the idea that Italy should resume control of it, as of Italian Somaliland. The reasons for this were of an immediate electoral kind: Truman wanted to win the Italian–American vote in the 1948 presidential elections, and to foster pro-American sentiments in the Italian general election of that year. But by 1950, when Haile Selassie had opportunely become ready to send his forces to fight with the USA in Korea, Washington favoured the federation of Eritrea with Ethiopia and helped the resolution to that effect through the UN.[3] From then onwards, the USA endorsed the territorial integrity of Ethiopia and refused to countenance any demand for Eritrean separation; indeed, it did not protest at the forced amalgamation of Eritrea with Ethiopia in 1962. While occasionally calling for a settlement of the dispute through negotiation, Washington continued to back the central government, providing the bulk of its arms. The USA claimed that it refrained from front-line involvement in Eritrea, leaving the main counter-insurgency work to the Israelis. But even this was less than the truth: after the Eritrean guerrillas had been active for three years, a counter-insurgency team was sent to Ethiopia and in 1966, over a hundred counter-insurgency advisers were brought in for two to three years, under a scheme known as 'Plan Delta'.

The official US view of its interests in Ethiopia was shortsighted. The US Ambassador to Ethiopia between 1963 and 1967 later described his government's policy in the following way: 'The US interest in Ethiopia was simple then for Washington. The Government defined it as "the unhampered use of Kagnew station". The facility was deemed then to be "strategically vital" to the United States, the only such military installation in Black Africa. We had 1,800 officers, men and civilians working there, plus 800 dependents; a total of 2,500 with plans well advanced during my briefing period to raise that number to 3,500 within a year, as

---

[3] Cao-Huy-Thuan, 'Les Etats-Unis et la question érythréenne', in Alain Fenet, Cao-Huy-Thuan, and Tran-Van-Minh, *La question de l'Érythrée*, Paris 1979.

did occur. The de facto price the United States paid for Kagnew was military aid, roughly $10 million to $12 million a year on the books. . . . The reports on the use of our military aid in Ethiopia were depressing. Much of the equipment was quickly ruined and junked by ill-trained soldiers. The Ethiopian army was regarded as little more than a rag trade force, and when I asked the briefing officer at the Pentagon what we were doing about it, he said that there wasn't much we could do with the Ethiopians, and it was really Kagnew rent money, and if the Emperor wanted it in "solid gold Cadillacs", that was his term, he could have it that way.'[4] It would appear that during the 1960s Washington made some attempt to encourage the Addis Ababa regime to introduce reforms. In Latin America, and in Middle East monarchies such as Saudi Arabia and Iran, the Kennedy and Johnson administrations promoted administrative reforms and urged land reform in order to stabilize regimes that would otherwise have been swept away by popular opposition. Under the pressure of events in Cuba and Vietnam, it was believed that reform was the way to prevent revolution. In this light, no country was more obviously in need of such reforms than Ethiopia, and between 1963 and 1967 the US Embassy in Addis suggested them. The guiding rubric was 'stability with progress'. The reforms included land reform, legal modernization, decentralization with greater rights for Eritrea, and a stronger role for the Ethiopian parliament. But the US initiative was unavailing in the end, and the policies that had worked in some other countries, such as Iran, were not implemented in any degree in Ethiopia. It was of the utmost importance that the USA, which was in a position to influence events in Ethiopia to a considerable extent, succeeded so little: the short-term price of sustaining the imperial state without reform was the suffering visited upon Ethiopia in the 1972–3 famine. The longer-run result was the 1974 revolution, and the change in Ethiopia's alignment.

In the early 1970s certain shifts in US–Ethiopian relations began to be evident. The break differed from those in Vietnam or Iran in that it pre-dated the revolution by some

[4] *Ethiopia and the Horn*, p. 36.

time. The Kagnew Base became less important, in the wake of developments in satellite communications. At the same time, the USA decided to construct a major new base, to include communications equipment, on the Indian Ocean island of Diego Garcia. Personnel at Kagnew fell from a peak of over 3,000 in 1971 to only thirty-five in 1976. As a result the USA lost one of the main reasons, if not indeed *the* main reason, for supporting Haile Selassie. This presaged the greater shift to an Indian Ocean policy that was to take place in the mid-70s, culminating in the USA's acquiring a base in Somalia in 1980. A further stage was reached with the Arab–Israeli war of October 1973, when Ethiopia, after years of Arab pressure, broke off diplomatic relations with Israel. It was now no longer so feasible for officials in Washington to argue for aid to Ethiopia on the grounds that the country was important for Israel's strategic posture. However, the immediate factor discouraging Washington from support for Haile Selassie was the manifest crisis through which his country was passing in 1972–3: the famine and the regime's inability to face up to the disaster. An upheaval was evidently looming in Ethiopia, of a kind that would sweep Haile Selassie away. It was therefore in Washington's interests to take its distance from the Ethiopian regime and to wait for events to run their course.

The first real indication of a cooling in relations was in May 1973, when Haile Selassie made the last of his several visits to Washington. Although he was promised ground-to-air missiles and a new brigade of armoured cars, his requests for new jets and M-60 tanks were refused. From January 1974 onwards, the USA was so concerned not to appear too close to the Emperor that it posted no ambassador in Addis Ababa; it was represented there during the critical months after January 1974 by a mere chargé d'affaires. The USA's hope was apparently that it would, despite its long-term association with the imperial regime, be able to recoup its position and establish ties with the new government, whatever form this might take.

In the period immediately after the fall of Haile Selassie, the Ethiopian armed forces were almost wholly reliant on US supplies, yet the USA itself no longer had any great military interest in the country. Economically, it was an important partner for Ethiopia but not vice versa: the USA provided aid valued at $36.4 million in 1974, out of a total of about $220 million, and was the largest single aid supplier. The USA also took most of Ethiopia's main export, coffee. But overall foreign investment in the country was low: the US total was about $20 million, under 10 per cent of the whole.

The dominant argument in Washington until early 1977 was that the US should continue to support the Derg. It rested on three basic premisses. The first was that if the USA cut off aid, Eritrea would become independent and aligned with the Arab world: this would give the Arab states control over both shores of the Bab al-Mandeb, the narrow mouth of the Red Sea through which Israeli-bound tankers and other shipping pass. The second was that if Eritrea broke away, and if the USA was seen to be permitting this, it would have a negative impact throughout Africa, where the permanence of existing borders was a matter of cardinal diplomatic and political importance. The third, and the one most used in public pronouncements, was that since Somalia was under Soviet domination, and was in particular armed by the Soviet Union, the USA should continue backing Ethiopia as a regional counter-weight, and as a guarantee of US credibility in the world as a whole.[5]

American arms sales and military aid was provided until the beginning of 1977. Washington continued to make cautious remarks about the Derg, while distancing itself from what it considered to be the unacceptable facets of Derg policy. It seems that the US Embassy had friendly relations with Brigadier Andom, the head of state in the period up to November 1974. When Brigadier Andom and dozens of other leading officials were killed on Bloody Saturday, November 23, 1974, US aid was suspended for a while. But in February 1975, military aid was re-authorized by Kissinger after a renewed Ethiopian request. In January 1976, under the impact of events in Angola, and with a confrontation looming with Somalia after France had announced that Jibuti would become independent, the Pentagon asked Congress for $22

---

[5] Farer resumes the arguments for and against continued US support for the PMAC.

million in military aid. It declared that it would intensify its programme of modernizing the Ethiopian army. Later, in the summer of 1976, the US Embassy seems to have exerted strong pressure on the Derg not to go ahead with the planned peasant march on Eritrea, and US officials claimed that they had played an effective role in persuading the Derg to stop it.

US Military Assistance to Ethiopia

	Grants in US$ (000)	Sales in US$ (000)	Personnel trained in USA
1970	10,494	6	
1971	11,763		140
1972	10,645	10	159
1973	9,439		156
1974	11,719	7,440	147
1975	12,999	22,127	130
1976	7,277	135,339	192

Source: *United States Arms Policies in the Persian Gulf and Red Sea Areas*, 172, 175

Until the end of the Republican Administration in January 1977 Washington officials were prepared to defend their policy of support to the Derg, both by evoking the three strategic reasons already mentioned, and by stressing the politically inchoate form of the Derg's policies. Kissinger's view seems to have been that so long as the Derg retained some pro-Western orientation it was important to back it in the face of the Soviet diplomatic and military build-up in Southern Africa and Angola. Speaking in August 1976 to a Congressional Committee, the Assistant Secretary of State for African Affairs, William Schaufele, stated: 'We believe we would incur much criticism from our friends in Africa and elsewhere were we to withdraw support from the Ethiopian Government during this time of difficulty – such a move would also be attributed to distaste for Ethiopia's brand of socialism. . . . Whether we can continue this degree of cooperation with Ethiopia will depend largely on the course finally taken by the new revolutionary regime which assumed power in 1974. It has deliberately decided to alter Ethiopia's previous reliance on the West, and has consequently strengthened its relations with the Socialist countries. To the extent that this does not lead to systematic opposition to the United States, it still leaves ample opportunity for continued cooperation, particularly as we are sympathetic to many of the new regime's ambitions to improve the living conditions of its people. But the situation is sufficiently volatile to bear close watching.'[6]

There were, however, voices raised against this policy. The paradox was that it was rightist elements inside the US state who favoured continued support for the Derg, for the conventional anti-Russian strategic reasons, whilst it was liberals who tended to oppose aid, pointing to the urban terror and the repression in Eritrea.[7] There was no strong movement against the Derg in Congress, as there had been, for example, against aid to Turkey after the 1974 invasion of Cyprus: Greek–Americans played an active role here. The problems faced by the USA were of another kind. First, it was not able in any systematic way to influence the Derg's policies: the Derg has been at best a loose executive body and, with the deaths of Andom and later Sisay, the Americans lost what contacts they had.[8] Secondly, there was opposition to US support for Ethiopia from one influential source – the conservative Arab states, led by Saudi Arabia. In any elementary tabulation of its economic and strategic interests, it was obvious that the USA had more reason to align with the Arab states now increasingly opposed to Ethiopia than with a beleaguered Derg. By the middle of 1977 a major policy shift had taken place and the long-standing link with Ethiopia had, apparently, been broken.

---

[6] *Ethiopia and the Horn*, p. 114.
[7] Ibid., p. 173.
[8] According to US calculations, at least twenty-two high-ranking Ethiopian officials were, in 1976, graduates of US training programmes. These included: Mengistu himself; Teferi Benti, chairman of the PMAC till February 1977; the Armed Forces Chief of Staff, Maj. Gen. Gizaw Belayneh; the Commander of the Ethiopian Ground Forces, Brig. Gen. Gahru Tofa, and the Commander of the Navy, Capt. Tesfaye Berhanu (*US Arms Policies*, p. 168). But despite this substantial training connection, it does not seem that US influence upon the military was at all substantial after 1974.

In February 1977 the new Secretary of State, Cyrus Vance, told a Senate committee that, as a result of human rights violations by the governments concerned, US military aid to Ethiopia, Argentina and Uruguay would be reduced as from the fiscal year beginning October 1, 1977. There was no immediate Ethiopian reaction, but on April 23, the Derg ordered all US-run installations in the country to close, with the exception of the Embassy and the AID office: within four days the remaining MAAG officers, as well as the last members of the Kagnew garrison, had gone. Radio Addis Ababa attacked Carter's decision on arms aid, pointing out that no military aid had been withdrawn when human rights were violated under Haile Selassie. Although only arms aid had been stopped officially, arms sales too had in practice already been blocked. Then on April 27, the Pentagon announced that all arms supplies to Ethiopia had been officially suspended. None of the F-5E fighter-bombers, M-60 tanks and ammunition approved under an early $65 million request had been in fact delivered. A further request for more ammunition made in the past two months had also been turned down. Within two months the USA had gone on to announce that it was prepared, by contrast, to sell arms to Ethiopia's rivals, Sudan and Somalia, and the new US policy of cooperating with Saudi Arabia to wean Somalia from the Soviet Union was under way. The break was now complete except for the rupture in diplomatic realtions.

In so far as it is possible to separate out the many strands involved, it would seem that four different developments in early 1977 combined to produce this change. In the first place, in January 1977 the Arab states took up a much more hostile stand towards the Derg. On January 20, the Sudanese President, Nimeiry, declared that Sudan supported the Eritrean movement, in terms far more explicit and committed than he had ever adopted before. In May there were reports of clashes along the Sudan–Ethiopian border. Sudan's new policy, coinciding as it did with a renewed Eritrean offensive on the ground, had the backing of Egypt and Saudi Arabia, with whom Nimeiry had signed a defence pact in July 1976. The shift in Nimeiry's stand came after Ethiopia was implicated, with Libya, in an attempt to overthrow his government.

The second development was the advent of the Carter administration. Although Nixon, Ford and Kissinger had had doubts about Haile Selassie and the Derg, they had continued to provide some aid to the Ethiopian state and had regarded the Emperor and the Derg as counters to a Soviet presence in Somalia. The Ford administration had decided to cancel military aid, but it never announced this, and it did not decide to block *sales* of military equipment. The Republican Administration had also not been too concerned about the issues subsequently subsumed under the term 'human rights'. Carter's policy marked a break with these previous tendencies. On the one hand, he was much less mesmerized by the Soviet–Somali connection; he also hoped to win Somalia, with Arab support, to the West, and did not continue the Republican policy of aiding regimes simply because they were in some way anti-communist.

The third development, which occurred within a fortnight of the first two, was the February 1977 dispute within the Derg, when controlling influence fell into the hands of Mengistu. The manner of Mengistu's consolidation of power was bloody; his new policies opened the way to closer ties with the Soviet Union and removed some of the doubts the Russians had till then harboured. For these two reasons, and even in the absence of the changes in Arab policy and in the White House, it would have been more difficult for the previous relationship to have been maintained.

The fourth and most important change was the switch in Somalia's position. Somalia had for some time been under pressure from Saudi Arabia to oust the Russians; and the regime in Mogadishu, whose attachment to the Soviet Union had always been of a rather pragmatic kind, was known to be willing to change its alignment. Since 1974, Somalia, a country where very few people speak Arabic as a first language, had been accepted as a member of the Arab League, as part of the rapprochement with the Saudis. During his visit to President Ford in October 1974, Siad Barre had actually offered the USA naval-base facilities at Kismayu in the south, to balance the Soviet facilities at Berbera in the north. Around the same time, the Saudis suggested to Washington that they could oust the Russians by offering large sums of aid to the impoverished Somalis. Both these offers were rejected by Washington on the grounds that such successes in Somalia would have weakened the case for the new US base on Diego Garcia.[9] In 1977 the climate was more favourable. Somalia strengthened its ties with the West and, after the failure of Fidel Castro's mediation between Ethiopia and Somalia in March, the door was open for a Western initiative. In May, the West offered to provide arms to Somalia.

These developments brought to an end an alliance that had begun in the early 1940s, and deprived Washington of what had, at one time, been its most important ally in black Africa. In one sense, however, Ethiopia was not 'lost': rather, it was thrown away by the Carter Administration, which placed the continuance of relations with the Derg below such priorities as the courting of Somalia and the human rights policy. The 'loss' of Ethiopia had nevertheless begun well before 1977, with the revolution itself and even before that, with the cooling of relations with Haile Selassie. Ultimately the USA 'lost' Ethiopia because the alliance depended upon the continuity of the absolutist regime: the failure of Haile Selassie's regime to resolve the contradictions within Ethiopian society, a failure in which the USA with its 'solid gold Cadillac' policy was implicated, was the cause of both the 1974 revolution and the subsequent rupture in US–Ethiopian relations.

The Somali Connection

The question of US relations with Somalia, in particular the extent of US support for the Ogaden invasion, is one of the most controversial of all in this context. In the Ethiopian view, the Somali invasion received the full support of the NATO powers. The Somalis too claim that they received undertakings from the West, which were then unilaterally revoked. The Americans, for their part, deny that they encouraged the Somalis. The evidence available suggests that

[9] The former US ambassador to Saudi Arabia, James Akins, blamed Kissinger for the US failure to pick up on the Saudi offer: see *Multinational Corporations and US Foreign Policy*, US Senate Sub-committee on Multinational Corporations, Part 14, Washington 1976, pp. 430–434.

the USA does bear considerable responsibility for the Somali invasion, even if this stops short of confirming the Ethiopian case.

From the first months of his administration, Carter expressed a clear desire to woo the Somalis away from the Soviet Union and to encourage them to oust the Russians stationed in their country. This was an activation of the policy previously advocated by the Saudis, and which Kissinger had refused. However, it corresponded to the new trilateral approach to the Third World favoured by Carter. This approach was less dominated by the concerns of a bilateral East–West policy and more disposed to seek the support of Third World countries such as Somalia that might at first sight appear to be hostile to the USA. The change of regime in Ethiopia in February obviously made such a switch easier, as did the subsequent deterioration in relations between Washington and Addis Ababa. In April 1977 the President was quoted as telling his Secretary of State, Vance, and his National Security adviser, Brzezinski, that he wanted them 'to move in every possible way to get Somalia to be our friend',[10] and in May 1977 the Western countries as a whole indicated for the first time that they would be willing to sell arms to Somalia.

On June 11, Carter issued a general foreign policy statement embodying the trilateral approach. 'My own inclination', he said, 'is to aggressively challenge, in a peaceful way of course, the Soviet Union and others for influence in areas of the world that we feel are crucial to us now or potentially crucial fifteen to twenty years from now.'[11] Among the countries where he thought such a challenge was possible were Vietnam, Iraq, Somalia, Algeria, China and Cuba. He went on to say that he was 'quite concerned' about the tensions in the Horn of Africa, 'involving Somalia and the Afars and Issas, Ethiopia, Sudan and to some degree Eritrea'. He said that his administration was seeking to improve relationships with Somalia and was 'trying to understand the

[10] *Sunday Times*, April 17, 1977.
[11] *International Herald Tribune*, June 13, 1977: given Carter's reputation for failure, it is worth pointing out that this policy met with considerable success. US relations with three of these six countries improved noticeably during his administration (Somalia, Iraq, China), while a fourth (Algeria) exerted itself to help the US out of the Iranian hostages entanglement.

Eritrean movement in Ethiopia'. A month later, on July 15, the USA officially announced that it was willing 'in principle' to supply defensive weapons to Somalia, following a report from a survey team which would, as was conventional in such cases, present its technical assessment to Washington.

All seemed to be set fair for a rapid US advance into a position of support and influence in Somalia, and the indications were that the Somali authorities were delighted at this prospect. But matters did not proceed as expected. The technical mission did not leave for Mogadishu, and within a few weeks, on August 4, 1977, the USA announced that it had placed its plan to sell arms to Somalia in abeyance. This turn of fate was due to two factors, whose precise contribution is hard to determine, especially as both were operative some time before the original July 15 announcement: one was the Kenyan objection to Somalia's having US arms, the other was the evident involvement of the Somali regular army in the Ogaden war. Whatever the exact causes, the result was that a US mission visited Somalia only in March 1978, *after* Somali forces had withdrawn from the Ogaden, and promised $15 million in military sales. But even that visit did not yield any agreement. It was two more years before a proper US–Somali military agreement was signed in August 1980, under which the USA took over naval facilities at Berbera and agreed to sell $45 million worth of weapons to Mogadishu in 1980–81.[12]

The official American case is that the offer to sell arms, made in mid-July 1977, was cancelled because, eight days after it was made, the Somali army went into Ogaden.[13] The USA knew about Somali guerrillas operating inside Ethiopia but had not foreseen that the regular army would be committed. It was not prepared to support such an action. Yet the Somalis have disputed this account. They claim that their Ambassador in Washington, Dr Abdullahi Ahmad Adu, a son-in-law of Siad Barre, met with Carter twice in May–June 1977 and that Adu's report back to Mogadishu was favourable. They also claim that they received assurances from Washington via Dr Kevin Cahill, a New York De-

---

[12] *US Security Interests in the Persian Gulf*, Report to the Committee on Foreign Affairs, US House of Representatives, March 16, 1981, p. 50.
[13] The following is based on interviews with the State Department Horn of Africa desk, April 1979.

mocratic politician and tropical medicine expert who had previously treated Siad Barre and who visited Somalia in June 1977. According to the Somalis, Cahill, in response to questions from their side, gave them two assurances: (a) that in the event of a Somali invasion of Ogaden the USA would not resupply Ethiopia; (b) that the USA would not 'look askance' at Somali requests for arms. American officials deny that the Adu meetings took place, and they initially denied the Cahill claims when they were first made by Siad Barre. But it later transpired that Cahill *had* consulted, prior to his visit to Somalia, with a high-ranking State Department Officer, the Legal Counsellor Matthew Nimetz, the Secretary of State's main trouble-shooter. Cahill is, in the words of one person who knows him, 'a man who does not get messages wrong'. It would seem that he had seen himself as an unofficial US envoy to Somalia.[14]

There can be little doubt that the Somalis, sensing the weakness of Ethiopia internally and internationally, and urged on by the Arab states, did believe that they had support from Washington. Siad Barre received offers of support during a secret visit to Saudi Arabia, but the Carter administration must also bear some responsibility for what subsequently occurred. Carter's public overtures to Somalia, combined with private assurances from Cahill, were read as a green light from Washington for an Ogaden invasion. Nor was this just a matter of Somali wishful thinking. American policy, for its part, was divided, with a pro-Somali faction taking initiatives that the indulgence of others was unable to prevent. It was only when the full scale of the Somali response, combined with Kenyan protests, was realized in early August that Washington as a whole drew back. Whilst US encouragement was not the only factor leading to the Somali decision to invade Ogaden, the shift in US posture from early 1977, as it was perceived in Mogadishu and as it affected conservative Arab advice to the Somalis, played a central role in detonating the Ogaden war and in creating the crisis into which the Soviet Union and Cuba later moved so decisively. It was a characteristic example of provocative

---

[14] On Cahill see the article by Jim Paul in MERIP, no. 62, November 1977, and *Newsweek*, September 26, 1977.

foreign policy conduct in Washington, uncoordinated and short-sighted but with dire long-term consequences elsewhere on the globe.

Although the USA and Britain publicly refused to supply arms to Somalia during its Ogaden offensive, some arms supplies were sent by the West and its allies through other channels: the Germans were grateful for Somali cooperation in freeing passengers from a hijacked Lufthansa jet at Mogadishu airport in October 1977 and ferried in material; Saudi Arabia and Iran also provided equipment, some of that provided by the latter probably being Russian weaponry purchased by Iran. The Shah's officials openly admitted that Washington had encouraged them to arm Siad. Egypt gave $30 million in Russian equipment; and at least $7 million worth of weapons is known to have been supplied in a covert operation by the CIA towards the end of 1977.[15] But no explicit support for the invasion of Ogaden was given. The major Western and Iranian commitment to step up aid was premissed on an Ethiopian occupation of Somali territory and, in the event, the Ethiopians stopped at the border.

In other respects, Washington pursued a cautious policy. If it had wanted to, it could have greatly increased its aid to other forces fighting the Derg – the EDU and the Eritreans – but although covert links no doubt exist between the EDU and the US government, the USA did not aid them in the way it aided, for example, the UNITA forces in Angola. The USA also avoided any assistance to Eritrea, although Washington may have been tempted to give some, not because it backed independence, but as a spoiling operation against the Russians, much as it was later to arm the Afghan rebels as a way of 'keeping the pot boiling'. The only known CIA connection with Eritrea was a covert propaganda campaign in the international press to use Soviet and Cuban involvement as a way of discrediting them in the eyes of their sympathizers.[16] The USA never publicly abandoned its historical position of support for the territorial integrity of Ethiopia; Carter's sympathetic remark about Eritrea in his June 1977

---

[15] *7 Days*, New York, March 19, 1978.
[16] Seymour Hersch in *International Herald Tribune*, June 2, 1978.

speech, and another during his visit to Nigeria in 1979, do not seem to have been taken further. Relations with the Derg itself continued at a low level: two Congressmen, Representatives Don Bonker and Paul Tsongas, met Mengistu whilst on a visit to Addis Ababa in November,[17] and in late February 1978 the USA announced that it was supplying a few jeeps and spare parts to Ethiopia, part of a $40 million consignment ordered the previous May.

The emphasis of US policy in the Horn was on denunciation of the Russian and Cuban roles, and this left little room for an improvement in relations with the Derg. The major initiative undertaken by Washington was in the closing stages of the Ogaden war when it negotiated with the Russians on the terms of a Somali retreat, the latter being agreed in return for Ethiopian commitments not to cross the frontier. How far the result was a consequence of the negotiation and how far it was a natural outcome we do not know: certainly the Ethiopians had enough reason to stop at the border, and the Somalis to pull out, without having to be coerced into doing so by either of the two major powers. A US initiative to ease the Somalis out was proposed in Washington in February 1978 but delayed because of bureaucratic wranglings. The judgement of one State Department official sums up the extent of US influence on the Somalis: 'We got them out', he told us, 'forty-eight hours earlier than they would have been thrown out'.[18]

The general worsening state of East–West relations in 1978–9 also had consequences for US policy in the Horn. Diplomatic ties with Ethiopia were kept open, and an ambassador, Frederic Chapin, was appointed in late 1978; but there was no agreement on military sales, or on the $20 million claimed by US firms as compensation for nationalizations in March 1975. Under Congressional amendments on

[17] *War in the Horn of Africa: A Firsthand Report on the Challenges for United States Policy*, Report to the Committee on International Relations, US House of Representatives, February 3, 1978, Washington 1978. Bonker and Tsongas advised: 'We should cease criticizing Ethiopia simply for accepting Soviet equipment. Faced with the well-trained and equipped Somali forces in the Ogaden, Ethiopia had no choice if it hoped to regain what it considers its territory' (p. 49).

[18] As note 13. The announcement of a Somali withdrawal from Ogaden was made in a statement by President Carter on March 9.

this issue, the USA was not only prevented from supplying aid, but was also enjoined to vote against aid to Ethiopia in international agencies such as the World Bank. In the fiscal year 1979, the USA provided only $10 million in development assistance to Ethiopia, plus $30 million in commodity assistance. In July 1980 Ambassador Chapin was expelled, amidst accusations by Ethiopia of US failure to honour its commitments. This was probably not the main reason, since underlying the stalemate and the 1980 crisis was the continuing US attempt to court Somalia. This culminated, after much wrangling, in a US agreement to aid Somalia militarily with $20 million in 1980 and $25 million in 1981. Although US officials insisted that the Somalis had promised not to cross the Ethiopian frontier or to use US equipment in such a venture, Mogadishu had in fact been trying in the previous months to activate the Ogaden resistance. In the spring of 1980, fighting had reached levels similar to those in the early summer of 1978. In the past the Somalis had shown themselves capable of overcoming similar pressure from the Russians and there was therefore a possibility that the new US commitment, achieved after six years of false starts, would embolden them to new action in Ogaden. More important than any alleged change in Somali policy, however, was the shift in world politics that led the US to seek base facilities in Somalia, along with Kenya and Oman and Egypt. The oldest reason for the Horn's significance, its coastline, was underlined in the USA's adoption of a military posture on the shores of the Indian ocean.

Middle Eastern Coordinates

The role of the USA in the Horn is inseparable from that of its Middle Eastern allies who have, in a variety of ways, played an influential role there over recent years. Both the Ethiopians and the Arab states tend to exaggerate the degree to which the politics of the Horn can be assimilated to those of the Middle East, the former by seeing all forces opposed to them as mere extensions of Arab regimes, the latter by presenting the peoples of Somalia, Eritrea and Jibuti as ethnic 'Arabs' – which they are not. Yet leaving such reductionism aside, the pattern is one of continued overlap with the politics of the Middle East, especially since the 1974 revolution in Ethiopia. For what has shaped this pattern of involvement is not just one conflict, the Arab–Israeli, but the much more complex skein of conflicts within the Arab world. The rivalries between different radical Arab regimes have been reflected in their competing support for local allies in the Horn. In particular the left–right conflict within the Arab world has involved as one of its components a split between the majority of Arab states opposing the Ethiopian revolution, and the minority who have, after 1974 and albeit with some reservation, lent support to Addis Ababa.

Until the mid-1970s, the Horn was influenced by the Arab–Israeli dispute in a mild, but straightforward, manner. Ethiopia, as a pro-Western, non-Arab state, where traditions of concern about a Muslim Arab menace run strong, maintained a low-level relationship with Israel.[19] The latter saw Ethiopia as a friendly state at the mouth of the Red Sea, and as the natural conduit for Israel's African policies. Israel used Addis Ababa's role as centre of the OAU to conduct a wider African policy, and Ethiopia was the largest recipient of Israeli economic aid in Africa. A number of Israeli firms also operated in Ethiopia and a regular trading route between Eilat and Massawa developed. The area of closest cooperation was in military affairs. From 1962 onwards, Israeli advisers trained the Emergency Police, an elite counter-insurgency group of 3,100 men established to operate in Eritrea. The official number of Israeli advisers is stated to have been around forty. The other important military concern was the Eritrean coastline along the Red Sea, where Israel was afraid of attacks on its shipping, either from Palestinian guerrillas (as happened, once, in 1971) or in the event of an Arab naval blockade during war (as happened in 1973). There is no doubt that Israel had and maintains a strategic concern to stop the Eritrean coastline falling into Arab hands: Israeli officials admit they would prefer a

---

[19] On the earlier economic link see *The Israeli Economist*, February–March 1972; on the military links see *Washington Post*, May 28, 1972. Israeli exports to Ethiopia ran at $4.4 million in 1975, $7.6 million in 1978 and $9.3 million in 1979 (*Statistical Abstract of Israel, 1980*, Central Bureau of Statistics, Jerusalem).

Russian to an Arab presence there. Israel and Ethiopia also had a common interest in the Sudan and, from 1969 until 1972, they cooperated in sending arms to the Anya-Aya rebels in the Sudanese south. Matters became more complicated in October 1973, when, under pressure from the Arab states, Haile Selassie terminated diplomatic relations with Israel. But it is by no means clear how far this led to a real break. Trading links via Massawa continued and at least some clandestine military contacts were maintained, until the relationship with the USSR and Cuba was fully developed. As late as 1977, a few Israeli technicians were still servicing Ethiopian jets, and in February 1978 Israel's Foreign Minister, Moshe Dayan, made the revelation that Israel had sold some spare parts for American equipment to the Ethiopian air force. But in any broader perspective Israel's role was a very small one. Israel was incapable of playing a significant role in the Horn and by 1978 its presence in Ethiopia had been terminated.

The demise of the Arab–Israeli dispute as a factor in Horn affairs was offset by an increased transposition into the Horn of the internal conflicts of the Arab world, between conservative and radical states, and within these two general groupings themselves. The expanded level of conservative Arab involvement suggested that the fear of a revolutionary regime in Ethiopia, however well disposed to the Arab cause against Israel, was considered a much greater threat to these states than an overtly pro-Israeli, but socially conservative, imperial Ethiopia. Prior to 1973, Saudi Arabia, Syria and Libya, and South Yemen gave some aid to the Eritreans, but this was on a modest scale. It did not preclude active diplomatic ties between Addis Ababa and a number of Arab capitals. Nasser and Haile Selassie collaborated in the context of the OAU and in 1972 Sudan and Ethiopia signed an agreement covering both Eritrea and southern Sudan, whereby both sides undertook not to aid dissidents in the other's country. Ethiopia broke its diplomatic ties with Israel in 1973, and other ties were progressively eliminated in the following years. Nevertheless, the level of Arab opposition to Ethiopia definitely increased, for weightier strategic concerns were now at work. The Saudis, able to play an influential role with their financial power, used this to strengthen conservative regimes in Sudan and Jibuti, and to assist Somalia's break with the USSR. At first pursued in tandem with Egypt, and then, after Camp David, separately, the Saudis, for reasons of geography and prestige, encouraged Ethiopia's enemies. Egypt, with a long historical association with the Horn and with a special concern about Sudan and the waters of the Nile, declared its hostility to the new Ethiopian government from 1976 onwards and played an active role in assisting Somalia, before and after the 1978 debacle.

Although employing a distinctive rhetoric, the policies of the radical nationalist Baathist governments in Syria and Iraq were hardly different from those of the Saudis and Egyptians in their effects on the Horn. Both declared it part of their pan-Arab duty to assist fellow 'Arabs' in the Horn: whilst competing with each other, they rallied to the Eritreans and the Somalis. Yet because of their factional rivalry, both imposed constraining conditions upon their local allies: in 1977, when the Iraqis sent pilots and spare parts for Russian equipment to the Somalis, the Syrians stopped their supplies to Mogadishu. Inside the Eritrean movement both exerted pressure on factions loyal to them, particularly within the ELF where Baathist connections were historically stronger. This must have contributed to the problems dividing the rebel organizations. By the end of the 1970s it seemed that both countries had, to some degree, modified their positions, under the influence both of the changing situation on the ground in the Horn and of discussions with the Russians and Cubans themselves. In 1980 the Iraqis threatened to cease aiding the Eritreans altogether, unless they united. The Syrians established diplomatic relations with Ethiopia in 1980 and appeared to favour some solution in Eritrea short of outright independence.

Two Arab regimes that did substantially alter their positions were Libya and South Yemen. The change in the Libyan position was partly a result of its conflict with Egypt and the Sudan – Qaddafi, like the Derg, supported the attempted coup in Sudan in July 1976. In justifying his change of position, Qaddafi argued, in a speech to Islamic foreign ministers in May 1977, that Muslims across the world should take an interest not just in Islamic minorities, such as that in Eritrea, but also in what he saw as an Islamic majority, that within Ethiopia as a whole. Since Libyan support had, in the past, been based upon the desire to overthrow the feudal regime there, and this revolution had succeeded, Libya now supported reconciliation between Ethiopia and Eritrea. South Yemen was in a different situation. It was geographically much closer to, and therefore more affected by, events in the Horn. Prior to 1974 it had acted as the main base area, with Sudan, for the Eritrean movement. It allowed the Eritrean groups to maintain their offices in Aden but from 1976 onwards it allied itself with the Ethiopian government, to the point of sending some troops and fighter planes to Ogaden and Eritrea in 1977. These troops were later withdrawn, partly because of opposition to such an involvement within South Yemen itself, but this did not lead to a fundamental change of policy.[20] In a May Day speech in Addis Ababa in 1979 the then South Yemeni President, Abdul Fatah Ismail, stressed that his country had supported the Eritreans against Haile Selassie, because the emperor's regime was sustained by 'reaction and imperialism'. Today, he said, South Yemen 'opposes any movement aimed at expansion or separation' and supports 'the right of nationalities to self-determination through peaceful negotiation. We are for the unity of progressive forces and for the unity of nationalities in the Horn of Africa'.[21] Both South Yemen and Libya attempted to mediate between the Ethiopian government and the Eritreans, and the South Yemenis also tried to mediate between Ethiopia and Somalia in 1977. Both argued that the objective context of the conflicts had dramatically altered since 1974, the one using an Islamic phraseology, the other an orthodox Leninist one.

The conservative Arab states acted not out of some permanent commitment to particular Horn policies, but

---

[20] South Yemen's policy was not shared by its otherwise close ally, the People's Front for the Liberation of Oman. PFLO continued to support the cause of Eritrean independence and retained a suspicion of left-wing military regimes. A PFLO delegation attended the EPLF conference in 1977 (*Saut al-Thawra*, Aden, no. 219, March 12, 1977).

[21] *Ethiopian Herald*, May 2, 1979.

according to their own internal politics. Whilst the Israeli presence in Ethiopia was certainly a concern, the revolution there, and the intervention of Soviet and Cuban forces, have been seen as a direct threat to the internal orders of the Arab states. Here lay the reason for the alarm shown in Saudi Arabia, Sudan and Egypt, and support for the Eritreans and Somalis as a function of this. Indeed, amidst all the Arab discussions of Eritrea, there is a consistent tendency to avoid the question of Eritrean independence as such. As with Palestine, the Arab states gain prestige by appearing to support a patriotic 'Arab' cause and they hope that such support will offset any radicalizing effects of these conflicts beyond their borders. For this reason time has brought about some change in conservative Arab attitudes. When, in 1976 and 1977, it seemed as if the Ethiopian regime might be overthrown, the Arab states seemed to favour outright opposition to it and they framed their policies in Eritrea and Somalia accordingly. But by 1978 the Ethiopian regime had found its feet again, and the policies of Somalia had led to the contrary result of a major Soviet–Cuban presence in Ethiopia. In such a situation the Arab states faced a dilemma: either to continue to back the opponents of Addis Ababa and in so doing to provide a justification for the continued Cuban presence in Ethiopia; or to abandon their previous policies and reach an accommodation with the Ethiopian regime. This dilemma had long been debated within the Saudi Arabian government, and the changes in Syrian and Iraqi policy, coupled with the reconciliation between Ethiopia and Sudan in 1980, indicated that for other Arab states too a similar policy choice was being faced.

At first sight the Horn would appear to have been an area where the Nixon doctrine of delegated counter-revolutionary activity was implemented with a considerable degree of success. Whilst its allies played an active part, the USA remained on the sidelines from 1974 until the Carter doctrine of 1980, which justified a greater direct American presence in the northern Indian Ocean and led to the Somali base agreement. The main support for Somalia came from the Arab states who financed and armed it, and Egypt continued to guarantee the stability of Sudan. As the US–Egyptian alliance developed, Egypt assumed greater responsibility for the Horn, stationing troops in the Sudan from 1976 onwards. The Shah of Iran also played a role, sending financial and military aid to Somalia in 1977 with US encouragement. Yet, although there was an overall convergence of policy, this coordination involved less delegated action than, say, the Shah's military actions in Pakistan and Oman, or Indonesia's role in East Timor. First, the conservative Arab states were much more militant on these issues than Washington, and frequently criticized the USA for its failure to confront Russia and Cuba in the Horn. It appears that US officials even placed restrictions upon the transfer by the Saudis of sophisticated military equipment, such as ground to air missiles, to the Eritreans. Second, some of the most active supporters of the Somali and Eritrean causes were not allies of the USA at all, but the Baathist regimes of Syria and Iraq who were, if anything, closer to the USSR. Most important of all, however, was the fact that these Arab–Iranian policies produced effects absolutely contrary to those desired by the USA: namely an increased Soviet–Cuban presence in the Horn and a more militantly anti-American Ethiopian foreign policy. Far from a success for US foreign policy and its allies, the Horn was a striking defeat. It was recuperable only by the abandonment of the Nixon doctrine in favour of a new, direct US presence, and by an alarmist campaign designed to place all the blame for the unfavourable course of events on the activism of the USSR.

The USSR and the Ethiopian Revolution

The policy of the Soviet Union in the Horn of Africa has been of immense importance, both in its effects upon local forces, in Somalia and later Ethiopia, and in the issues of political principle that it has raised. Since the autumn of 1977, when Soviet support for the Ethiopian government was greatly increased, the course of Soviet and Cuban policy has been the object of criticism both on the international right, and on much of the left, provoking opposition not only from China, but also from a number of European Communist parties. Yet the Soviet policy towards the Horn from 1977 onwards was not, as at first it appeared, a reversal of such a sudden or uncharacteristic kind. It reflected options adopted considerably earlier by the PMAC, that only later came to fruition. It reflected the maturing of changes within Somalia, as well as a wider international context that encouraged such a change. It also reflected long-standing priorities in Soviet policy that went back through policy in the 1960s to the very first years of the Bolshevik regime. Indeed, if it raised questions of political principle, these were as much about Soviet policy prior to 1977 as they were about policy subsequent to the massive intervention of that year.

Throughout its three phases of strategic importance, the Horn of Africa has occupied a curious place, intermittent and discomforting, in the attentions of the international socialist movement. In the 1880s and 1890s, the young Italian workers' movement derived internationalist inspiration from the defeats inflicted upon Italian colonialism at Dogali (1887) and Adowa (1896) by the Ethiopian forces. In the 1930s, opposition to Mussolini's assault upon Ethiopia was for a time a rallying-cry of the European workers movement, and in July 1935 at the Seventh Comintern Congress, prior to the actual Italian invasion, the Italian Party leader, Togliatti, issued an internationalist appeal for an Ethiopian victory.[22] Although the movement of solidarity petered out in 1936, after the defeat of the Ethiopians, and was overtaken by the more immediate concerns of the civil war in Spain, the Italian Party retained interest in Ethiopia and dispatched a small team of guerrilla experts to help the Ethiopians in their resistance to fascist occupation.[23] Yet even in this period the Horn was an object of dissension, because of the refusal of the Soviet Union to impose oil sanctions upon Italy and its obstruction, through the Comintern, of a joint communist–socialist campaign on the issue. Stalin had by March 1936 dismissed the Ethiopian war as 'an episode'. Given what was later to occur in Poland and Greece, where the USSR failed to provide support for left-wing forces, one

---

[22] Giuliano Procacci, *Il Socialismo internazionale e la guerra d'Etiopia*, Rome 1978, provides an illuminating and critical study of this period.

[23] Eric Hobsbawm, *Revolutionaries*, London 1973, p. 40.

may doubt whether Soviet policy would have been more forthcoming had there been an identifiable left movement in Ethiopia. But in the absence of such a force to whom socialists elsewhere could relate it was certainly all the easier for the cause of Ethiopia to be relegated in the wider interest of Stalinist accommodation. Fearful of what an overly enthusiastic collaboration of communists with socialists in support of Ethiopia might lead to, and anxious to prevent a complete identification of Italy with Germany, Stalin seems to have decided that the cause of Ethiopia was not one to which the communist movement should attach great importance.[24]

In the post-war period the Horn was at first of little importance to the Soviet Union. The first major concern was the disposal of Eritrea where, in line with Soviet policy on Italian colonies generally, the Russian position favoured first a UN trusteeship, and then independence. The guiding principle seems to have been not Eritrean rights, but hostility to imperialists or their allies. In 1950, at the UN Debate on Eritrea, the Soviet delegate insisted: 'The USSR delegation objects to the proposal for the federation of Eritrea with another state, as such a federation would disregard the right of the Eritrean people to self-determination by preventing the Eritreans from exercising that right.' He continued: 'The only just solution to the problem of the future of Eritrea is to grant independence.'[25] When in 1952 the General Assembly voted through the federation proposal, the USSR voted against it. But, later in the decade, the USSR began to develop formal relations with Haile Selassie. Embassies were exchanged in 1956 and in 1959 Haile Selassie visited Moscow, the first African head of state to do so. The Soviet Union provided a loan of $102 million to Ethiopia. During the 1960s Soviet aid concentrated on building the country's only oil refinery, at Assab, which was completed in 1967, and on training Ethiopian personnel.[26] Above all, the Soviet Union ac-

[24] Procacci, p. 221.
[25] Bereket Habte Selassie, p. 177.
[26] Aryeh Yodfat, 'The Soviet Union and the Horn of Africa', *Northeast African Studies*, part one, vol. 1, no. 3, winter 1979–80, part two, vol. 2, no. 1, spring 1980, part three, vol. 2, no. 2, fall 1980; Charles McLane, *Soviet–African Relations*, London 1974. For a Soviet view of the earlier contacts see Anatoli Gromyko,

knowledged Ethiopia's place in African politics and sought, during two later visits by Haile Selassie to Moscow, to win him to a non-aligned position and to some criticism of US policies in Vietnam. But the initial hopes of the 1959 visit were not fulfilled: the Russians preferred their alliances with Egypt and Somalia and criticized the presence of US bases in Ethiopia.

Nonetheless, in this context of limited diplomatic courtship, the Soviet Union was not interested in overtly supporting opposition to the Ethiopian regime. There was no communist party or other identifiable pro-Soviet group with whom party-to-party relations might have been established.[27] In 1960, when Mengistu Neway and his fellow officers tried to oust Haile Selassie during his visit to Brazil, *Pravda* reported warmly on Haile Selassie's return to his capital after the defeat of the coup attempt and reprinted an article from the Ghanaian press in which the rebel officers were characterized as 'imperialist agents'.[28] When the Eritrean movement began to develop, Soviet policy was to ignore it. The original 1950 position was not, it seems, reiterated, and it appears that at no time prior to 1974 did the Russians ever publicly endorse, or privately support, the Eritrean movement.[29] The Russians must, however, have known about aid given by some of their allies: some military aid was provided

---

'USSR–Ethiopia: Traditions and Contemporaneity', *Asia and Africa To-day*, Moscow, vol. 1, 1980. In pre-revolutionary times Ethiopia had exercised a certain fascination for Russia: contacts between the two sectors of eastern Christianity were established in the nineteenth century, a flourishing branch of Ethiopianist scholarship developed in Russia, and during the Italo–Ethiopian conflicts of the 1890s a Russian medical mission was sent to Ethiopia. The poet Pushkin's grandfather was an Ethiopian, Abram Hannibal, who had served as an artillery officer in the army of Peter the Great.

[27] Although a number of works of Russian literature were translated into Amharic, it seems that no works of Marxist or Leninist theory were published: one result was the lack of any indigenous theoretical vocabulary for Ethiopian socialist writers: see above pp. 135–39.

[28] *Pravda*, December 19, 1960, quoted in *Current Digest of the Soviet Press*, hereafter CDSP, vol. XII, no. 51.

[29] Eritrean sources report that one student delegation visited the USSR prior to 1974; if so, this was not reported in the Soviet press. TASS correspondent Valentin Korovikov told the authors in Addis Ababa in 1978 that no contacts had ever been established.

by Bulgaria and Syria, and in 1968 a number of Eritreans received military training in Cuba.

At this time, Soviet policy in the region paid more attention to two of Ethiopia's neighbours, Sudan and Somalia. Soviet support for the regime of President Nimeiry, who seized power in 1969, was linked to the support given to Nimeiry's first government by the Communist Party; when, in July 1971, Nimeiry executed the Party leadership after a failed left-wing coup, relations deteriorated. Indeed, one major consequence of the Sudanese events was that it hardened Soviet suspicion of military regimes, which was already growing in relation to Egypt, and thereby delayed the development, later on, of close relations between Moscow and the PMAC. In the Somali case, relations were developed in the mid-1960s; they were predicated not on the regime's supposedly progressive credentials but on Somalia's need for military support that the West would not supply. However, when the Somali military seized power in October 1969 and then in 1972 embarked upon what they called a 'socialist' path of development, the Russians did not demur, and for some time in the mid-1970s Somalia was held up as one of the exemplary Third World states embarked upon the 'non-capitalist road'. During the drought in early 1970s, a Soviet airlift saved the lives of many thousands, and in 1974 the two countries signed a twenty-year friendship treaty. In addition to providing Somalia with substantial military and economic aid, the Russians also acquired military facilities at Berbera, on the northern Somali coast, and at two other points.

When, in 1976, Siad established the Somali Socialist Revolutionary Party, the Russians welcomed this as 'a new, important step in the development of the Somali revolution, and as evidence of the resolve of Somalia's working people, under the leadership of their militant vanguard, to struggle for national independence, freedom and the building of a socialist society'.[30] Despite the warm tones in which the two sides spoke of each other, however, there was no indication that the USSR agreed with Mogadishu on the important issue of Somalia's boundaries. The Somalis seem to have inter-

---

[30] *Pravda*, August 10, 1976, in CDSP, vol. XXVII, no. 32.

preted the clauses of the 1974 treaty condemning imperialism
and colonialism as an implicit endorsement of their claim to
Ogaden, which they saw as a 'colonial' issue. But no Russian
statements ever confirmed this. Rather, *Pravda* was keen to
emphasize that the 1974 treaty was 'not directed against any
third country' and that both parties to the agreement
supported a policy of 'peace, friendship and good neighbour-
liness'. Such a gloss was inconsistent with support for Somali
desires in Ogaden.[31] There is no evidence that the Russians
backed the Somalis primarily or even coincidentally in order
to press the claim to Ethiopia. Rather they backed them
because of Somalia's position as a strategic counter-weight to
a pro-American Ethiopia and later because of what were
regarded as progressive developments inside Somalia itself.
The issue of Ogaden was, in public at least, left out of the
discussion: it would appear that the Russians hoped that their
restraining influence, plus the overall superiority of the
Ethiopians, would keep the Somalis in check, and prevent the
ambiguity of their position coming to the test.

The initial Soviet response to the Ethiopian revolution was
cautious. During 1974 the Soviet press reported the general
strike and the movement against the emperor. As early as the
first week in July, *Izvestia* reported on the formation of the
Derg, describing it as not 'an egotistical group' but composed
of 'patriots'.[32] Later, after the PMAC was formed, the Soviet
press also reported on the 'national democratic' reforms the
military proclaimed in 1975 and 1976. Yet even in these
guarded analyses a number of significant qualifications may
be noted, reflecting the lack of Soviet knowledge and a general
wariness of army regimes. First, time and again, the Soviet
commentators stressed the complexity and retarded social
conditions of Ethiopia and counselled against precipitate
reforms. In March 1975, just after the proclamation of land
reform, *Pravda* warned of the need to go slowly: 'There is still
an enormous amount of explanatory and upbringing work to
be done amongst the workers, particularly the peasants who

---

[31] During Haile Selassie's visit to the USSR in 1970 the Russians declared their
support for Ethiopia's 'territorial integrity'. On differences in interpreting the 1974
Soviet–Somali treaty see Yodfat, part 2, p. 34.

[32] *Izvestia*, July 6, 1974, in CDSP, vol. XXVI, no. 27.

must be drawn into administrative and economic activities'.[33] In May 1976, after the proclamation of the NDR, *Pravda*, whilst generally welcoming this statement, again warned: 'about 90 per cent of the population lives in the villages. The great majority of the people are illiterate. The country's per capita income is very low, and religious prejudices are still strong. All this demands a more careful and realistic appraisal of the situation by the authorities, as well as the unity of the anti-feudal and anti-imperialist forces'.[34] These same reports, in addition to stressing the need for care in reforms, thus pressed the need for maximum political unity and for the establishment of a party: in August 1975 and again in May 1976 *Pravda* was found welcoming the progress being made in establishing a party – encouragement that Ethiopia's leaders appear to have disregarded at that time.[35]

This overt Soviet caution towards the PMAC on the pace of social and political change was not, however, marked by any such dissent on another major political issue, namely Eritrea. As early as February 1975, in the immediate aftermath of the Eritrean assault on Asmara, the Soviet press began reporting on Eritrea for the first time in a quarter of a century. After discussing what it termed 'acts of sabotage', *Izvestia* gave a brief résumé of Eritrean history, endorsing the 1952 federal act and the 1962 annexation, and passing over in silence early Soviet support for Eritrean independence.[36] It went on to blame the imperial regime for the crisis in Eritrea and to report, in a favourable manner, the desire of the PMAC 'to resolve the problem through peaceful means, following the principles of preserving national unity and the territorial integrity of the state'. In July 1976, following the visit to the USSR of a high-level Ethiopian delegation, the Russians again endorsed what were termed 'the actions being undertaken by the government to effect a peaceful settlement of the Eritrean problem'.[37] Finally, in March 1978, a *Pravda* article on Eritrea reported that the 'secessionists' in Eritrea were being

[33] *Pravda*, March 29, 1975, in CDSP, vol. XXVII, no. 13.
[34] *Pravda*, May 16, 1976, in CDSP, vol. XXVII, no. 20.
[35] *Pravda*, August 16, 1975, in CDSP, vol. XXVII, no. 33, and previous note.
[36] *Izvestia*, February 9, 1975, in CDSP, vol. XXVII, no. 6.
[37] *Pravda*, July 14, 1976, in CDSP, vol. XXVII, no. 28.

used by imperialists to weaken Ethiopia and deprive it of its access to the sea.[38] Whilst this clear support for the Ethiopian government's stand came after the establishment of full relations between the two countries, the line of argument that *Pravda* pursued in March 1978 was the same as that of February 1975. From the beginning, therefore, there was no overt disagreement between Ethiopia and Russia on this issue. The one element of divergence between Soviet statements and Ethiopian practice was, of course, the Soviet insistence that the solution in Eritrea be 'peaceful'. But since the Ethiopian government persisted in the pretence that it too supported a peaceful solution, and since the Soviet press did not alert its readers to the difference between Ethiopian statements and deeds, there was no evident reason to suppose that the Russians had the same reserve about PMAC policy in Eritrea as they had on matters of social and economic policy.

Soviet reserve towards the new regime was not matched on the Ethiopian side. Indeed one of the few major policy questions upon which the PMAC was not divided was that of relations with the USSR, which attracted army officers not merely as a result of an automatic suspicion of Haile Selassie's longtime protector, the USA, but also because Ethiopian military personnel were aware of the comparatively greater assistance given by the Soviet Union to Somalia. From the very first meetings of the PMAC, in September 1974, it was decided to request substantial military assistance from the USSR.[39] Yet these publicized appeals were not at first successful and, for the first two years, Soviet assistance was limited to economic aid and the provision of short courses in the USSR for selected Derg members: the first six PMAC personnel went to Russia in 1975. Soviet reserve was motivated by several factors. The character of the new regime was as yet unclear, and the lessons of military repression of the left in Sudan, Egypt and Indonesia were fresh in Russian minds. The Derg retained links with Israel and the USA. The reckless nature of the reforms appeared to confirm the PMAC's instability. The Russians were also keen not to antagonize the Somalis, and

[38] *Keesings Contemporary Archives*, May 26, 1978, p. 28994.
[39] Yodfat, part two, p. 32; this was confirmed to us by a former high-ranking civilian in the revolutionary regime.

indeed signed a major arms deal with them in 1975. They also sought to avoid conflict with Arab regimes such as Iraq or to give Sadat another reason for pushing on to the final breach.

Relations improved considerably during 1975 and 1976, and the Ethiopian delegation that visited Moscow in July 1976 signed the first agreement on Russian military supplies. It appears, however, that the Russians delayed delivery of these supplies, because they were suspicious of the overall direction of the Derg, divided as the latter was at that time. Only when Mengistu came to power in February 1977 and went on an important visit to Moscow in May of that year were the reservations of the earlier period overcome. By now the main links with the USA and Israel had been broken; there was little risk in antagonizing Egypt and the Sudan, both of which had by then expelled the last Russian advisers; Somalia appeared to be moving towards the conservative Arab states; and the political character of the Derg was more defined. All this was prior to, and largely independent of, the Somali decision to attack Ethiopia.

The improvement in relations between Ethiopia and the USSR was not, as it is conventionally portrayed, a simple switch of support from a smaller country, Somalia, to a stronger one, Ethiopia. The Russians could certainly see the strategic advantages of having an ally in Ethiopia. But they had never supported Somalia's claim to Ogaden and they tried, in the early months of 1977, to reconcile the two states. This initiative seems to have won them little credit in the Horn, but it was a serious attempt to resolve the conflict between the two countries on a peaceful basis. In March 1977 Fidel Castro visited the Horn and, after holding separate discussions with Mengistu and Siad Barre, arranged a meeting in Aden between these two leaders, and the South Yemenis. A month later the Soviet President, Podgorny, visited both countries and again tried to mediate: he had to leave Mogadishu on the afternoon of the day he arrived.[40] The precise details are not known; but in both cases some

[40] Castro's own account of his mission is given in *Afrique–Asie*, May 16, 1977, and in his speech on Cuba's military role in the Horn, *Granma*, March 26, 1978. Details of Podgorny's mediation are not available, but soon after his return to the USSR he was dismissed: how far his failure in Africa contributed to his fall is not known.

form of federal solution was proposed, in which Ethiopia and Somalia, and, according to various other accounts, also South Yemen, were to participate. Some versions suggest that Eritrea and Ogaden were to be given separate status within such a federation. Some reports even suggest that it was Siad Barre who first proposed a federation, in 1976. Whatever the precise details, all accounts agree that it was the Somalis who rejected the proposal, insisting that Ogaden be transferred to them. With the failure of the Castro and Podgorny missions, the stage was set for the Ogaden war. By late May, Somali irregulars were moving into Ogaden and in July the Somali army crossed the frontier.

Even after the war began, the Soviet Union did not simply abandon the Somalis. It appears that the Russians initially believed they could restrain the Somalis and informed the Ethiopians of this: the result was that the first supplies of Soviet tanks, which arrived in Ethiopia in June 1977, were transferred north, to the Gondar and Gojjam areas where the conservative EDU was fighting; as a result, the south-eastern frontier was left relatively underdefended. In August, Siad Barre visited the Soviet Union in a vain attempt to win the Russians over to his point of view. It was not until late October that the USSR announced that it had ceased supplying arms to Somalia. Yet until that time the level of Soviet assistance to Ethiopia was limited, and there were no Soviet or Cuban personnel fighting on the ground. What fully tipped the balance was the Somali decision, on November 13, 1977, to expel all Soviet and Cuban advisers from Somalia and to break relations with Cuba. Thirteen days later, on November 26, a large-scale airlift of Soviet equipment to Ethiopia began, the largest such operation ever carried out by the Soviet armed forces in the Third World, and in December Cuban troops began arriving in Ethiopia. In January 1978 the first major Ethiopian–Cuban counter-offensive began, and by March the Somalia forces had withdrawn from Ogaden.

The Soviet assessment of the Ogaden war was given in a *Pravda* article of March 19, 1978. 'The Soviet Union's attitude toward the events in the Horn of Africa has long been well known', it said. 'Our country did everything possible to avoid an armed conflict between the two neighbouring African states. In so doing the Soviet Union proceeded from the obvious fact that such a conflict could not be in the interests of either of these African countries. . . . The Ethiopian leadership is taking a responsible approach to the solution of problems of vital importance to the Horn of Africa and feels that, though the present war was inflicted on its country, there exists no sense of enmity between the peoples of Ethiopia and Somalia'.[41]

The Ogaden war cemented a military alliance between Moscow and Addis Ababa and led to an estimated $1.5 billion worth of Soviet equipment being supplied to Ethiopia. So long as the Somalis maintained their claim to Ogaden there remained a need for this alliance on the Ethiopian side. A Soviet economic aid agreement was signed in September 1978 and in November the links between the two countries were further consolidated by a twenty-year Friendship and Cooperation Treaty. In addition to promising to expand cooperation, this agreement stressed respect for 'territorial integrity and inviolability of frontiers'. Yet despite these ties, there remained several areas of disagreement between the two states, such that once again the relatively large room for independent manoeuvre of local states was underlined. Soviet pressure for the establishment of a party, evident in 1975 and 1976, continued, and in May 1978 the Russians were apparently implicated in an attempt to revive the fortunes of ME'ISON. The delay in party formation through 1978 and 1979 was in part attributable to the desire of Mengistu and his associates to prevent those PMAC members most sympathetic to Moscow from gaining control of a new party. Mengistu's talks with Soviet leaders in November 1978 were described as 'frank', a sign of some disagreement. On the economic front the Soviet Union provided aid and equipment, but the Ethiopians were critical of both its quantity and quality and continued to direct most of their foreign trade to the West. It appeared that by 1978 some agreement on repayment of Ethiopia's military debt had been worked out, but this was phased over a number of

[41] *Pravda*, March 19, 1978, in CDSP, vol. XXX, no. 11.

years and was not such as fundamentally to realign its foreign trade links.[42]

In theory Soviet policy on Eritrea remained what it had been since 1975: support for a peaceful solution within a unitary Ethiopian state. Yet the situation had changed by early 1978. First, as the *Pravda* editorial of March 15 indicated, the Russians, under the impact of their fate in Somalia, were now laying greater stress on the links between the Eritreans and the conservative Arab states. Secondly, the situation on the ground had changed, because the Ethiopian army was now rearmed and supported in such a way that it could launch an offensive in Eritrea and redress the setbacks of 1976–7. The Russians were not prepared to prejudice their overall relationship with Ethiopia by adopting a publicly dissonant position on Eritrea, and throughout 1978 and 1979 they continued to supply Ethiopia with the military equipment it needed to sustain the Eritrean war. It is not clear how far Soviet military personnel were actively involved in Eritrea, but it does seem that some officers took part in late 1978. Overall, the Ethiopian military campaign in Eritrea would have been impossible without the initial and continuing agreement of the Russians. The latter had shown themselves capable, in the case of Somalia, of cutting off arms supplies to an ally whose military campaigns they opposed, and their failure to do so in the case of Eritrea must therefore have denoted at least some measure of assent.

The Soviet Union was, nevertheless, subjected to other diplomatic pressures. Its original 1950 position on Eritrea seems not to have been recalled, but a number of Soviet allies in the Arab world – the PLO, Iraq, Syria – did try to persuade the Russians to moderate their stand on Eritrea. As a result, a number of Eritrean delegations were invited to talks. While EPLF delegations visited East Berlin on three occasions in 1978, an ELF delegation visited Moscow in 1978 and again in 1980.[43] Both the ELF and the EPLF directed appeals to the

---

[42] Ethiopia was to pay for the Soviet arms over ten years, in hard currency, and with 2 per cent interest charges.

[43] Ahmad Nasser reported on his second Moscow visit as follows: 'They said they are against any attempt to solve the Eritrea question militarily and agreed with the ELF exposition that continuation of military escalations can only complicate the

Soviet Union asking it to alter its stand on Eritrea. Throughout, the Soviet Union continued to emphasize its support for a 'peaceful' solution in Eritrea along the lines of Marxist–Leninist nationalities policy, and it appears that Soviet contacts with the Eritrean groups in 1979 and 1981 provoked disagreement between the Kremlin and the PMAC. Yet these diplomatic moves were in themselves ineffectual: the Eritrean and Ethiopian positions remained irreconcilable, and the Soviet Union was not prepared to use its military leverage on the Ethiopians to force a halt to the campaigns in Eritrea. The balance of Soviet policy was therefore clear enough: on the one side appeals for a peaceful settlement and exploratory negotiations with the Eritreans, on the other continued provision to the Ethiopians of the material means by which to combat the guerrillas. The argument that the USSR does not publicly criticize the internal affairs of its allies is not sustainable. It is not a justifiable policy, if Soviet aid is used by that ally for reprehensible purposes. Nor is it a true argument: the USSR was to show no such reticence over Poland in 1980.

Much of the criticism made in the West of Soviet policy in the Horn was unfounded. The Soviet action was not in any sense illegal: the Ethiopian government was an internationally recognized authority, entitled to ask for assistance against external aggression of the Somali variety. Soviet support of the territorial integrity of Ethiopia was merely continuing a policy upon which successive Western governments and in particular the USA had insisted under the imperial regime. There is no evidence that the Soviet intervention was motivated by calculations of economic gain; rather, the relationship with Ethiopia promised to be deficitary for many years to come. The charge that the Soviet Union now controlled Ethiopian government policy, or that Ethiopia was now in some sense a Soviet 'surrogate' was contradicted by

---

matter. The USSR confirmed that it supports our initiative for a peaceful and democratic solution which serves the interests of both the Eritrean and Ethiopian peoples. However, the USSR side did not suggest any solution to the problem, believing that a solution can be worked out only by the Eritreans and the Ethiopians themselves' (*The Eritrean Newsletter*, April 1980).

the evidence. The Soviet assertion that a profound revolution was occurring was quite justified.[44] More problematic were two other aspects of Soviet policy: their characterization of the PMAC regime, and their nationalities policy. As will be discussed in chapter 7, the Soviet theory of the 'non-capitalist road' and its later refinements have tended to misrepresent the internal processes of Third World countries, with the result that Soviet policy suffers rebuffs when these processes reach a certain point of maturity. There is no need to look further than Somalia, once the prime Soviet ally in Africa, to see this. With the consolidation of the post-revolutionary regime in Ethiopia in the early 1980s there were signs that the PMAC too might be considering a new foreign policy, less aligned with the USSR and more open to the West. The Soviet policy on nationalities did not begin in Ethiopia: it was the product of many precedents where the unity of a multi-national revolutionary state was given priority over the demands of a particular nationality for self-determination. These policies, combined with the endorsement of a centralized party, raised somewhat more substantive problems than the issues in terms of which criticism of the Soviet role was normally framed.

Cuba's Interventions

Cuba's role in support of the Ethiopian government was in

[44] One point upon which Russian commentators insisted was the depth of the Ethiopian upheaval, in contrast to the superficial changes introduced by coups elsewhere in Africa. In the words of the Soviet ambassador to Ethiopia in 1977 Anatoli Ratanov, formerly Ambassador in Guinea: 'Ethiopia is different from most African countries. If there were a revolution in Niger, everything would be over in one night. Political life there exists only among an elite of a hundred people. You could change the government, and the people wouldn't notice even. But in Ethiopia there has been a class society with well-established boundaries between classes. It has been an independent state. There was a nobility, which was a landowning class. There was an old monarchy and an old outworn Church. In other words, there was an organic society – a body with a head, trunk, arms and legs. Here it was not possible to change the head without changing the body. It was not so different from Russia in 1917. At the root of the revolution was a popular movement against injustice. You had explosive material for a popular uprising by students, or workers, or the Army. As it happened, the Army was the leading force. It played the role of the Party. Not that there was a military coup, or action by the general staff. Instead, the thrust came from below – the sergeants.' Joseph Kraft, 'Letter from Addis Ababa', *New Yorker*, July 31, 1978, pp. 54–5.

some domains as important as that of the Soviet Union, and earned it as much criticism, from both left and right. Like the Russians, the Cubans were accused of having 'betrayed' their former allies, the Somalis, and of changing sides on Eritrea. In addition the Cubans were cast as mere agents of a policy dictated in Moscow. Since they were already heavily committed, from 1975, in support of the Angolan revolution, their decision to send several thousand troops to Ethiopia in December 1977 not only multiplied the ire of the Western world, but must also have placed serious strains upon the resources and the security of the Cuban state. The controversies surrounding the Cuban role were used by its enemies to try to isolate it from its international political following. Yet the conventional critical picture of Cuban policy is not tenable: Cuban policy tried to avert both the Ethiopian–Somali conflicts and the continued war in Eritrea, and its policy statements were somewhat different in tone and substance from those of the USSR.

Prior to 1974 Cuba had given support to the Eritrean movement. Eritrea was not mentioned in the statements of the Tricontinental Conference, held in Havana in 1966, but the ELF sent about 130 guerrillas to Cuba for training in 1968, and the publications of the Tricontinental organization endorsed not only the legitimacy of the Eritrean movement against Haile Selassie and the USA but also the Eritrean demand for independence.[45] In 1970, however, the Cubans suspended military aid to the Eritreans, on the grounds that where a split occurred in a liberation movement, and this was not evidently along clear lines of progressive and conservative (as was the case in Angola), then aid should be so withheld. For the remaining years of the imperial regime, the Cubans continued to give political support to the Eritreans. Yet in his speech to the non-aligned conference in 1973 Castro

---

[45] *Tricontinental* (Bulletin) nos. 22–3, January–February 1968; ibid., no. 39, June 1969; ibid., no. 71, February 1972; *Tricontinental* (Bimonthly), no. 15, November–December 1969. These reports support the Eritrean struggle for independence, but describe it as a movement against feudalism and US domination. It would seem that ELF–Cuban relations were established via Syria, which worked closely with Cuba when the left fraction of the Baath headed by Nureddin al-Atassi came to power in December 1966; al-Atassi was ousted in 1970.

refrained from mentioning the Eritrean movement.⁴⁶ And Cuba no longer provided military aid. On the other hand, the Cubans established another link in the Horn in July 1972, when they exchanged diplomatic recognition with Somalia, and in January 1974 they signed a number of agreements with Mogadishu. Cuban doctors and sugar refinery experts were working in Somalia by the mid-1970s, as were military experts helping to train the Somali militia. In 1976 Siad Barre startled the Western embassies in Mogadishu by saying that if necessary he would have no hesitation in calling in the Cubans to help his country defend itself, just as the Angolans had done.⁴⁶

Despite their previous involvements with Eritrea and Somalia, the Cubans' response to the Ethiopian revolution was an enthusiastic one. The upheaval in this ancient and romantic land, which also occupied a special place in the non-aligned movement, seems to have captured Castro's imagination and in a speech in March 1975 he expressed his enthusiasm for the events in Ethiopia, which were, he said, 'of great interest and historic importance'. Castro went on, however, to say: 'Unfortunately, a fratricidal struggle between the new government which broke the old structures and a national liberation movement is being waged within that very state. This situation in which two causes of progressive trends are confronting each other is complex. Therefore, what is the duty of the Non-Aligned? Is it perhaps to cross our arms or support one side to the detriment of the other? Urge on the war? Decidedly not. The least that should be done is to make a serious effort and seek a peaceful and just solution that would be acceptable to the parties in the conflict which is separating and confronting the Ethiopian revolutionary process and the Liberation Movement in Eritrea.'⁴⁷ Nothing came of this appeal, and in March 1977, when Castro visited the Horn, his main efforts were devoted to trying to negotiate a settlement between Ethiopia and So-

⁴⁶ Philippe Decraene, *L'Expérience socialiste somalienne*, p. 136. Siad Barre can hardly have expected that, within two years, it would be his Ethiopian rivals who would follow the Angolan example.
⁴⁷ 'The non-aligned countries will know how to fulfil the duty that the present demands of them', Havana, 1975, p. 13.

malia. Three months later, Somali forces were in the Ogaden. In November the Somalis not only expelled all Cuban personnel from Somalia, but also broke off diplomatic relations, a measure they were not prepared to take against the USSR. In December, several thousand Cuban troops arrived in Ethiopia.

From 1978 onwards, the Cubans maintained their troops in Ethiopia, but they were confined to bases in the Ogaden region and were not used in the renewed conflicts of 1980. At the same time, Cubans provided Ethiopia with substantial amounts of civilian aid. Over 300 Cuban doctors had been brought to staff Ethiopian hospitals by 1978; they were apparently shocked by the survival of pre-revolutionary distinctions between different grades of patient and refused to accept these. Cuban personnel were involved in building a dam on the Benbela river at Debre Zeit; and around 2,500 Ethiopian children went to study in the children's educational project on the Isle of Pines in Cuba.[48] There were also several important exchanges of visits – Mengistu visited Cuba in May 1978 and again in September 1979, for the non-aligned conference, whilst Castro made a second visit to Ethiopia in September 1978.

Cuban policy towards Eritrea was less enthusiastic than the Ethiopians may have wished, and, as in the pre-revolutionary period, it differed from the Russians'. The Cubans never publicly criticized Ethiopian policy there, but Castro's 1975 statement, defining the Eritreans as 'progressive' and as a 'national liberation movement', clearly diverged from the official stance in both Addis Ababa and Moscow. Through their contacts with the Arab world the Cubans were made aware of hostility to Ethiopian policy: Iraq and the PLO in particular tried to get the Cubans to intervene with the PMAC.

[48] Up to 2,400 Ethiopian children went to study on Cuba's Isle of Pines (*Ethiopian Herald*, November 18, 1979), where they were joined by children from Angola, Mozambique and Namibia. The *escuelas africanas*, or African Schools, were staffed by teachers from Cuba and the African countries concerned. Cuba also developed a wide-ranging programme of medical assistance to African countries, in line with the belief of Fidel Castro, himself a doctor, that doctors were the best ambassadors – good administrators, able to get close to the people, and of practical help. In 1979 Cuba had an estimated 2,250 medical personnel in sixteen African countries (*The Guardian*, April 23, 1979).

Neither of the official Ethiopian–Cuban communiqués of 1978 make any mention of Eritrea. There is some evidence that in the period immediately after the defeat of Somalia, in March 1978, some Cuban forces were moved to Eritrea, but if this did occur they seem to have been withdrawn a few months later.[49] Inside Ethiopia itself, Cuban policy seems to have been one of avoiding the issue as far as possible, consistent with overall support for the Ethiopian revolution. Cuba neither endorsed nor opposed Ethiopian policy; it regarded it as an 'internal affair' in which they would criticize Ethiopia. Whilst continuing to urge a political solution, Cuba was not prepared to cause a full rupture in relations with the PMAC over the question.

The Cuban role in Ethiopia covers three separate policy issues – the revolution itself, Somalia, and Eritrea. From the first months, Cuba enthusiastically supported the Ethiopian revolution and in 1977 we find Castro comparing the Ethiopian to the French and Russian revolutions. Mengistu's advent to power in February 1977 seems to have strengthened ties, and Castro went out of his way several times to give personal endorsement to the Derg chairman. 'I consider Mengistu to be a true revolutionary and the revolution now taking place in this country is a true revolution', he told one interviewer.[50] The level of the Cuban commitment to Ethiopia's economic development says much for Castro's view of the revolution as a whole. Yet whilst Castro's support for the revolution itself was justifiable, his fulsome praise for Mengistu is less so, and may have struck an unwelcome note among Ethiopian audiences.[51]

[49] John Duggan reports that Cuban forces protected Asmara in the early part of 1978, and that Cuban advisers helped with Ethiopian artillery, and flew air strikes ('International Aspects of the War in Eritrea', unpublished manuscript, May 1980). Officials in Havana denied that Cuba was playing any direct role in Eritrea (*Washington Post*, June 23, 1978).
[50] *Afrique–Asie*, May 16, 1977, p. 16.
[51] An official Cuban view of the Ethiopian revolution was given by Central Committee member Raul Valdes Vivo, in *Ethiopia. The Unknown Revolution*, Havana 1978. This concealed a number of questionable political judgements behind a veneer of journalistic impressionism. Apart from a few asides, it did not mention the problem of Eritrea at all, and it endorsed the PMAC's account of such matters as the Aman Andom killing and the red terror. This was in contrast to the more balanced and cautious evaluation contained in the chapter on the revolution

The Somali issue is one where the Cubans did their utmost to avoid the conflict of 1977: the charge that they 'betrayed' the Somalis is baseless, since it was Somalia that went back on its commitment not to invade Ethiopia. Had the Cubans really wanted to punish Somalia, they could easily have taken advantage of their predominant military position in March 1978 to inflict serious damage on Somali territory itself. Where the Cubans may have erred in regard to Somalia is in the opposite direction, in giving too much credit to the Siad Barre regime in the first place. In his account of the Cuban involvement in the Ogaden war, Castro identified a left and a right current inside Somalia, the implication being that the left was opposed to the Ogaden war.[52] But what the Cubans and the Russians sought to protect by such an account was their own earlier endorsement of the Somali regime. What Castro's account could not make clear was why a regime that Cuba had supported so strongly and which had not, contrary to his account, changed its political character, should have decided to launch the Ogaden offensive. One factor may have been an underestimation by the Cubans of Somali nationalism. Like Ethiopian nationalism, this took a form far more forceful than anything they had encountered in Latin America and they may have been induced to underestimate its virulence. But the later evolution of the Somali regime must also call into question the very theory of the 'non-capitalist' path of development upon which the Cubans and Russians based their support for Siad Barre in the first place.

Cuban policy in Eritrea was, as we have seen, one of restrained disagreement. Not only did Cuba refuse to play its expected military role in the campaigns that unfolded against the Eritreans from June 1978 onwards, but it pointedly abstained from the political endorsements that Moscow was quite willing to provide. Cuba's pre-1974 record, and

---

appended to the standard East European study, the two-volume history of Ethiopia published by the Polish authors Andrzej Bartnicki and Joanna Mantel-Niecko (*Geschichte Äthiopiens*, Berlin 1978). This stressed the divisions within the PMAC and avoided factional views on both Aman and the civilian opposition. It included some reflections on the clergy's opposition to reform (pp. 616–17): these were presumably regarded as being of special relevance to a Polish readership.

[52] *Granma*, March 26, 1978.

Castro's 1975 description of the Eritreans as a national liberation movement, marked Cuban policy off from that being pursued by Moscow and Addis Ababa. Yet on any overall balance-sheet, Cuban policy was not simply one of neutrality. First of all, the very help that Cuba was providing to Ethiopia in Ogaden inevitably had consequences in Eritrea, by the simple fact of Cuba's forces releasing Ethiopian resources that would otherwise have been committed to the defence of Ethiopian territory against Somalia. No doubt some of the forces trained by the Cubans were also later used in Eritrea. A second major problem concerns the Cubans' public political position: however much they refrained from overt support for the Ethiopians, and however much they privately regretted what was happening in Eritrea, their overall stance of support for the Ethiopian government combined with the absence of criticism over Eritrea meant that, on balance, they were seen as supporting Ethiopian policy. As with the Russians, so with the Cubans: the test of their support for the peaceful solution of the Eritrean question was whether they were prepared, clearly and publicly, to distance themselves from what the Ethiopians were doing. Yet at no point did they ever disown Ethiopian policies in Eritrea. If in overall terms, therefore, the Cuban role in the Horn was a positive one, involving defence against Somali aggression and substantial assistance in social and economic programmes, their policy in regard to Eritrea was, in the end, collusive with the PMAC's repression.

Interested Spectators: China and the Communist Movement

Prior to the 1960s, China did not have an active policy in Africa. It was inevitable that even when it initiated one, the initiatives it undertook would be determined by the consideration that dominated its foreign policy elsewhere – its contest with the USSR. Alternatively phrased in 'left' and 'right' terms, this critique provided the general line by which China judged the rest of the world, including Africa. At the same time, its initiatives in Africa underlined something that neither the Chinese themselves, nor their opponents, were the first to identify: that despite its prestige and demographic weight, China is not in any serious sense a world power. It lacks the military and economic weight to play a major role in areas away from its immediate geographical periphery, and its political influence is far less than the stridency of its statements or the expectations of its admirers might at first suggest.

China's relations with the Horn began in 1964 and formed a curious chapter in the foreign relations of the states concerned.[53] In January 1964 Chou En-lai embarked upon a major tour of Africa and on January 30 he visited Haile Selassie. The emperor declared himself willing to establish diplomatic relations and to support China's attempt to regain its seat in the United Nations. Yet, in violation of the norms of international diplomacy to which Chou so carefully adhered, he delivered a public lecture to his visitor on the iniquities of China's foreign policy, accusing the People's Republic of stirring up trouble throughout Africa. In addition, Chou was received not in Addis Ababa, the Ethiopian capital, but in what was formally a provincial town. The town happened to be Asmara, and there can be few who missed the symbolism of the Ethiopian emperor trying to win implicit Chinese acceptance of the annexation which had occurred but two years before. Chou went on from Asmara to Mogadishu, where he delivered himself of his famous judgement that 'an excellent revolutionary situation exists in Africa'. It was a rather inappropriate remark to make in what was then one of the more conservative African countries. His Somali hosts greeted him with slogans calling for support for the liberation of Ogaden; but since there had just been a small war between Ethiopia and Somalia, this appeal for Chinese support was probably just wishful thinking, and there is no evidence that China, then or later, ever endorsed Somali claims.

As it turned out, nothing substantial came from Chou's two visits in 1964: relations with Somalia remained low-level, and under US pressure Haile Selassie refrained from honouring his promise to recognize the People's Republic. For its part, China began to give covert aid to the ELF and by the late 1960s

---

[53] Bruce Larkin, *China and Africa 1949–1970*, London 1971; 'Chou En-lai on Safari', W.A.C. Adie, *The China Quarterly* no. 18, April–June 1964.

the Chinese press was openly supporting the Eritrean movement. However, the shift in Chinese foreign policy after the end of the cultural revolution in 1969 led to a new accommodation with the conservative rulers of the Third World; the benevolence that the Shah of Iran and General Pinochet were later to enjoy was also bestowed upon the Ethiopian emperor and, after negotiations in Khartoum, diplomatic relations were established in December 1970. All aid to the Eritreans ceased, and in October 1971 Haile Selassie visited Peking where he was received by Mao Tse-tung and given $84 million in aid. China's relations with Somalia were, on the other hand, somewhat reserved: whilst the Chinese agreed in 1972 to build a 600-mile north-south road in the interior of the country, running near the frontier with Ethiopia, they were evidently suspicious of the growing ties between Moscow and Somalia and in particular of the Soviet naval facilities at Berbera. When Siad Barre followed Haile Selassie to Peking in 1972 he was not graced with an interview with Chairman Mao.

China initially responded to the Ethiopian revolution with guarded support, and the generally sympathetic attitude to China amongst Ethiopian left-wing circles added an additional element of potential friendship in relations between the two states. But by the time of Mengistu's advent to power and the strengthening of ties with the USSR, this warmth had begun to pall, and, guided by its general hostility to the USSR, China began to show more favour to Somalia. China did not publicly endorse the Ogaden war, but commented selectively on it: it welcomed the Somali expulsion of Soviet and Cuban advisers, saluting it as a 'just action of great significance in combatting hegemonism'.[54] Although it always denied that it exported arms, there were reliable reports of some Chinese equipment including Mig-21s being sold to Somalia and China took over construction of the Faroli dam from the Russians.[55] But, whilst China continued to attack the Russians and Cubans for their role in the Horn and to blame the whole conflict on them, Peking also stressed the need for

---

[54] *Peking Review*, November 18, 1977.
[55] *US Security Interests*, p. 50.

such conflicts to be resolved by peaceful discussions. They were not therefore willing to go all the way in support of Somalia, and while trying to derive tactical advantage, their formal position on Ogaden was no different from Moscow's or Havana's.

However, China's sympathies for Somalia led in 1978 to a major attack on its policy by Mengistu. Speaking on the occasion of the fourth anniversary of the overthrow of Haile Selassie, he accused China of arming the EPRP, the Eritreans and the Somalis.[56] Later, mass meetings were held throughout Ethiopia to condemn China's role. This Ethiopian outburst was in general provoked by China's support for Somalia, but it may also have had two other functions: one, to express support for Fidel Castro, who was at that time visiting Ethiopia and whose policies were daily denounced by the Chinese; and secondly, to intimidate domestic political forces, especially the Was League, who were sympathetic to China and were believed to be complicating the party-formation policies of the PMAC.

China's response was not to attack Mengistu or the Ethiopian government directly, but to denounce Castro for his statements made whilst in Ethiopia; in 1978, however, the Chinese press began, for the first time in nine years, to publicize the Eritrean struggle,[57] and there were unconfirmed reports that some Eritreans were being trained in China once again. However, the material impact of China's renewed backing for Eritrea, as of its support for Somalia, was extremely limited and was of little more than symbolic importance in the overall conflict in which China was engaged with the USSR. Even its political positions were incomplete, fragments selected for use in a polemic rather than general analyses of the situation. It was a strange picture that the Chinese press presented of the Somali situation, since it did not mention the Somali attempt to regain the Ogaden and carefully avoided anything that might be construed as support of it. At the same time its discussion of

[56] *Ethiopian Herald*, September 12, 1978. Mengistu included China among the 'thirteen' countries which had, he claimed, supported Ethiopia's enemies. Attempts by the authors to acquire a list from Ethiopian diplomatic personnel of these thirteen countries have been unsuccessful.

[57] *Peking Review*, December 15, 1978; ibid., September 14, 1979.

Eritrea skirted the issue of whether or not the Eritreans had the right to independence: they were praised for fighting *against* the Russians and Cubans, but what they were fighting *for* was left purposely vague. Just as China had ended support to the Eritreans in 1970 in order to include Haile Selassie in its world-wide front of countries hostile to the Soviet Union, so it was now keen to restart aid to them, and to give partial support to the Somalis, in pursuit of a similar goal. In sum, China's policy choices were guided by factors external to the Horn of Africa itself and had only a moderate impact upon it.

The conflicts in the Horn attendant upon the Ethiopian revolution not only involved the post-revolutionary states, but found a considerable echo within the left in Africa and the advanced capitalist countries. The Communist parties were led to adopt positions on the conflicts in Ogaden and Eritrea, whilst on the non-Communist left there was almost complete opposition to Soviet and Cuban policies in Ethiopia. This disarray was especially striking because it occurred in the wake of the Cuban intervention in Angola, which had commanded widespread support on the left, and only two years after the triumph of the Vietnamese revolution, in which so many on the left had endorsed or at least tacitly supported the Soviet role. This controversy was also at first sight surprising, given the fact that the Horn was an area in which the left had traditionally shown very little interest, but the presence in Europe and North America of politically active communities of Ethiopian and Eritrean students and the links of some Communist parties to Somalia helped bring the issues to the fore, as did the right's response to events. The issue of Somali–Ethiopian relations and even more so the question of Eritrea became causes of division on the left, of a kind unparalleled in relation to any other recent Third World question, with the possible exception of the Arab–Israeli dispute.

In Africa, the two parties most directly concerned were the Communist parties of the Sudan and of South Africa, the former the largest party in the Arab world, located in a country bordering Ethiopia, the latter with a directing role and publishing programme such that it acted as an influential guide for Communists throughout the sub-Saharan area. The

Communist Party of Sudan had already faced issues comparable to those in Ethiopia: it had had its own bitter experience of a supposedly progressive military regime, and had had to confront the problem of the secessionist movement in the southern Sudan, which Haile Selassie had supported. Whilst it supported the Ethiopian revolution it stressed the need for 'a free and voluntary alliance' of all those forces who made the revolution, including the EPRP, and it favoured the establishment of a fully democratic system, in which parties and trade unions would be permitted, and the right to strike guaranteed.[58] Its own policy on the southern Sudan had been one of opposition to the secession of the south, and support for regional autonomy. Yet when it came to the Eritrean question, the Sudanese CP gave support to the right of the Eritreans to self-determination, including full independence, provided Ethiopia was guaranteed a safe exit to the sea. This clear policy was all the more remarkable because Sudanese CP members were in private rather suspicious of the Eritreans, whom they regarded as being dangerously close to the Sudanese authorities and to a number of Arab governments.

The Communist Party of South Africa, without the direct regional pressure of the Sudanese party, was at first reserved on the question of the Ethiopian revolution: there were those within its following who shared the general scepticism about military regimes derived from the experiences of Sudan, Egypt, Indonesia and elsewhere and who favoured the programme of the EPRP and the right of the Eritreans to self-determination. By 1977, however, the issue had been decided in favour of a more orthodox endorsement of the PMAC, and the CPSA's journal, *The African Communist*, was publishing articles that supported the official Addis Ababa line.[59] The

[58] *The Sudan Bulletin*, issued by the Central Committee Communist Party of the Sudan, no. 3, April 1978, 'Resolution on the Situation in the Red Sea Region', pp. 51–4.
[59] *The African Communist*, no. 74, 1978. Initial coverage of the Ethiopian revolution in *The African Communist*, nos. 60 and 63, 1975, stressed the limits of military regimes; but while supporting the Eritrean struggle against 'Ethiopian colonialism', it called for a negotiated settlement within the confines of a united Ethiopia. Its first full analysis of events in Ethiopia was W. Jones, 'Problems of the Ethiopian Revolution', no. 69, 1977.

paradox was, therefore, that the African party with most direct contact with the Ethiopian experience, namely the Sudanese, adopted a far more critical stance on the issues of the Ethiopian revolution than the one which, from a less immediate standpoint, might in principle have been expected to take up a more measured stance.

The European Communist party most concerned with Ethiopia was, naturally, the Italian, which also saw in the Horn an issue on which it could develop its foreign profile independently of the USSR. The Italian party had already established links with Somalia, and the PCI-controlled cooperative movement from Ravenna was involved in development projects in Somalia. At the same time the PCI was in close touch with the EPLF, whose representatives in Rome had acquired considerable influence throughout the Italian left. The official party position on the Ogaden conflict was that this should be resolved peacefully. The PCI opposed any military solution in Eritrea, whilst stressing the need for Eritreans to be given self-government within the confines of Ethiopia. PCI delegations were actively involved in 1977 and 1978 in attempts to defuse the two conflicts, and in February 1980 the Party hosted secret Derg–ELF talks in Rome.[60] Yet the PCI's initiatives were not successful: neither they nor the others who tried to mediate between Somalia and Ethiopia were effective, and the Ethiopians took no more notice of them than they did of the Cubans and the Russians, who called for a peaceful solution in Eritrea. At the same time the official policies of the party leadership met with strong criticism from within the PCI: there remained considerable sympathy for Somalia and those espousing this wanted PCI support for the Ogaden claim; at the same time, the pressure from the outright pro-Eritrean sections of the party remained considerable.[61] Whilst able to resist these international pressures, the PCI had by the end of 1978 to respond to events in the

---

[60] On PCI policy in the Horn see Carlo Pajetta, 'Interview on Ethiopia and Somalia', *New Left Review*, 107, January–February 1978; *The Guardian*, February 22, 1978; Gina Carlo Pajetta in *Rinascita*, February 17, 1978, and the correspondence that followed; *Africa Confidential*, July 30, 1980.

[61] Strong support for the Eritrean cause came from the veteran Italian socialist Lelio Basso; see his interview in *Dritte Welt Magazin*, Bonn, July–August 1978.

Horn itself and to issue a strong attack on the Ethiopian government for pursuing the military solution in Eritrea.[62]

Elsewhere on the left there was also disarray on the issue of Ethiopia. Normally less prone to diverge from the CPSU, the French Communist Party added its voice to those calling for a peaceful solution to the Eritrean question within the confines of Ethiopia, but did not experience the internal disputes of the PCI.[63] The British party, which had close relations with the former British colony of Somalia and which had had informal contact with the EPRP in the period immediately after the revolution, was as divided as the Italian party and took its lead from Rome. Its press gave favourable coverage of the Eritrean movement.[64] Most of the non-Communist left in Europe and North America was even more favourable to the Eritrean cause: it tended to discount the Ethiopian revolution itself, whilst giving credence to the more loyalist interpretations of the Eritrean movement.

Most of those on the left who adopted positions on the Horn of Africa did so by means of simplifications of greater or lesser scale. Those who accepted the validity of an Ethiopian revolution tended to allow themselves to be taken in by some of the less credible and more macabre exaggerations of the PMAC. By a twist of political logic, 'internationalist' support for the Ethiopian revolution entailed endorsement of the PMAC's chauvinist policies at home. Those who supported the PMAC's opponents tended all too often to deny that there had been a revolution in Ethiopia at all, and to point to such features as the terror, the military regime or the policy on the nationalities as evidence for their position. Many of those who supported Somalia did so by whitewashing the social and national characteristics of the Mogadishu regime, whilst backing for the Eritrean movement tended to be reduced to support for one or other group, usually the EPLF, which was

---

[62] *Le Monde*, December 12, 1978.

[63] *L'Humanité*, April 25, 1978; August 19, 1978.

[64] *Morning Star*, May 10, 1979. See also the article by Jack Woddis, head of the international department of the CPGB, calling for a negotiated settlement between Ethiopia and Somalia, *Morning Star*, February 20, 1978. Woddis held a number of discussions with EPRP representatives in 1974–5; he recalled that at one point they said to him: 'Now we have overthrown the emperor, what should we do next?' (conversation with the authors, February 1978).

then presented as the genuine representative of the whole movement. The EPRP too had its supporters who, with varying degrees of information at their disposal, purported to see it as the revolutionary party that had made the revolution and was now representative of the Ethiopian working class. Behind all these debates lay both a tendency to reduce the complexities of the Horn to simpler shades, and varying preconceived ideas, pro and con, about the foreign policy of the Soviet Union.

Ethiopia in World Affairs: Object and Subject

The crisis of 1977–8 had implications not just for the Horn, but for the overall climate of world politics. It formed one component of the deterioration in international relations that began with the revolution in Angola in 1975 and which continued through the crises over Shaba, Iran and Afghanistan. Western politicians saw Soviet policy in the Horn as one of the major examples of a new 'expansionism' in Moscow, and as a reason for replacing détente by a tougher policy. Some US officials took to reminding their listeners that the Second World War began in Ethiopia and that the Third might do so as well. The clearest exponent of this view was Carter's National Security Adviser, Zbigniew Brzezinski, who, both during the Horn crisis and in subsequent statements, argued that the USA should have taken a more combative position. In early 1978 he advocated sending a naval task force to the waters off Somalia, although, by all accounts, he was unable to say what the task force would have done.[65] The Ethiopian restraint, in not invading Somalia in March 1978, removed the need for that particular US response; but Brzezinski continued to criticize Soviet and Cuban actions in Ethiopia and, through the concept of 'linkage', used these actions as a reason for slowing down negotiations with the Russians. The draft treaty on limiting strategic arms, SALT-II, was, claimed Brzezinski, 'buried in the sands of Ogden'.[66] And many another conservative

---

[65] *New Yorker*, May 1, 1978, contains an account of the dispute over Horn policy.
[66] *International Herald Tribune*, December 4, 1980.

commentator would cite the Ethiopian case as one of the several instances – including Angola, South Yemen, Iran and Afghanistan – where Soviet conduct in the Third World had undermined East–West relations.[67]

This position did not go unchallenged within the US government. Carter's UN Ambassador, Andrew Young, voiced the opinion that the Soviet presence in Ethiopia might have some beneficial effects. Secretary of State Cyrus Vance warned at the time against automatic responses to Soviet policy, and later challenged the view that the Ogaden war was a case of Soviet misconduct: 'We got what we wanted', Vance was to say later, pointing out that the Americans warned the Russians and Cubans not to invade Somalia and that they did not.[68] But neither Young nor Vance was able to prevail: Young was sacked in 1979 for meeting with Palestinian representatives at the UN and Vance resigned in 1980 in protest against the attempt to use force to rescue the hostages in Iran. It appeared that Soviet 'misconduct' in the Horn had become an established part of the bill of indictment in the Second Cold War. Yet, as with the other components of this bill, the Ethiopian example proved far less than was generally believed. It did reflect a new Soviet capacity to provide military assistance to allies far removed from its frontiers: the airlift of November–December 1977 was, in both strategic and technical terms, a breakthrough for the Russians, who had been unable, seventeen years beforehand, to provide comparable aid to the beleaguered revolutionary regime in the eastern Congo. It also exemplified a new Soviet confidence in its ability to meet demands for assistance from the Third World, a confidence that was in part born of the overall strategic parity which it had by then achieved with the USA. But the charges of 'misconduct' and 'violation of détente' were of little substance. The Russians were, after all, only doing what the West had been doing for decades – providing aid to allied governments who requested it. Despite claims that the Russian and Cuban policy was 'illegal', even an 'illegal invasion',[69] there was nothing illegal about it: Somalia

[67] Henry Kissinger, *For the Record*, Boston 1981, p. 175.
[68] As note 66.
[69] Secretary of State Alexander Haig, *The Sunday Times*, February 8, 1981.

had invaded Ethiopia, and the Russians and Cubans were only helping the Ethiopians to repel the attack. And both Washington and Moscow were committed to the territorial integrity of Ethiopia.

In more general terms, the US charges are confused. They leave out of account the role that US forces played in provoking the 1977 crisis – just as comparable charges over Angola omit the responsibility of the West and its allies in that conflict. The allocation of blame for the deterioration in international relations uniquely to the USSR is unsustainable: the climate had to some extent begun to deteriorate far earlier, and for many reasons. The focus on the Ogaden war, in conjunction with one or two other Third World crises, obscures the deeper international causes of the crisis in Soviet–American relations that matured at the end of the 1970s.[70]

The longer-run international effect of the Ethiopian revolution may be not so much in its impact on East–West relations, or in the manner in which outside powers have become involved in the Horn. It may, rather, lie in the fact that revolutionary Ethiopia has itself become a significant factor in African and Third World affairs, inheriting and transforming the role that the emperor had played for so long. Ethiopia retains those attributes that gave it influence in the past: its population is the third largest in Africa, it is the seat of the OAU and the only African state not to have been colonized. To these attributes is now added the fact that it has undergone the most profound social revolution in contemporary African history, and possesses the largest and most experienced black army south of the Sahara.[71] In the first years after 1974, the Ethiopian authorities were concerned with maintaining their international positions – preventing the removal of the OAU from Addis Ababa, rallying support against Somalia, and trying to find assistance in resolving the

---

[70] For an elaboration, see Fred Halliday, *Soviet Policy in the Arc of Crisis*, Transnational Institute, Washington 1981.

[71] Ethiopia enjoyed the support of the great majority of African countries in its conflicts with Somalia and over Eritrea. This arose from the OAU's position of respecting the existing colonial boundaries. One partial exception was Mozambique, where the press was at times sympathetic to the EPLF.

Eritrean question.[72] Even amongst Arab states disposed against the PMAC, there was considerable success, as the close relations with Libya and South Yemen, and the gradual rapprochement with Sudan showed. However, as the new government gained confidence, it also began to play a role in politics to the south, and Ethiopian support was given in substantial quantities to Mugabe's forces during the last years of the Zimbabwean struggle. Further afield, in the west African state of Liberia, radical junior officers who seized power in April 1980 openly proclaimed their model to be that of Ethiopia. Even those Western countries who had kept their distance since 1974 were, in the end, willing to reopen relations and in April 1981 the Italian Foreign Minister Emilio Columbo visited the country. Whether or not rumours of a possible shift away from the Russians prove substantial, there is no doubt that the new confidence of the PMAC will lead it to play a more active international role and to become one of those more influential Third World countries – such as Algeria and Nigeria in Africa, or Mexico in Latin America – whose combination of demographic weight and political character give them a particular influence in world affairs. The implications for the rest of Africa, whether in terms of revolutionary example or in terms of concrete military assistance in the continuing conflicts of the south, remain to be seen.

---

[72] Authors' interview with Foreign Minister Feleke Gedle-Giorgis, Addis Ababa, December 1977.

7
Conclusions: A State of Socialist Orientation?

The opening chapter of this study argued that the Ethiopian revolution could be seen as located in two distinct revolutionary 'times', that of the overthrow of absolutist monarchies, of which it is a late example, and that of social revolution in the post-colonial world, of which it may be one of the earlier instances. The dimensions of the first 'time' were explored in chapter 2, which discussed those factors within the old order that led to the revolution of 1974. The depth of the revolution and its subsequent direction were, in part, attributed to the fact that it occurred within a society that had not been restructured by colonial domination, where class relations were highly articulated, and which therefore retained important similarities with the societies of absolutist Europe. Chapter 2, and the chapters that followed, also explored the second 'time', and the manner in which the Ethiopian revolution was catapulted into a new historical conjuncture – its radical social reforms, its public adherence to a socialist transition, its dramatic shift in international alignments. The socio-political coordinates of this process and the constitution of a new state were explored in chapters 3 and 4. The ethnic and regional problems, both a feature of the revolution and an obstacle to the consolidation of a stable post-revolutionary order, were explored in chapter 5, and the next chapter detailed the changing international connections of the PMAC, in particular the emergence of its alliance with the USSR.

The aim of this final section is to address, in summary form, the issue raised by the second revolutionary 'time'. In particular, it discusses the question of Ethiopia's possible

Conclusions: A State of Socialist Orientation?

transition to a socialist mode of production. These remarks will, therefore, draw together issues raised in the preceding chapters. Insofar as the transformation of Ethiopian society is still very much in its early stages, no definitive answer to this question can be given. The outcome of the Ethiopian revolution could be that the country embarks upon a transition to socialism. Alternatively, Ethiopian society could, after a period of oscillation, become one in which capitalist social relations predominate. The reasons for caution are self-evident. The revolution itself was not led by an avowedly socialist movement or organization and the new regime's ability and determination to implement its programmes must remain in doubt. The history of other Third World countries over the past two decades has given more than enough instances of self-proclaimed 'socialist' regimes that were soon replaced by overtly capitalist ones or which, in response to some combination of internal and external factors, themselves decided to abandon any claims to socialism. Even the definition of socialism itself has to be clarified when it is used to describe the post-revolutionary societies of Eastern Europe, the USSR, China, and so on, to which they are conventionally applied. Socialism is a period of transition between capitalism and communism. It is characterized by the abolition of private ownership of the means of production, the social redistribution of the product, and control by the direct producers over political and economic decision-making. In other words, socialism involves both economic and political conditions in its commitment to the socialization of the economy and of political power. Societies such as exist in Russia and China can be termed 'socialist' insofar as private appropriation has been abolished, but not in their political systems. While they can no longer accurately be termed 'capitalist', they fail to satisfy the criteria of socialism.[1]

---

[1] There exists a large and contentious body of literature concerning the definition of 'socialism' and how far the societies that claim to be socialist merit this title. It is not our concern to enter into this debate here, beyond registering the fact that countries such as Russia and China can be considered socialist in some, but not all, of their characteristics. The phrase 'actually existing socialism' as developed by Rudolf Bahro (*The Alternative in Eastern Europe*, London 1978) draws attention to what must be the two components of any analysis of these societies: on the one hand, a critique of their claim to have realized socialism; on the other, a concern with the mechanisms that govern them, with how these societies actually work.

The dimensions of the problem as they relate to Ethiopia were outlined at the end of the discussion of the concrete transformations of the state in chapter 4. There it was stated that Ethiopia could begin a transition to socialism if all of three conditions were fulfilled: first, that the conflict within the state itself was resolved in favour of those supporting a socialist transition; second, that the balance of class forces inside Ethiopian society was such as to favour this transition; and third, that the international conditions for such a transition were favourable. The factors that might encourage or impede such a process can be assembled from the discussions of the previous chapters. Within the state itself, power is concentrated in the hands of a group of radical military officers who have proclaimed their intention to lead Ethiopian society in a socialist direction. Their commitment to some form of radical change and their determination to implement what they proclaim are not, by now, in doubt. Within Ethiopian society itself, there are factors favouring such a transformation: the inability of the existing capitalist forces openly to oppose a socialist transformation, and a widespread mobilization of formerly oppressed social groups in support of the regime's goals. Internationally, the PMAC can rely on the support, military, ideological and in some degree economic, of the USSR and its allies. By improving relations with the Arab states, it may at least prevent them and also the West from giving substantial support to groups overtly opposed to the new Ethiopian order.

The forces against such a transformation are of equal force and potential determination. Within the state there remain many personnel opposed to socialism and who are able to lessen the impact of any reforming decrees from above. Apart from this civilian sector, in the main resistant to a socialist transformation, there are also those within the PMAC itself who are cautious about such radical changes. Moreover, quite apart from the supposed intentions of political factions vying for power within the state, there is the broader question of the processes of class formation that have accompanied the constitution of a post-revolutionary order. The pattern in some other Third World states has been for radical army officers to use their positions of power to acquire control over means of production, especially land, and

Conclusions: A State of Socialist Orientation?

thereby to constitute themselves, in collaboration with the civilian bureaucracy, as a new ruling class. For all these reasons, the outcome of the conflict within the Ethiopian state apparatus cannot be a foregone conclusion. Yet even if this first condition is met, there remains the second problem, of the limits set to the capacity of the state to bring about the desired transition. While the relative autonomy of the state enables it to promote changes in social relations and not merely reflect them, the interventionist character of the state should not be mistaken for omnipotence. It cannot voluntaristically induce transformations that do not find some corresponding support in the society. Large areas of the countryside, indeed the majority of the Ethiopian population, remain subject to conditions of subsistence agriculture; the survival of these pre-capitalist relations sets limits to what reforms from above can achieve. At the same time, small-scale petty commodity production has been on the increase since the revolution, particularly in the rural sector. This spread of market relations, combined with the existence of inequalities in land tenure, will, unless countered, provide the conditions for the development of capitalist class relations and forces. On the other hand, there is a basis for development towards socialism, given the fact that the 1974 revolution has also created a state sector – in industry, finance and agriculture – and has, through the mass mobilizations and the planning system, increased its overall ability to direct the economy. Any further progress on the path to a transition to socialism would involve expanding the state's control over the economy and in particular a substantial transformation of agrarian relations. Here, the most important internal obstacle to a socialist transition remains: the predominance of pre-capitalist, petty commodity and capitalist social relations and the inevitability of clashes with the classes benefiting from these relations. The weakness of a capitalist ruling class in Ethiopia was one of the factors accounting for the radical character of the revolution to date: but the advance towards a socialist transition can be carried out only through major social conflicts, which would, inevitably, find their reflection within the state apparatus, military as well as civilian. The dangers of reforms imposed from above, without recognition of the social limits of such policies, have been dramatically illustrated by the case of Afghanistan in the latter half of the 1970s.²

The international alignments of the new regime appear, at first sight, favourable to an attempted transition to socialism. Yet, in a number of respects, this is a more complex matter than might appear. First, the type of social order being encouraged by the USSR, and which enthusiasm for the Soviet model would induce the Ethiopian leadership to follow, cannot be accepted as a full model of socialism, in the combined political-economic sense identified above. At best, it would involve creating in Ethiopia a society exhibiting some of the features of socialism. It would have the economic features of that mode of production, but would also exhibit political deformations, denying appropriate freedoms to both the working class and the peasantry, and to the nationalities. Even this outcome, however, will encounter serious difficulties. Such a process involves a major transformation of economic and social structures in Ethiopia, which can only be achieved with substantial economic aid from abroad. Yet aid of this kind is simply not available from the USSR and its allies, who have over the years found it increasingly difficult to meet their Third World allies' requests for economic support. Both classical Marxist theory concerning states leaping over the capitalist stage, and current Soviet theories of such a path of development, stress the essential character of external aid, as also does orthodox development economics. It is a precondition which, in Ethiopia as in most of the rest of the Third World, the Soviet Union and its allies are not in a position adequately to fulfil. Ethiopia could, certainly, turn to the West and to multilateral agencies for economic assistance, and there is no reason, in principle, why this should be accompanied by a distortion of its socio-economic programme. Indeed there is evidence to suggest that in Ethiopia,

---

² Since so much of the literature on 'socialist' regimes in the Third World has been concerned, often rightly, with criticizing these regimes for being less socialist than they claim, it is important to register the other problem – of regimes that try to accelerate the process of the transition to socialism and in doing so pay too little heed to the reality of precapitalist and capitalist social relations persisting within them. A critique of the record of Egypt or Iraq should not obscure the mistakes such as arbitrarily imposed land reform committed in Afghanistan in 1978–79.

Conclusions: A State of Socialist Orientation? 273

as elsewhere, the USSR has encouraged an allied government in the Third World to supplement its income by seeking aid from these quarters.³ But such an option will strengthen the political influence of forces within Ethiopia, in both state and society, who favour a capitalist path of development. Such a tendency will be strengthened, if it is also accompanied by corresponding changes in the international political sphere, namely a shift of Ethiopian foreign policy away from its close alliance with the USSR. The reasons for this alliance, detailed in chapter 6, owe much to temporary factors, to the particular military needs of the Ethiopian state: were such needs to be lessened, by an improvement of its relations with its neighbours and a lessening of conflict in Eritrea, then the possibility of a more autonomous foreign policy would certainly arise. The examples of Somalia and Egypt, both of which turned to the West for foreign policy reasons, are pertinent. The underlying current of nationalism among Ethiopian state personnel, combined with a tendency to blame the Eastern European countries for some of the problems experienced by post-revolutionary Ethiopia, might lead to a new diplomatic opening to the West. Whilst distinct from and in some degree autonomous of changes in internal policies, such a shift would, like a greater economic availability of Western economic support, nonetheless assist a less radical (that is, capitalist) evolution inside Ethiopian society.

The nature of Ethiopia's post-revolutionary social system is increasingly seen within the country in terms of the theory advanced by Soviet writers of the 'non-capitalist path of development'. Originally formulated in the mid-1950s, this concept was designed to identify a group of countries not yet

---

[3] The conventional anti-imperialist assumption that all forms of economic contact with the capitalist world are to be avoided is both unrealistic and naive: unrealistic because trade and aid from these countries is necessary for economic growth in the Third World, given the limits of support from other quarters, and naive because it assumes that all forms of contact must inevitably undermine the economies involved. Provided the terms of trading and aid are governed by the Third World country, such contacts can be beneficial and need not involve a restoration of capitalism. Hence Angola's sale of oil to the West, or Cuba's attempts to diversify its international trade, can be seen as strengthening, not weakening, the post-revolutionary systems in these countries. The converse view, that nationalization of foreign property itself breaks capitalist domination is equally false: in both cases, the key question is the nature of social relations within the country.

in transition to socialism, but which were considered to be laying the basis for such a transition. In the face of considerable theoretical criticism, and in the face of quite a number of cases where such states moved away from policies that were even verbally 'socialist', Soviet theorists have produced a later, more refined version, the theory of 'states of socialist orientation'. A survey of Soviet literature in the late 1970s suggests that there were nineteen countries in the world falling into this category, among them Ethiopia.[4] Ethiopia therefore provides an illustration of this theory of 'non-capitalist development', whilst analysis of the theory may provide some insight into the direction of post-revolutionary change in that country.[5]

Although drawing upon certain earlier themes in Marxist thought, the concept of the 'non-capitalist road' was first elaborated in coordination with a shift in Soviet policy in the mid-1950s, away from neglect of the Third World and towards a positive evaluation of some nationalist regimes in Africa and Asia which were marked by a strong state control of the economy and opposition to Western policies. A clear statement of the theory is contained in the Declaration of the 1960 Conference of Communist Parties: 'After winning political independence, the peoples seek solutions to the social problems raised by life and to the problems of reinforcing national independence. Different classes and parties offer different solutions. Which course of development to choose is the internal affair of the peoples themselves. As social contradictions grow, the national bourgeoisie inclines more and more to compromising with domestic

[4] These were: Ethiopia, Guinea, Benin, Malagasy, Congo, Tanzania, Angola, Mozambique, Guinea-Bissau, Cape Verde, São Tome, Algeria, Syria, South Yemen, Libya, Afghanistan, Burma, Nicaragua, Grenada.

[5] Analysis of this school is given by Joe Slovo in 'A Critical Appraisal of the Non-Capitalist Path and the National Democratic State in Africa', *Marxism Today*, June 1974; Karen Pfeifer 'State Capitalism and Development', MERIP no. 78, June 1979, and Marina Ottaway, 'Soviet Marxism and African Socialism', *Journal of Modern African Studies*, vol. 16, September 1978. Elaborations of the Soviet theory can be found in K.N. Brutents, *National Liberation Revolutions Today*, 2 vols, Moscow 1977, and I. Andreyev, *The Non-Capitalist Way, Soviet Experience and the Liberated Countries*, Moscow 1977. For historical background to the emergence of this theory see Hélène Carrère d'Encausse and Stuart Schram, *Marxism and Asia*, London 1969.

reaction and imperialism. The people, however, begin to see that the best way to abolish age-long backwardness and improve their living standards is that of non-capitalist development. Only thus can the peoples free themselves from exploitation, poverty and hunger. The working class and the broad peasant masses will play the leading part in solving this basic social problem'.[6] On the foundations of this assertion, that there existed a non-revolutionary path to socialism, the Soviet Union gave support to a variety of regimes in the Third World, the most prominent among them being Egypt.

The difficulties involved in showing how such 'non-capitalist' regimes would begin to make the transition to socialism, combined with the political disappointments that the USSR experienced in its relations with such countries, had led by the mid-1970s to a new theory, that of the 'states of socialist orientation'. This theory was much more explicit about the non-socialist features of the societies in question: it stressed the disconnection of state and society, and the retarding potential of the latter on any group within the state committed to a socialist transition; whereas the earlier theory had expressed the view that the people themselves would urge the 'non-capitalist' path, this later formulation emphasized that the masses were not capable of exercising full power, and called for a greater stress on education as a precondition for popular decision-taking. Military officers as well as progressive civilians were now seen as capable of playing a vanguard role in such situations. Where earlier theories had stressed the need for correct class composition in the formation of the new parties, the new theory laid at least equal stress on the need to rid the party of tribal and personal factors that might continue to dominate it. Earlier theories had not given so much attention to possible forms of reversal of the 'non-capitalist' course, apart from predictable allusions to imperialist intervention and counter-revolutionary action. The later theories did take the possibility of reversal more seriously, attributing such reversals to a much wider range of factors including the process of class formation under statist regimes. Indeed, by the late 1970s, there had emerged a much more sober

[6] G.F. Hudon and others, *The Sino–Soviet Dispute*, London 1961, p. 194.

evaluation of the possibilities for socialist transition in the Third World. Far from resting on an undisputed orthodoxy, Soviet discussion of these Third World states reflected differing theoretical and political evaluations of the latter. Some writers drew attention to the possibilities of private accumulation open to office-holders in Third World statist regimes. Others underlined the ideological confusions inherent in such doctrines as 'Arab nationalism'. Others again stressed the need for the USSR to seek military access in the Third World, rather than place its hope in some more profound and permanent socio-economic transformation. Soviet theory on these 'states of socialist orientation' may have reflected overriding strategic considerations: but this did not preclude an element of diversity about how best to secure Soviet state interests, and a growing realism about the restricted possibilities of such 'non-capitalist' states' embarking upon a transition to socialism.[7]

That possibility nonetheless existed, and there were some positive instances to point to. The first Third World state to embark upon a 'non-capitalist' path after its revolution in 1921, namely Mongolia, did later proceed to a transition to socialism. The first Latin American state to begin this 'non-capitalist' process, namely Cuba, also did so: both instances showed that, under certain conditions, social revolutions not led by communists could develop into processes where the state encouraged a transition to socialism. Marx's own writings discussed the possibility of such a transition in societies that had not undergone the full process of capitalist development, and the theory of the 'non-capitalist road' built on these early speculations. The theory was also justified in the way it sought to differentiate between various forms of Third World nationalist regime and to identify a group whose internal and foreign policies were distinct from those of conventional capitalist states. Thus Algeria is not Morocco, Tanzania is not Kenya, South Yemen is not Oman, Burma is not Thailand: the level of state intervention in the economy, the implementation of land reform, the degree of inequality

---

[7] Sylvia W. Edgington, '"The State of Socialist Orientation" as Soviet Developmental Politics', *Soviet Union, Union Soviétique*, autumn 1981; V. Chirkin and Y. Yudin, *A Socialist Oriented State*, Moscow 1978.

Conclusions: A State of Socialist Orientation? 277

of distribution of goods and services, the extent of foreign capital's control of the economy – all differ radically from one group to the other. These may not, however, be socialist-oriented states, only comparatively more progressive capitalist ones: the same variety that exists within the advanced capitalist countries between, say, a Sweden and a USA may also exist in the developing capitalist world.

The theory of 'states of socialist orientation' identifies a set of tendencies which are said to be laying the basis for a transition to socialism in these states. 'They are countries which, while not yet socialist, reject capitalism as the system for their further social development and regard socialism as their goal'. Among these defining tendencies are: 'liberation from capitalist monopoly domination and the achievement of tangible economic independence; the abolition of the exploitation of man by man, the creation of public ownership and the creation of conditions which exclude the taking over of positions in the economic and social spheres by capitalist elements; the promotion and expansion of the state sector in the economy on an anti-capitalist basis, the subordination of various existing modes to the development of the leading mode of a socialist nature, and the creation of social and economic conditions for its triumph; agrarian reforms carried out in the interests of the broad sections of the peasants and a cooperative movement launched on democratic principles; a democratized state machine, the involvement of representatives of the working people in government, and the granting of genuinely democratic rights and freedoms to the peoples; the establishment of a vanguard party of scientific socialism; a cultural revolution, the abolition of illiteracy, progress in public education, the moulding of the new man of the socialist future, and the total abolition of the remnants of tribalism'.[8] The theory does not, however, ascribe such advances uniquely to the internal workings of such societies; rather it stresses that 'the main and decisive condition for the success-

---

[8] Anatoly Dinkevich, 'Principles and Problems of Socialist Orientation in the Countries of Africa and Asia', *Soviet News*, October 16, 1979. For an example of Soviet writing on Ethiopia as an exemplar of this development path see M. Barinov, 'Socialist Ethiopia Moves Confidently Ahead', *International Affairs*, Moscow, no. 11, 1980.

ful development of these countries is the fundamental change in the world balance of forces in favour of socialism'. However, even in its later, more realistic and conditional form, this theory raises a number of difficulties. While it points to a number of tendencies developing in these societies, it avoids the important issue of how these will yield a process of socialist transition. However 'autonomous' the state may be, it exists within constraints imposed by the social and political structures of these countries. Hence a process of socialist transition must encounter opposition stemming from the interests embodied in the class structures of the 'socialist orientation' phase. These theories play down any mention of class struggle: yet far from a smooth progression being possible, there will be sharp conflicts between those forces favouring and those opposed to a socialist transition, with inevitable international involvement in the resistance of the social groups threatened with dispossession. Apart from the resistance of such pre-existing classes, the 'non-capitalist' process has its own social consequences, which may themselves result in the formation of a new possessing class. In other words, the 'non-capitalist' programme, with its emphasis upon state control and expropriation of foreign capital, could prepare the ground not for a socialist transition, but for a strengthened capitalist system. The practical effects of state policies rarely amount to securing the conditions for a transition to socialism. What such policies achieve is instead a dismantling of the pre-capitalist social order and the establishment of new social relations, involving a combination of different forms of social system. Whether capitalist, or socialist or hybrid relations prevail, depends on a variety of factors, already summarized under three general headings: the conflict within the state, the balance of class forces in the society, and the international conjuncture. In most countries that have undergone this process, the result has been the forging of a new social order in which capitalist social relations are at least as important as socialist ones. In the aftermath of land reform, a class of small farmers generally emerges, whilst a burgeoning class of traders flourishes in the urban sector. They interlock with the upper sections of the civil service, who enjoy possibilities for private accumulation

Conclusions: A State of Socialist Orientation? 279

through their privileged position in the state apparatus. The mere fact of nationalization of large sectors of industry and finance does not preclude this development in the longer run. Whilst forming part of any genuine process of socialization, such measures do not constitute sufficient conditions for the establishment of socialist relations of production. They can, on the contrary, secure the conditions for the development of national capitalism.

This is, indeed, the empirical pattern seen in a number of countries hailed at one time or other as exemplars of the 'non-capitalist' road. In some of these countries the regimes were overthrown, by coups, and replaced by more overtly pro-Western ones (Indonesia 1965, Ghana 1966, Mali 1968). Such setbacks certainly pose a difficulty for the theory; they cast doubt on the degree of popular support enjoyed by the statist regimes and on the supposed weakness of conservative classes. But the major challenge arises in the case of those countries where no such break in political continuity has occurred, but rather a change in orientation by governments continuous with those previously categorized as pursuing the 'non-capitalist' path. The cases of Egypt, Iraq and, in the area of the Horn, Somalia and the Sudan, fall into this category. Here the apparently 'non-capitalist' path of development concealed a process of class formation that laid the basis for a new acceptance of capitalism, with the necessary changes in internal social structure and international alignment. Other areas of the theory are also problematic, as can be seen by reference to the Ethiopian case. The claim of the 'socialist orientation' theory is that in societies such as Ethiopia the state machine and political life are being democratized. Certainly, the range of recruitment to leadership positions widens in such regimes, and considerable efforts are made to mobilize popular support. The great emphasis on literacy campaigns is motivated in part by this concern to bring the masses into political life.[9] It is also true that the social policies implemented by such regimes tend to bring benefits to the mass of the population that free-market capitalist regimes

---

[9] Soviet and Ethiopian writers frequently cite Lenin's observation that 'an illiterate person is outside politics'.

generally do not: the assault on illiteracy, ill health, bad housing is carried out with some determination. In the sense of objectively benefiting the population, the new state machine is in varying degrees democratic, and some Soviet writers specify that this is what they mean.[10] But if 'democratic' is understood to involve an element of mass control over political decisions and a degree of freedom even for those not committed to the revolutionary process then the term is not applicable. This absence of political controls from below may correspond to the logic of 'revolution from above' and to what are perceived as being the imperatives of transformation in societies as tumultuous as Ethiopia. But they involve the risk that those exempted from political control will impose changes that alienate the social support required for their success, and will take advantage of their exemption to acquire social privileges and possibilities for accumulation which will lead to the formation of a new possessing class.

This centralist tendency can be seen in three particular respects – the party, the nationality question, and policy on women. The emphasis in recent Soviet writing upon the autonomy of the state has gone together with increased emphasis on the central role of the revolutionary or vanguard party in leading these states to the socialist transition. The implication is that the existence of a determined and ideologically sound vanguard is a decisive factor in deciding the fate of the 'non-capitalist' states. Ideologically hybrid entities of the 'Arab Socialist' variety, as seen in Egypt or Iraq, are unable to complete this process. Whatever the precise development of COPWE, it will be seen as the main instrument for ensuring that Ethiopia does attempt a socialist transition, and it is for this reason that the Soviet Union persisted in

[10] 'In the countries of socialist orientation, the ruling revolutionary-democratic parties, and the state power carry out radical social reforms which are consonant with the interests of the overwhelming majority of the population, the working people. That, and not the number of parties or election procedures, is the yardstick of genuine social democracy. Of course, in the conditions of a revolutionary regime, of sharp class struggle, some aspects of political democracy are restricted. The revolution must be able to defend itself. But, as the resistance of reaction is suppressed, political democracy develops and broadens'. Veniamin Chirkin, '"Political Modernization" or Social Orientation of the Developing Countries?', in *Political Systems: Development Trends*, Proceedings of the XIth World Congress of Political Scientists, p. 189.

Conclusions: A State of Socialist Orientation? 281

encouraging its establishment for so long. Yet the dangers of over-emphasizing the vanguard are evident: the imposition of socialist programmes upon a peasantry that will not produce, or at least part with its surplus produce, and upon a working class that will not work, can only alienate the population. It will lead to the frustration of plans for transformation and to the discrediting of the goal of socialism. The question of the nationalities is similar in kind: orthodox theories of the 'socialist orientation' programme tend to understate the importance of this in the Third World. Yet, in terms of its place in the minds of the populations of these countries, and in terms of the obstacles that such conflicts can place in the way of a post-revolutionary consolidation, nationality issues may play a role at least as great as class struggles, or problems associated with the end of foreign domination. A revolutionary Third World state that proved able to solve this problem in a voluntary manner, consistent with the maintenance of its own territorial unity, would set an important example. Although it invokes the example of the USSR, Soviet writing on nationalities tends to adopt a policy that is in fact different, defending the unity of Third World states without any concession to the principle of secession, and advocating what is in reality a multinational solution within existing post-colonial boundaries. We have argued that this policy comes not from Lenin, from whom Soviet theories of nationality normally derive, but from the Austro-Marxist currents associated with Otto Bauer. Although just in its emphasis upon the dangers of fragmentation, it is another case of how a supposedly 'democratic' and 'class-based' policy can involve a new centralization that overrides the consent of the population concerned.[11]

A similar elision of class with non-class factors can be seen in the case of women. Like the nationalities, they occupy only a marginal place in theories of 'socialist orientation' and yet are handled by reference to a body of theory and practice derived from the USSR. In Ethiopia, the imposition of orthodox Soviet theory on this issue has involved a distinct ideological retreat from the earlier positions, which did

---

[11] Georgi Galperin, 'Ethiopia: Some Aspects of the Nationalities Question', *Asia and Africa To-Day*, November–December 1979, and chapter 5 above.

recognize that women were oppressed by factors other than class – by male domination. The mobilization of women in the organizations of the Ethiopian state will henceforward be based not on an elaboration of this theory, but on the much more limited and reductionist account of women's emancipation embodied in Soviet writings.

The third empirical challenge engages the theory's emphasis on the positive role to be played by the USSR in encouraging these 'non-capitalist' states. One of the preconditions identified by Marx himself for by-passing capitalist development was that the transition to socialism in such countries be assisted by a victorious proletariat in more developed societies.[12] Thus the USSR's ability to provide Third World states with economic assistance and the military wherewithal to defend themselves against attack, can assist these states to continue a transition to socialism. But the reality is less persuasive. First, the provision of Soviet aid has been determined primarily by the given country's foreign policy – its stance in East–West relations – not by its level of socio-economic transformation; its internal policies are treated with as much indulgence as the facts will allow, once such an international correspondence has been established. Soviet aid to countries like India and Turkey has assisted the consolidation of overtly capitalist regimes; and aid to the Afghan monarchs in the 1950s and 1960s permitted the survival of a pre-capitalist monarchy. Aid to countries like Egypt, Iraq and Somalia, whilst justified on the grounds that they were 'non-capitalist', depended in practice upon the international positions adopted by these comparatively progressive capitalist states. It was not conditional upon, nor did it contribute to, a transition to socialism. Second, while the ability of the USSR to provide military aid to Third World states has developed greatly in the 1960s and 1970s, its capacity to provide economic assistance is far weaker, and is still no match for the West: both in quantity and in quality, Soviet aid is far inferior to that of the USA and its allies, just as Soviet consumer goods exert a minimal attraction in the Third World, compared with those from the advanced capitalist countries. If the ability of the USSR to provide a real

[12] See Slovo, for the discussion of this.

Conclusions: A State of Socialist Orientation? 283

alternative to the capitalist world is '*the main and decisive condition for the successful development*' of the non-capitalist countries,[13] then economically this condition is a long way from being met. In terms of economic competition and assistance in the Third World, the balance of forces is still in favour of the advanced capitalist countries, now assisted by the rise of new capitalist financial or industrial powers in the Third World itself.[14]

The cases of successful progress towards a socialist transition underline the peculiarity of the conditions in which this can take place. In Mongolia and Cuba, the indigenous ruling classes had been severely shaken by the initial revolutionary processes and discredited by their association with foreign powers – the Tsarists and imperial China in the one case, the USA in the other. The revolutionary movements that emerged were operating in relatively small and ethnically homogeneous societies, not riven by the nationality and tribal problems of so much of the Third World. The USSR was also able to provide a level of development assistance that transformed the internal possibilities for social and economic growth – a level, however, that it cannot provide to order, in a generalized policy. The radical nationalist forces who came to power saw that their only hope lay in transforming their own society and in adopting the international alignments they did. Ethiopia has certain major advantages in attempting to pursue such a path, but the forces acting against this, both inherited from the old order and promoted by the new, are also substantial. Asia and America have already yielded one example of the progress from 'socialist orientation' to 'socialist transition'. It remains to be seen whether Africa's first major social revolution will follow a similar path.

---

[13] Dinkevich, p. 337 (our italics).
[14] The limits on Soviet development aid arise from several factors. These include: the lack of hard-currency foreign exchange; the overall constraints on Soviet action arising from the shortage of funds within the Soviet economy; Soviet weaknesses in key areas of development technology, especially those related to agriculture; the unpopularity of foreign aid with a Soviet population itself exposed to consumer shortages; political refusal to take responsibility for what are seen as the consequences of capitalist imperialism; a distrust of the Third World regimes in question. Growing Soviet scepticism about the possibilities of sustained progressive development in the Third World, beyond an initial burst of 'anti-imperialist' militancy, is discussed in Jerry F. Hough, *Soviet Leadership in Transition*, Washington 1980 pp. 164–6.

Abbreviations

AALC	African–American Labor Centre
AEPA	All-Ethiopian Peasant Association
AETU	All-Ethiopian Trade Unions
AFL-CIO	American Federation of Labor–Congress of Industrial Organization
ANLM	Afar National Liberation Movement
CDSP	Current Digest of the Soviet Press
CELU	Confederation of Ethiopian Labour Unions
CIA	Central Intelligence Agency
COPWE	Commission for Organizing the Party of the Working People of Ethiopia
ECHA'AT	Oppressed People's Party of Ethiopia (in Amharinya)
EDU	Ethiopian Democratic Union
ELF	Eritrean Liberation Front
ELF–PLF	Eritrean Liberation Front–Popular Liberation Front
EMALEDH	Union of Marxist–Leninist Organizations (in Amharinya)
ENLF	Ethiopian National Liberation Front
EPLF	Eritrean People's Liberation Forces (1971–6) Eritrean People's Liberation Front (1976–)
EPRA	Ethiopian People's Revolutionary Army
EPRP	Ethiopian People's Revolutionary Party
ESUE	Ethiopian Students' Union in Europe
ESUNA	Ethiopian Students' Union in North America
ICFTU	International Confederation of Free Trade Unions

Abbreviations

MALERED	Marxist–Leninist Organization of Ethiopia (in Amharinya)
ME'ISON	Mela Etiopia Socialist Netanake (All-Ethiopia Socialist Movement)
NDR	National Democratic Revolution Programme of 1976
NSC	National Security Commission
OAU	Organization of African Unity
OPEC	Organization of Petroleum Exporting Countries
OLF	Oromo Liberation Front
PCI	Partito Comunista Italiano
PDRY	People's Democratic Republic of Yemen
PLO	Palestine Liberation Organization
PMAC	Provisional Military Administrative Council (the Derg)
POMOA	Provisional Office for Mass Organization Affairs
REWA	Revolutionary Ethiopian Women's Association
SALF	Somali–Abo Liberation Front
TLF	Tigray Liberation Front
TPLF	Tigrean People's Liberation Front
WSLF	Western Somali Liberation Front

Short Bibliography

(a) Books and Articles

Abir, Mordechai, *Oil, Power and Politics: Conflict in Arabia, the Red Sea and the Gulf*, London 1974
Addis Hiwet, *From Autocracy to Revolution*, London 1975
—, *From Autocracy to Bourgeois Dictatorship*, 1976
—, *The Nationalities Question in Ethiopia and the Horn*, 1978
All-Ethiopian Socialist Movement (ME'ISON), *Programme*, n.d.
Alula Abate and Tesfaye Teklu, 'Land Reform and Peasant Associations in Ethiopia', *Northeast African Studies*, vol. 2, no. 2, Fall 1980
Amnesty International, *Human Rights Violations in Ethiopia*, London 1977
Bartnicki, Andrzej and Mantel-Niećko, Joanna, *Geschichte Äthiopens*, 2 vols, Berlin 1978
Baxter, P.T.W., 'Ethiopia's Unacknowledged Problem: The Oromo', *African Affairs*, vol. 77, no. 308, July 1978
Bereket Habte Selassie, *Conflict and Intervention in the Horn of Africa*, New York 1980
Cao-Huy-Thuan, Alain Fenet and Tran-Van-Minh, *La question de l'Érythrée*, Paris 1979
Chaliand, Gérard, 'The Horn of Africa's Dilemma', *Foreign Policy*, no. 30, Spring 1978
Cliffe, Lionel, Basil Davidson and Bereket Habte Selassie, *Behind the War in Eritrea*, Nottingham 1980
Crummey, Donald and C. Stewart, *Modes of Production in Africa*, London 1981

Darch, Colin, *A Soviet View of Africa, an Annotated Bibliography on Ethiopia, Somalia and Djibouti*, Boston 1980
Davidson, Basil, 'Notes on the Revolution in Somalia', *Socialist Register 1975*
Decraene, Philippe, *L'Expérience socialiste somalienne*, Paris 1977
Eritrean Liberation Front, *Political Programme*, Beirut 1977
Eritrean People's Liberation Front, *National Democratic Programme*, n.d.
Ethiopian People's Revolutionary Party, *Political Programme*, 1975
Ethiopian Revolutionary Information Centre, *Ethiopia in Revolution*, Addis Ababa 1977
—, *The Ethiopian Revolution and the Problem in Eritrea*, Addis Ababa 1977
Farer, Tom, *War Clouds on the Horn of Africa: The Widening Storm*, Washington 1979
Gadaa Melbaa, *Oromia, A Brief Introduction*, 'Finfine' 1980
Gilkes, Patrick, *The Dying Lion*, London 1975
—, 'The Nationalities Policy of the PMAC' *in* Lewis, ed. (see below)
Jones, A. and Elizabeth Monroe, *A History of Ethiopia*, Oxford 1978
Kaplan, Irving, et al. *Area Handbook for Ethiopia*, Washington 1971
Kraft, Joseph, 'Letter from Addis Ababa', *New Yorker*, July 31, 1978
Lefort, René, *Éthiopie, La révolution hérétique*, Paris 1981
Legesse Lemma, 'The Ethiopian Student Movement 1960–1974', *Northeast African Studies*, vol. 1, no. 2, 1979
Legum, Colin, *Ethiopia: The Fall of Haile Selassie's Empire*, London 1975
—, and Bill Lee, *Conflict in the Horn of Africa*, London 1977
—, and Bill Lee, *The Horn of Africa in Continuing Crisis*, London 1979
Levine, Donald, *Greater Ethiopia, The Evolution of a Multiethnic Society*, London 1974
Lewis, I.M., *A Modern History of Somalia*, London 1980
—, *Somalia Culture, History and Social Institutions*, London 1981

—, ed., *National Self-Determination in the Horn of Africa*, London 1982
Markakis, John, *Ethiopia: Anatomy of a Traditional Polity*, Oxford 1974
—, 'Garrison Socialism in Ethiopia', *MERIP Reports*, no. 79, July 1979
—, and Nega Ayele, *Class and Revolution in Ethiopia*, Nottingham 1978
Mengistu Haile-Mariam, *Report Delivered to the First Congress of COPWE*, Addis Ababa, 1980
—, *On the Acts of Aggression Committed Against Ethiopia Through Foreign Intervention*, Addis Ababa 1977
—, *The National Revolutionary War in the North*, Addis Ababa 1978
Molyneux, Maxine, 'Algunos Problemas en el Análisis de la Revolución Etíope', *Estudios de Asia y Africa*, Vol. XIV, No. 3.
Nadel, S.F., *Races and Tribes of Eritrea*, Asmara 1944
Nwafor, Azinna, 'Revolution and Socialism in Ethiopia', *Omenana*, vol. 2, nos. 1–2, Winter–Summer 1980
Ottaway, David and Marina, *Ethiopia, Empire in Revolution*, New York 1978
Pajetta, Gian Carlo, 'Interview on Ethiopia and Somalia', *New Left Review*, 107, January–February 1978
Perham, Marjory, *The Government of Ethiopia*, Evanston 1969
Pestalozza, Luigi, *The Somali Revolution*, Paris 1974
Pliny The Middle-Aged, 'The PMAC: Origins and Structure', Part One, *Ethiopianist Notes*, vol. 2, no. 3, 1978; Part Two *Northeast African Studies*, vol. 1, no. 1, 1978
—, 'Eclectic Notes on the Eritrean Liberation Movement: E Pluribus Unum?', *Ethiopianist Notes*, vol. 2, no. 1, 1978
Pool, David, *Eritrea, Africa's Longest War*, London 1979
Provisional Military Administrative Council, *Basic Documents of the Ethiopian Revolution*, Addis Ababa May 1977
—, *Ten Year Investment Programme 1980/81–1989/90*, Addis Ababa 1981
Rubenson, Sven, *The Survival of Ethiopian Independence*, London 1976
Sabbe, Othman Saleh, *The History of Eritrea*, Beirut n.d.

Saint-Veran, Robert, *A Djibouti, avec les Afars et les Issas*, Cagnes sur Mer 1977
Senay Likke, *The Ethiopian Revolution: Tasks, Achievements, Problems and Prospects*, n.d.
Sherman, Richard, *Eritrea, The Unfinished Revolution*, New York 1980
Thomson, Blair, *Ethiopia, The Country That Cut Off its Head*, London 1975
Trevaskis, Kennedy, *Eritrea, A Colony in Transition*, London 1960
Ullendorf, Edward, *The Ethiopians*, London 1973
US Congress, House of Representatives, Committee on International Relations, *War in the Horn of Africa: A First-hand Report on the Challenges for United States Policy*, Washington 1978
—, *United States Arms Policies in the Persian Gulf and Red Sea Areas: Past, Present and Future*, Washington 1977
US Congress, Senate, Committee on Foreign Relations, *Ethiopia and the Horn of Africa*, Washington 1976
Valdelin, Jan, 'Ethiopia 1974–7: From Anti-Feudal Revolution to Consolidation of the Bourgeois State', *Race and Class*, vol. 19, no. 4, Spring 1978.
Vivó, Raul Valdes, *Ethiopia: The Unknown Revolution*, Havana 1978
Yodfat, Aryeh, 'The Soviet Union and the Horn of Africa' (three parts), *Northeast African Studies*, vol. 1, no. 3, Winter 1979–80, vol. 2, no. 1, 1980, vol. 2, no. 2, 1980.

(b) Journals and Newspapers

Abyot (EPRP)
Africa Confidential (London)
Altrafrica (Rome)
Challenge (Journal of the Ethiopian Students Association in North America)
Combat (Journal of the Ethiopian Students Union in North America)
Eritrea Information (Rome, EPLF)
Eritrea Newsletter (Beirut, ELF)

Eritrea Review (Beirut, ELF–PLF)
Ethiopian Herald (Addis Ababa)
Ethiopian Marxist Review (EPRP)
Forward (World-wide Federation of Ethiopian Students, pro-EPRP)
Horn of Africa (Summit, New Jersey)
International Affairs (Moscow)
Le Monde (Paris)
MERIP Reports (Washington)
Meskerem (Addis Ababa, COPWE Journal)
Modern African Studies (Cambridge, England)
New Times (Moscow)
Northeast African Studies (East Lansing, Michigan)
Peking Review
Review of African Political Economy (London)
Vanguard (Rome, EPLF)
Voice of the Masses (ME'ISON)

Maps

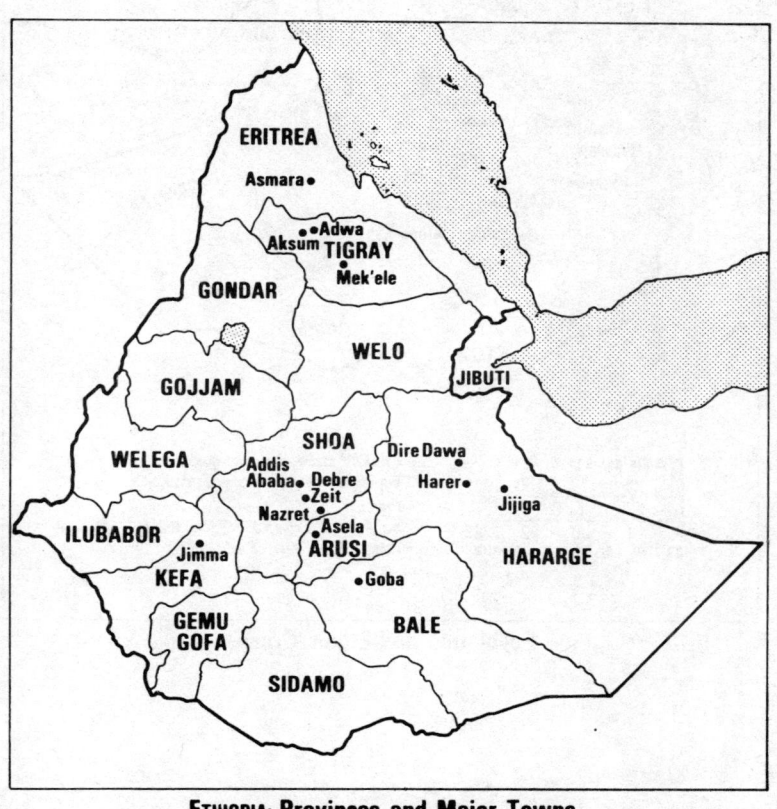

ETHIOPIA: Provinces and Major Towns

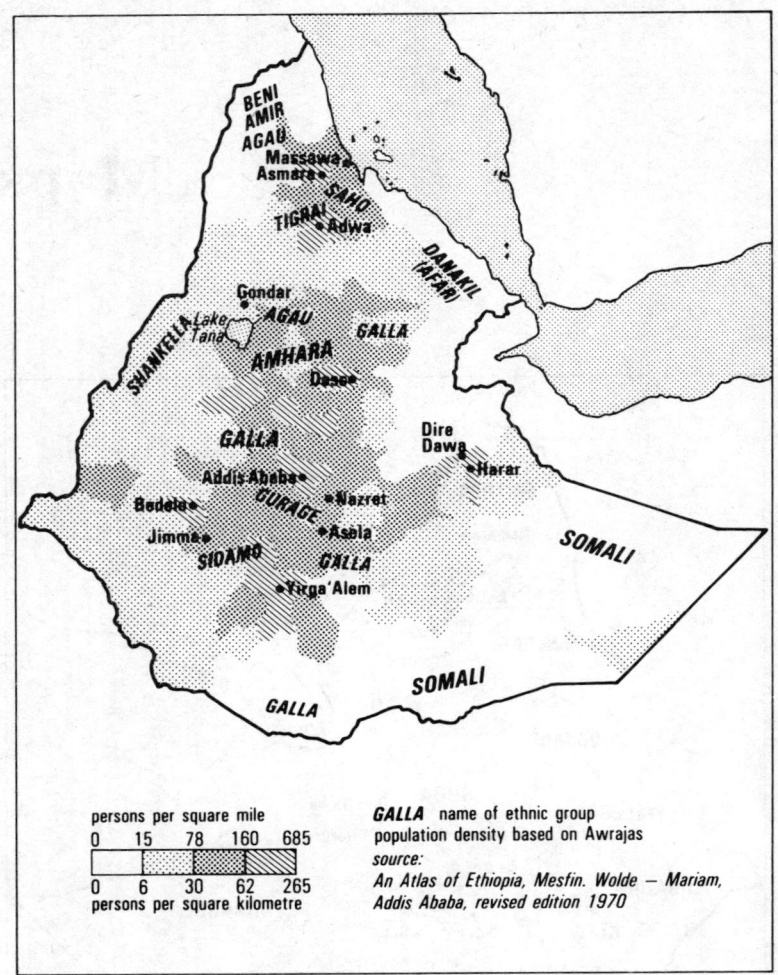

Population and Ethnic Groups

Map 293

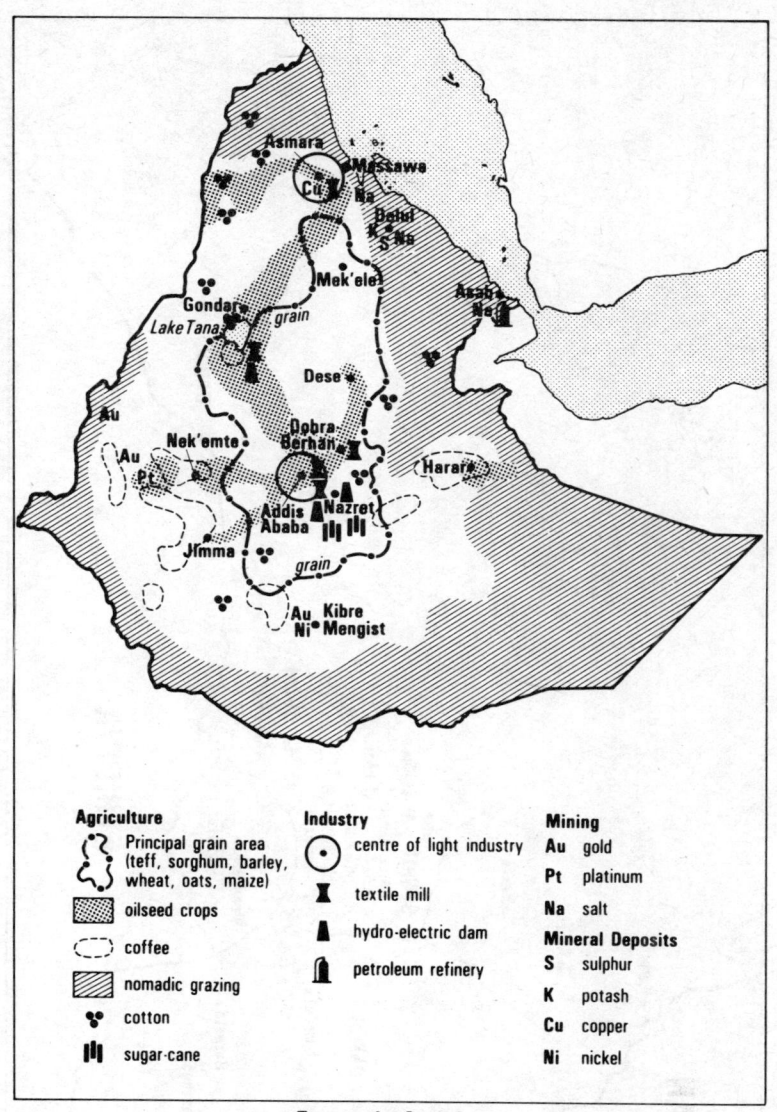

Economic Activity

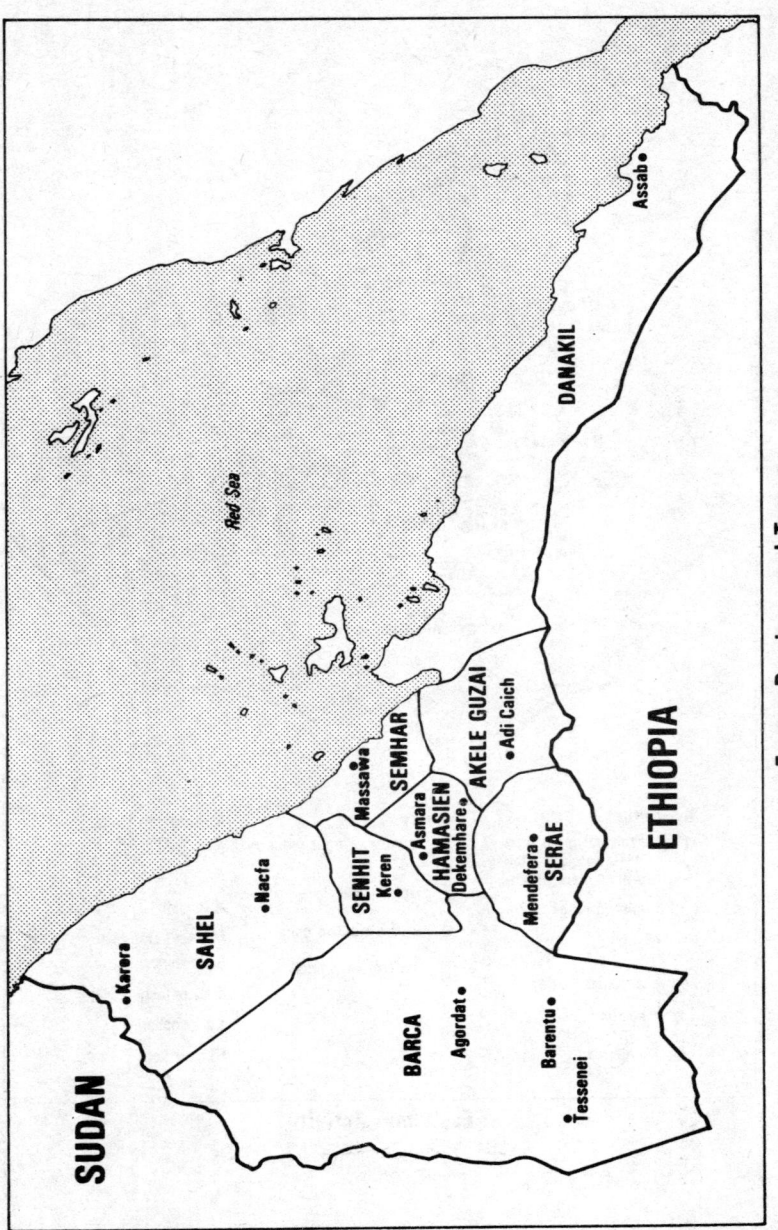

ERITREA: Provinces and Towns

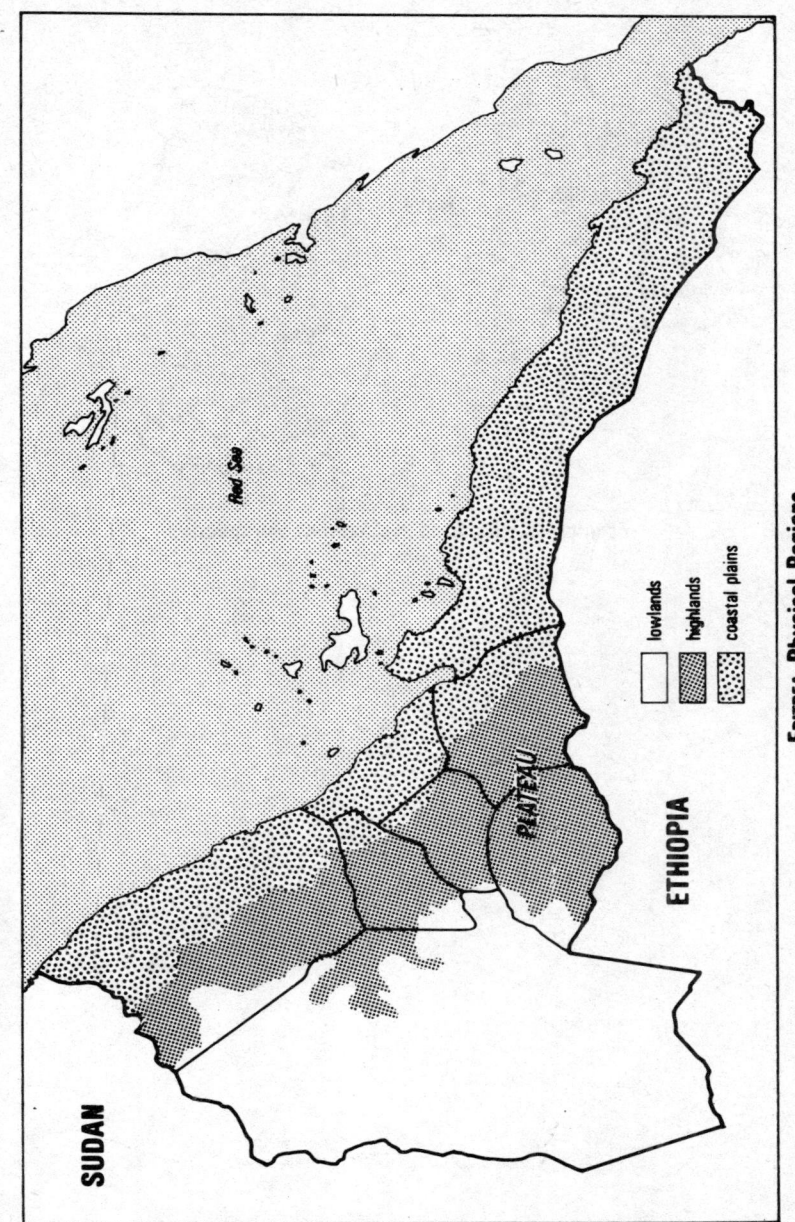

Eritrea: Physical Regions

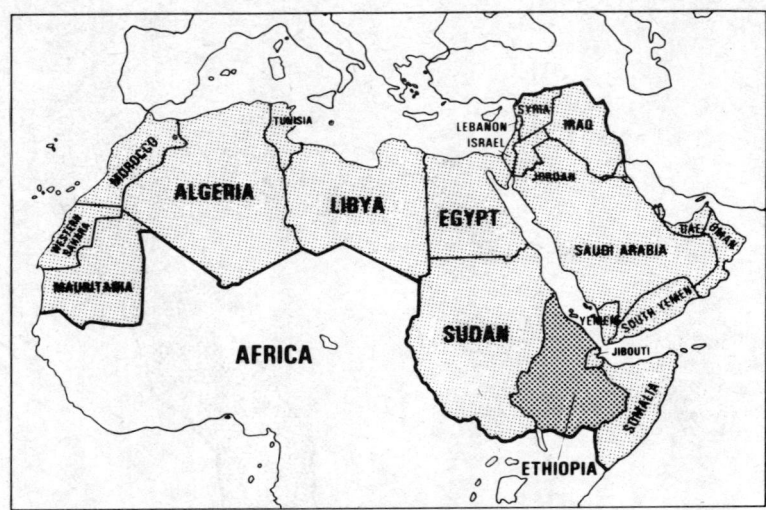

Ethiopia in the Arab Nationalist Perspective

Index

Abbe Youlou, 33
Abdul Fatah Ismail, 235
Abdullahi Ahmad, 227
Abyotawit Etiopia Waim Maut, 153
Abyotawit Seded, 129, 130, 131
Addis Ababa, 29, 47, 48, 55, 63, 65, 66, 67, 68, 71, 76, 77, 78, 80, 83, 84, 85, 86, 89, 92, 94, 110, 119, 120, 121, 123, 124, 128, 132, 137, 140, 150, 156, 159, 179, 191, 193, 196, 203, 214, 216, 218, 223, 226, 232, 233, 236, 247, 253, 256, 257, 261, 266
Addis Tedlay, 118
Aden, 235, 245
Adola, 67
Adowa, 56, 57, 238
Afars, 105, 164, 165, 168
Afar Liberation Front, 195
Afar National Liberation Movement, 195
Afghanistan, 19, 20, 21, 23, 24, 30, 33, 34, 39, 41, 54, 56, 139, 229, 264, 265, 272, 282
Africa, 19, 24, 41, 50, 61, 69, 70, 103, 139, 147, 148, 175, 181, 212, 213, 214, 215, 216, 217, 221, 232, 240, 247, 250, 256, 257, 260, 262, 266, 267, 274, 283
African-American Labour Centre, 82
African Communist, 261
Age of the Princes, 174
Agordat, 184
Agricultural and Industrial Development Bank, 73
Ahmad Mohammad Nasser, 184
Akele Guzai, 178, 184

Aklilu Habte Wold, 83, 84, 85, 91
Albania, 126
Alexander the Great, 52
Algeria, 24, 77, 216, 226, 267, 277
Ali Mirah Anfere, 164, 195
Ali Mohammed Said Berhatu, 182
Ali Musa, 115
All-Ethiopian Peasant Association, 144
All-Ethiopian Socialist Movement, 78, 128
All-Ethiopian Trade Union, 121, 143
Alvarez, Francisco, 54
Aman Andom, 88, 93, 113, 160, 172, 220, 222
Amazons, 52
Amhara, 55, 58, 60, 61, 63, 64, 72, 75, 76, 93, 95, 115, 116, 117, 133, 137, 138, 153, 162, 164, 165, 170, 193, 194, 195, 196, 197, 198, 199, 208
Amharinya, 55
Anatolia, 29
Anglo-Ethiopian campaign, 57
Anglo-Ethiopian Treaty of 1897, 200
Angola, 18, 24, 183, 211, 220, 221, 229, 251, 252, 260, 264, 265, 266
Angola-Russian Treaties, 56
Arab World, 44, 46, 47, 49, 61, 118, 124, 133, 139, 158, 159, 163, 165, 180, 181, 183, 184, 186, 187, 188, 189, 190, 192, 204, 208, 212, 213, 214, 219, 222, 223, 224, 228, 231, 232, 233, 235, 236, 237, 245, 248, 253, 260, 261, 267, 270, 270, 277, 280
Arabian Peninsula, 55
Argentina, 223

297

Arlington, 216
Armenians, 68
Arussi, 76, 198
Anya-Aya, 233
Asfa Wossen, 83
Asia, 19, 51, 211, 274, 283
Asmara, 68, 81, 84, 89, 171, 172, 173, 177, 179, 183, 184, 184, 206, 215, 216, 243, 257
Assab, 56, 165, 171, 173, 175, 239
Atatürk, Kemal, 29
Atnafu, 86, 114, 153
Austro-Hungarian Empire, 167
Austro-Marxists, 167, 281
Awash Valley, 66
Axum, 55, 174

Baath parties, 189, 234, 237
Bab al-Mandeb, 220
Baghdad, 184
Baher Negast, 174
Bale, 76, 83, 156, 194, 197, 198, 199
Balkanization, 166
Bangladesh, 166, 204
Barca, 178, 183, 184, 185, 200
Baru Tumsa, 129
Batista, 24
Bauer, Otto, 281
Begemdir, 105
Belgium, 41
Benbela, 253
Beni Amer, 179, 184
Berbera, 224, 227, 241, 258
Berhanu Bayih, 118
Berhanu Salem, 123
Berlin, 77
Biafra, 166
Birhane Meskel Reda, 78, 125
Bloody Saturday, 220
Bolsheviks, 124, 167, 168, 169, 239
Bonker, Don, 230
Bragmans, 52
Brazil, 79, 240
Britain, 41, 43, 49, 56, 57, 65, 75, 76, 80, 137, 175, 176, 199, 200, 201, 215, 229
Brzezinski, Zbigniew, 226, 264
Bulgaria, 241
Burma, 116, 276

Cahill, Kevin, 227, 228
Cairo, 183
Cambodia, 18, 272
Camp David, 234
Canada, 41
Carter, Jimmy, 223, 224, 225, 226, 228, 229, 237, 264, 265
Castro, Fidel, 225, 246, 251, 252, 254, 255, 256, 259
Central Intelligence Agency, 82, 229
Chapin, Frederic, 230, 231
Chile, 33
Chilot, 70
China, 19, 39, 45, 67, 105, 126, 131, 137, 141, 180, 183, 204, 215, 227, 237, 256–264, 269, 283
Chou En-lai, 257
Christianity, 52, 64, 175, 212
Christians, 60, 63, 64, 72, 105, 115, 163, 165, 177, 179, 183, 184, 185, 187, 188, 195, 197, 198, 199, 207
Cold War, 211, 265
Columbo, Emilio, 267
Commission for Organizing the Party of the Working People of Ethiopia, 102, 117, 118, 130, 131, 142, 143, 148, 169, 280
Communist Labor Party, USA, 129
Communist Manifesto (Marx), 60, 138
Communist Party of Great Britain, 263
Communist Party of South Africa, 261
Communist Party of the Soviet Union, 263
Communist Party of Sudan, 127, 261
Confederation of Ethiopian Labour Unions, 81, 87, 91, 92, 101, 119, 120, 121, 121, 124, 143
Conference of Communist Parties, 274
Congo, 33, 80, 265
Congress (US), 221, 222
Ethiopian Democratic Union, 106
Coptic Church, 174, 176, 195, 205
Corsica, 117
Council of Ministers, 115, 116, 118
Cromwell, Oliver, 39
Crown Council, 70
Cuba, 19, 24, 44, 48, 77, 163, 173, 180, 193, 197, 202, 205, 211, 213,

215, 218, 226, 228, 230, 233, 234,
  236, 237, 241, 246, 250–256, 258,
  260, 265, 266, 276, 283
Cyprus, 222

Danakil, 55, 178
Darod, 201
Debre Zeit, 84, 253
Demissie Kassaye, 143
Democrazia, 124
Denikin, Anton, 169
Derg See Provisional Military
  Administrative Council
Diego Garcia, 219, 225
Dien Bien Phu, 56
Dire Dawa, 120
Dogali, 238

East Berlin, 248
East Germany, 130
East Timor, 237
Eastern Europe, 137, 142, 144, 269,
  273
Egypt, 26, 29, 30, 33, 35, 36, 38, 59,
  68, 174, 180, 184, 205, 213, 214,
  223, 229, 231, 234, 236, 237, 240,
  241, 244, 245, 261, 273, 279, 280,
  282
Egypt's Free Officers, 80
Eilat, 232
El Dorado, 52
El Salvador, 69
Emergency Police, 232
Endela Tessema, 114
Endalkatchew Makonnen, 75, 84, 85,
  86, 87, 92
Eritrea, 44, 61, 65, 72, 75, 93, 115,
  127, 135, 152, 184, 194, 199, 200,
  203, 212, 214, 217, 220, 221, 227,
  231, 232, 234, 235, 246, 249, 252,
  254, 256, 259, 260, 262
  external relations of, 47, 124, 126,
    185, 194, 201, 216, 229, 233, 236,
    237, 239, 240, 241, 244, 249, 251,
    255, 258
  guerrillas, 160, 162, 163, 171, 178,
    182–193, 195, 217
  national question, 46, 113, 125, 127,
    159–171, 186, 205, 207, 252, 267
  repression in, 30, 39, 45, 148

Ethiopian relations with, 38, 41, 48,
  77, 81, 88, 93, 101, 118
revolt in, 80, 83, 94, 132, 156, 158,
  171–182, 241, 243
Eritrean Democratic Movement, 182,
  188
Eritrean Liberation Front, 75, 172,
  181, 182, 183, 185, 186, 187, 188,
  189, 190, 192, 206, 235, 248, 251,
  257, 262
Eritrean Liberation Movement, 75,
  133, 182
Eritrean People's Liberation
  Forces/Front, 121, 127, 172, 181,
  182, 183, 185, 186, 187, 188, 190,
  192, 206, 207, 248, 262, 263
Eritrean People's Revolutionary
  Army, 90
Eritrean Liberation Front-Popular
  Liberation Front, 184, 185, 187
Eritrean People's Revolutionary Party,
  190, 263
Eshatu Chole, 120
Ethiopian Democratic Union, 169,
  190, 229
Ethiopian National Liberation Front,
  76
Ethiopian People's Revolutionary
  Party, 119, 120, 121, 123, 124, 125,
  126, 127, 128, 129, 238, 141, 144,
  145, 150, 153, 159, 259, 264
  actions of, 121, 122, 132
  conflict with, 97, 101, 112, 129, 49,
    153
  programme of, 119, 120, 122, 125,
    134, 141, 261

Fallul, 188
Fikre Merid, 128, 131
Fikre-Selassie Wogderess, 118, 142
Finland, 39, 168
Fisseha Desta, 116, 118
Ford, Gerald, 224
France, 14, 15, 16, 39, 45, 46, 52, 54,
  56, 82, 93, 199, 220, 254
Friendship and Cooperation Treaty,
  247

Gara Huleta, 57
Gebbi, 153-4

Georgia, 117, 169
Germane Neway, 79
Germany, 26, 239
Gesesse Wolde-Kidan, 118
Getachew Shibeshi, 124
Ghana, 139, 240, 279
Girma Kebede, 123, 132
Gojjam, 75, 105, 207, 246
Gondar, 55, 63, 121, 174, 246
Great Kahn, 52
Greece, 68, 222, 238
Guinea-Bissau, 18
Haile Fida, 77, 78, 128, 132, 134
Haile Selassie, 16, 23, 24, 29, 44, 51, 54, 56, 58–59, 64, 65, 67, 71, 74, 75, 77, 78, 79, 80, 81, 83, 84, 86, 91, 93, 111, 119, 126, 153, 156, 163, 171, 177, 187, 200, 202, 203, 207, 212, 216, 217, 219, 223, 224, 233, 235, 239, 240, 244, 244, 251, 257, 258, 259, 260, 261
Halewa Sewra, 188–9
Hamassien, 178
Hamatic Agau people, 55
Harar, 57, 71, 80, 90, 114, 118, 149, 198
Hararghe, 76, 118, 194, 195, 199
Havana, 251, 259
Herui Tedle Bairu, 188
Holeta, 80, 114, 116, 149
Horn of Africa, 44, 45, 46, 47, 48, 61, 117, 159, 190, 199, 211–214, 227, 230, 231, 232, 233, 234, 235, 236, 237, 238, 239, 245, 246, 247, 249, 252, 256, 257, 258, 260, 262, 263, 264, 265, 266, 279
Hungary, 204

Ibrahim Idris Totil, 184
Imperial Guard, 79
India, 39, 41, 68, 175, 204, 283
Indian Ocean, 212, 219, 231, 236
Indo-China, 181, 211
Indonesia, 33, 237, 244, 261, 279
Inner Mongolia, 204
International Confederation of Free Trade Unions, 82
Iran, 14, 19, 21, 22, 25, 33, 39, 41, 108, 157, 159, 209, 215, 218, 237, 264, 265

Iraq, 30, 33, 35, 36, 139, 166, 180, 184, 186, 189, 209, 226, 234, 236, 237, 245, 248, 253, 279, 280, 283
Ireland, 39
Isais Afeworki, 183
Islam, 55, 59, 64, 115, 195, 235
Isle of Pines, 253
Israel, 213, 216, 220, 232, 233, 237, 244, 245, 260
Italian invasion, 58, 59–60, 65
Italo-Ethiopian Treaty of 1908, 200
Italy, 46, 49, 51, 53, 56, 68, 69, 70, 80, 82, 174, 175, 176, 177, 178, 184, 199, 200, 201, 212, 217, 238, 262, 263, 267
Izvestia, 242, 243

Jaafar Nimeiry, 75
Japan, 26, 27, 28, 29, 31, 51
Jerusalem, 53
Jubuti, 165, 200, 220, 231, 234
Jimma, 85, 90, 120
John, Prester, 52
Johnson, Lyndon Baines, 218
Judaism, 52

Kagnew, 215, 217, 218, 219, 223
Kassala, 180
Kay Fanu, 130
Kebede Menguesha, 128
Kebeles, 97, 99, 100, 110, 112, 122, 123, 124, 131, 132, 140, 144
Kennedy, John F., 218
Kenya, 200, 227, 228, 231, 276
Kenyatta, Jomo, 52
Keren, 166, 183
Khartoum, 77, 172, 180, 187, 258
Khediv Ismail, 205
Kiros Alemayehu, 113
Kismayu, 224
Kissinger, Henry, 220, 221, 224, 226
Kolchak, Admiral Aleksandr, 169
Koranic, 183
Korea, 80, 217
Kremlin, 249
Kuomintang, 39
Kurds, 166, 186, 209
Kuwait, 180, 185

Labour Code, 111
Labour Party, 181

Index

Land reform, 46, 97, 99, 101, 105–111, 112, 125, 126, 277
Laos, 18
Latin America, 19, 218, 255, 267, 276
League of Nations, 58
Lebanon, 68
Legassie Asfaw, 142
Lenin, Vladimir Ilyich, 136, 167, 168, 235, 281
Liberia, 267
Libya, 139, 180, 223, 233, 234, 235, 267
Lij Jasu, 55, 57
Liquidation Committee, 187
Los Angeles, 77
Lumumbria University, 137

Makele, 206
Mali, 103, 279
Manka, 188
Mao Tse-tung, 126, 137, 195, 206, 207, 258
Mareb, 191
Mareb Mallash, 174
Marxism, 136, 184, 195, 249, 272, 274, 276, 282
Marxist-Leninist Organization of Ethiopia, 129, 131
Massawa, 183, 184, 232, 233
May Day 1975, 123
Mela Ethiopia Sosialist Netanake (All-Ethiopian Socialist Movement, ME'ISON), 120, 121, 127, 128, 129, 130, 131, 132, 133, 135, 138, 141, 145, 159, 197, 198, 247
Menelik II, 47, 55, 57, 175, 194, 199, 206
Mengistu Haile-Mariam, 102, 114, 118, 120, 143, 245, 247, 253, 258, 259
 background, 86, 98, 116–7, 196
 emergence as leader, 97, 114, 116, 136, 153, 245, 254
 his politics, 98, 117, 120, 122, 126, 129, 134, 142, 153, 162, 163, 224
Mengistu Neway, 240
Mexico, 19, 267
Michael Imru, 87
Middle Ages, 52

Middle East, 137, 212, 215, 216, 218, 231–237
Ministry of Industry, 99
Ministry of Labour, 81
Ministry of the Pen, 70
Mobutu, 216
Mogadishu, 76, 196, 198, 200, 201, 202, 203, 224, 227, 228, 231, 234, 241, 245, 253, 247, 263
Mohammad Dirye Urdah, 203
Mongolia, 276, 283
Morocco, 216, 276
Moscow, 239, 241, 245, 247, 248, 251, 253, 255, 256, 259, 264, 266
Moscow Foreign Language Press, 138
Dayan, Moshe, 233
Mugabe, Robert, 267
Muslims, 60, 92, 105, 163, 165, 176, 177, 178, 180, 184, 185, 189, 195, 196, 199, 205, 212, 213, 232
Mussolini, 238

Naktu, 173
Narkomnats, 168
Nasser, 36, 38, 233
Nasser Pasha, 184
National Assembly, 70, 123
National Democratic Revolution, 100, 120, 128, 129, 130, 131, 133, 136, 139, 142, 150, 160, 161, 162, 163, 165, 169, 198, 200, 243
National Revolutionary Economic Development Campaign, 102, 103, 109, 110, 118
National Security Commission, 85, 86, 92
Negede Gobeze, 128
Neghelle, 84
Negus, 58
Nepal, 54
Nicaragua, 19, 21, 22, 23, 25
Nigeria, 40, 166, 213, 230, 267
Nile, 212, 234
Nimeiry, 126, 173, 223, 241
Nine Point Statement on Eritrea, 160, 163, 198
Nixon, Richard, 224, 236, 237
Nkrumah, Kwame, 51–2
North Atlantic Treaty Organisation, 24, 225
North Yemen, 54, 211

Ogaden, 50, 54, 57, 101, 133, 156, 159, 173, 194, 199, 200, 201, 202, 203, 204, 205, 207, 212, 225, 227, 228, 229, 230, 231, 235, 241, 242, 245, 246, 247, 253, 255, 256, 257, 258, 259, 260, 262, 264, 265, 266
Organisation of Petroleum Exporting Countries, 84, 104
Old Testament, 53
Oman, 231, 237, 276
Oppressed People's Party of Ethiopia (ECHA'AT), 128–9, 130–1, 159, 197, 198
Organization of African Unity, 52, 80, 213, 216, 232, 266
Oromo, 55, 58, 63, 64, 72, 73, 76, 93, 105, 115, 116, 117, 118, 127, 129, 133, 138, 153, 157, 164, 193–207
Oromo Liberation Front, 198
Orthodox Church, 59
Osman Saleh Sabbe, 184, 185
Outer Mongolia, 204

Pahlavi monarchy, 21
Pakistan, 24, 40, 41, 166, 237
Palestine, 185, 190, 232, 236, 265
Palestine Liberation Organization, 248, 253
Paris Commune, 117
Parti Communiste Français, 263
Partito Communista Italiano, 262
Peasants, 62, 65–7, 97, 99, 100, 105, 106, 107, 108, 143, 163, 165, 221
Peasant Associations, 106, 108, 109, 110, 111, 131, 140, 144, 152
Peasant Association Decree, 107
Peking, 126, 258
Pentagon, 218, 220, 223
People's Democratic Party of Afghanistan, 34
People's Democratic Party of Yemen, 172
Perón, Juan, 139
Persia, 56
Peru, 29, 30, 33
Philippines, 216
Pinochet, Augusto, 258
Plan Delta, 217
Podgorny, Nikolai, 245, 246
Poland, 238, 249

Popular Revolutionary Party, 181
Pravda, 240, 242, 243, 244, 246, 248
Progressive Dictionary, 137, 138
Provisional Military Administrative Council (the Derg), 29, 31, 39, 59, 78, 86, 86, 87, 92, 93, 96, 107, 111, 112–118, 143, 171, 172, 192, 198, 207, 208, 209, 220, 247, 250, 254, 261
  actions of, 92, 96, 148, 151
  Central Committee, 115
  composition of, 29, 88, 93, 97, 98, 100, 112, 114, 115–8, 143, 149, 196, 197
  divisions within, 25, 112, 139, 142, 153, 154
  external relations of, 159, 222, 223, 224, 229, 230, 234, 241, 243, 244, 249, 253, 267, 268, 270
  and Eritrea, 93, 156, 158, 157, 159–171, 173, 177, 191, 192, 193, 194, 208, 244, 254, 263
  Interior Ministry, 168
  policies of, 25, 38, 39, 44, 87, 88, 93, 95, 107, 113, 135–139, 140, 155, 158, 159–171, 167–8, 173, 193, 214, 221, 238, 245, 256, 259, 263
  reforms carried out by, 25, 99–102, 105, 110, 151, 160
  relations with civilian politics, 25, 37, 92, 96, 97, 119–135, 140, 145, 159, 200
  Security Committee, 118
  Standing Committee, 113, 115, 118

Qaddafi, Colonel Muamar, 234

Ramadan Nur, 183
Ras Kebede Tessema, 116
Ras Makonnen, 57
Ras Mengesha Seyoum, 206, 207
Rases, 53, 89
Ras Tafari, 50, 55
Red Sea, 55, 56, 59, 180, 191, 212, 213, 220, 232
Revolutionary Ethiopia's Women's Association, 145
Romanov Tsars, 168
Rome, 262, 263
Rumania, 204

Rushaida, 180
Russia, 14, 15, 16, 39, 45, 46, 51, 82, 90, 105, 254

Sadat, Anwar, 245
Sahara, 260, 266
Sahel, 173, 178, 183, 200
Saho, 184, 200
Saudi Arabia, 54, 180, 185, 204, 218, 222, 223, 224, 226, 228, 229, 233, 234, 237
Schaufele, William, 221
Second International, 167
Second World War, 65, 70, 74, 166, 215, 265
Semhar, 178, 183
Senate (US), 223
Senaye Likkay, 129
Senghor, Leopold, 52
Senhit, 183, 184
Serae, 178, 184
Seventh Comintern Congress, 238
Shaba, 264
Shah of Iran, 24, 43, 229, 237, 258
Sheba, 52, 59
Sheikh Jarra, 197, 198
Shkria, 180
Shoa, 63, 105, 121, 165, 177, 195, 205, 207
Shoan nobility, 55, 57, 60, 70
Shums, 53
Siad Barre, 201, 202, 203, 204, 205, 224, 227, 228, 229, 245, 246, 252, 255, 258
Sidamo, 57, 67, 194
Sisay Habte, 113
Sisay Kiris, 120, 222
Skočpol, Theda, 45
Solomon, 52, 59
Somali Socialist Revolutionary Party, 241
Somalia, 24, 29, 33, 36, 42, 44, 46, 47, 48, 49, 55, 58, 76, 88, 98, 126, 132, 133, 134, 137, 149, 153, 158, 159, 165, 173, 193–207, 208, 214, 220, 223, 224, 225–231, 234, 236, 237, 240, 241, 242, 244, 245, 246, 247, 248, 249, 250, 251, 252, 253, 254, 256, 257, 258, 259, 260, 262, 263, 264, 265, 266, 267, 269, 282

Somali-Abo, 197
Somoza, Anastasio, 21, 22, 23, 24
South Africa, 260
South Yemen, 180, 233, 234, 235, 245, 246, 265, 267, 277
Spain, 41, 238
Stalin, Josef, 126, 238, 239
State Department (US), 230
Strategic Arms Limitation Talks II, 264
Sudan, 35, 55, 58, 106, 171, 172, 178, 179, 180, 184, 190, 200, 205, 223, 233, 234, 235, 236, 237, 241, 244, 245, 260, 261, 262, 267, 279
Sun Yat-sen, 39
Sweden, 277
Syria, 180, 189, 197, 233, 234, 236, 237, 241, 248

Taffera Taclaeb, 86
Tamrat Fedree, 114
Tanzania, 139, 276
Tatek, 132
Teferi Benti, 93, 113, 197
Ten-Year Plan, 102, 104, 109
Tesfaye Gebre-Kidan, 118
Tewodros, 55, 56, 153
Thailand, 19, 54, 276
Third World, 11–50, 151, 166, 167, 168, 175, 181, 211, 226, 241, 246, 250, 258, 260, 264, 266, 267, 269, 270, 272, 273, 274, 275, 276, 281, 282, 283
Tibet, 54
Tigray, 105, 109, 118, 120–1, 125, 126, 127, 154, 174, 175, 193–207
Tigray Liberation Front, 206
Tigrean People's Liberation Front, 121, 125, 127, 195, 206
Tigrinya, 55, 60, 63, 64, 72, 78, 178, 181, 183, 188
Togliatti, Palmiro, 238
Trades Unions, 152
Transylvania, 204
Tricontinental Conference, 251
Trimberger, Ellen J., 27, 28, 29, 30, 31
Trotsky, Leon, 124, 137
Truman, Harry, 217
Tsarists, 283

Tsongas, Paul, 230
Turkey, 26, 27, 28, 29, 31, 174, 180, 223, 282

Union of Marxist-Leninist Organisations (EMALEDH), 130, 131, 164
UNITA, 229
United Nations, 46, 177, 201, 216, 239, 257, 265
Uruguay, 223
United States of America, 21, 23, 25, 43, 52, 79, 116, 135, 141, 211, 213, 237, 251, 260, 264, 265, 277, 283
   aid from, 79, 136, 204, 205, 233
   relations with, 17, 29, 44, 46, 48, 49, 69, 124, 126, 133, 137, 214–231, 242, 244, 245, 264
Union of Soviet Socialist Republics, 19, 21, 36, 49, 117, 118, 126, 130, 167, 169, 170, 202, 205, 209, 224, 229, 233, 236, 237, 253, 256, 258, 259, 262, 265, 269, 272, 273, 274, 275, 276, 280, 281, 282
   aid from, 44, 48, 100, 104, 135, 136, 173, 205
   relations with, 17, 23, 98, 104, 114, 118, 126, 137, 142, 155, 163, 166, 172, 193, 212, 213, 214, 217, 223, 226, 229, 230, 231, 234, 237–250, 251, 256, 260, 266, 268, 270

Vance, Cyrus, 223, 226, 265
Vendée, 207

Vietnam, 18, 24, 29, 116, 141, 215, 218, 226, 240, 260
Virginia, 216
Voice of the Masses, 128

Waku Guta, 76, 197, 198
Was (Labour) League, 129, 131, 137, 259
Washington, 214, 217, 218, 219, 220, 221, 224, 226, 227, 228, 229, 230, 237, 266
Welega, 198
Weo, 55, 83, 105, 109
West Bengal, 204
West Indies, 51
Western Somalia Liberation Front, 76, 195, 201, 202, 203, 204
White House, 224
Wollamo, 116
Women's Associations, 152
World Bank, 69, 231
Woubshet Dessie, 118

Yekatit 66, 122, 130, 131, 142, 143
Yohannes II, 55
Young, Andrew, 265
Yugoslavia, 105

Zaire, 40, 211, 216
Zara, Yacob, 83
Zauditu, 56
Zimbabwe, 18, 187, 267